Ethics in Medicine

Jennifer Jackson

polity

First published in 2006 by Polity Press

Polity Press
65 Bridge Street
Cambridge CB2 1UR, UK

Polity Press
350 Main Street
Malden, MA 02148, USA

ISBN: 0–7456–2568–1
ISBN: 0–7456–2569–X (pb)

A catalogue record for this book is available from the British Library.

Typeset in 10.5 on 12 pt Plantin
by Servis Filmsetting Ltd, Manchester
Printed and bound in Great Britain by MPG Books Ltd. Bodmin, Cornwall

The publisher has used its best endeavours to ensure that the URLs for external websites referred to in this book are correct and active at the time of going to press. However, the publisher has no responsibility for the websites and can make no guarantee that a site will remain live or that the content is or will remain appropriate.

Every effort has been made to trace all copyright holders, but if any have been inadvertently overlooked the publishers will be pleased to include any necessary credits in any subsequent reprint or edition.

For further information on Polity, visit our website: www.polity.co.uk

DA

To the memory of my mother

Clara Marion Farrell Jackson Brooke, 1902–2005

who, fortunately for me at least, ignored medical
advice not to risk another pregnancy

Contents

Contents

Acknowledgements

I have been working on this book for some half-dozen years, and throughout that time have benefited hugely from regular discussion of the ideas and issues with my students. Friends and colleagues at the University of Leeds and elsewhere have provided valuable comment on drafts or portions of these at various stages. I particularly wish to thank the following for their helpful advice: Professor Nigel Biggar, Dr Emma Cave, Professor Maureen Dalton, Dr Heather Draper, Professor Jim Drife, Dr Jim Eccles, Mr Bruce Lawson, Dr Robert Ruston, Professor Jim Thornton, and my son, Alexander Coope. I have also to thank the readers for the publisher, one of whom kindly advised on more than one draft. As ever, my biggest debt is to my husband and colleague, Christopher Coope. If there is anything that is neatly expressed or insightful in what follows it most likely bears his stamp and he has saved the reader from many of my ineptitudes and muddles.

Introduction

The philosopher, Peter Singer, opened a recent book with the triumphant announcement: 'After ruling our thoughts and decisions about life and death for nearly two thousand years, the traditional western ethic has collapsed.'[1] He appears to be confident that the new ethic, which like-minded philosophers are now developing to replace the old, will provide a better framework for doctors to rely on when making life and death decisions than did the 'traditional' ethic with its alleged religious and Hippocratic underpinnings. Not everyone will share his optimism. But whether we welcome or deplore the involvement of philosophers in shaping views on these matters, we should at least pay attention to what they are up to. I think that we should take the pessimists (who include philosophers as well as doctors and nurses) seriously. It has to be admitted that 'Trust me, I'm a philosopher!' has a somewhat comical ring.

There are five sorts of misgivings about the role of philosophy in medical ethics that deserve mention. First, there is the view that even if clinical experience is not sufficient for solving the problems of medical ethics, it is at least necessary. This sentiment is voiced in a *Lancet* editorial: 'Departments of ethics that are divorced from the medical profession, wallowing in theory and speculation, are quaintly redundant.'[2] Secondly, isn't philosophy essentially a somewhat wayward enterprise – the very last thing to place trust in when seeking to lay down an ethical framework for clinicians? Thirdly, that aside, aren't individual philosophers quite likely to be seriously mistaken on some ethical issues, however well-intentioned they are? Fourthly, isn't the current state of ethical theory just in too unsatisfactory a state to be 'applicable'? Fifthly, philosophers need to find some common ground as their starting point from which to work out a new ethic. But in our present-day world *is* there enough common ground? Let us take up these points in turn.

Consider first the complaint against academic 'ethicists' who are not members of any of the health professions – the implication being that they do not know what they are talking about. The charge may stick against some, depending on what kinds of claims they make and how they defend them. But no one seriously believes that we are competent to pass moral judgement only on practices of which we have personal or professional direct experience. We do not need to have personal, first-hand experience of slavery, rape or torture to know that these are ethically indefensible. We do not need to have witnessed an execution to be able to discuss sensibly the morality of capital punishment. That said, obviously first-hand experience does sometimes lead us to think differently – and, sometimes, better.

The second and third grounds for misgiving are closely related and will receive the same answer: proceed with caution. The second warns us of the waywardness of philosophical enquiry – the oddity of what philosophers of good standing have said and still say. The third warns us that individual philosophers in this field sometimes instruct us incorrectly about what is ethically defensible or indefensible (and not just over relatively small matters). Consider, for example, the controversy over routine testing of new drugs on animals before using them on humans. Some philosophers denounce this practice, others defend it. However well-intentioned, both sides to the dispute cannot be right. One side will be teaching us wrongly about what is ethically defensible or indefensible.

So our teachers in this subject can be presumed to be both wayward and sometimes, indeed, corrupting. This is uncomfortable, but must be faced. It shows that we can by no means take for granted that philosophers, brought in to teach doctors and nurses, will do more good than harm. This is no new thought. 'Beware lest any man spoil you through philosophy and vain deceit!' One way of containing the risk, is to preserve a little distance between the academic philosophers and those in positions of power – to beware of philosopher-kings, and also, more appositely, of philosophers who don white coats and adopt the role of on-call hospital ethicists.

Another way of containing the risk, is to recognize that the subject can be done piecemeal. We do not have to accept a whole package. And a guide who is wayward or corrupt in one way may still be sound in another – think of the slave-owners in the Old South before the American Civil War: they were wrong about slavery (a huge injustice), but they were not all at sea about morality, or even about justice.

The remaining grounds for misgiving suggest not just that we need to be careful and critical in studying what philosophers have to say on matters in medical ethics, but that the very idea of counting on them at all for guidance is wrong. The fourth ground for thinking this points up the unsatisfactory state that moral philosophy is in: too confused and contentious to be able to provide reliable instruction. The fifth ground for thinking this points up the unsatisfactory state that our societies are in: too divided and unhomogeneous for the project of working out a shared moral vision on which to peg resolutions of contentious matters of policy or practice in health care.

Consider, then, the fourth worry: is there no sense in attempting to 'apply' moral philosophy, given its current state? Should we wait till it has sorted itself out? And is that at all likely in the next 2,000 years? What help is it to a doctor or nurse to be presented with a confusing medley of conflicting views, theories or approaches, none of which is established?

One way round this worry has been offered by Beauchamp and Childress in their well-known and widely studied *Principles of Biomedical Ethics* (now in its 5th edition). They survey various ethical 'theories' (each of which, they say, contains insights but is problematic), and then propose a way forward that aims to spare health professionals the need to wrestle with the arguments among philosophers over these. They call their approach 'pluralist'. Rival theories are all to be accommodated, because their four foundation principles are based on 'values' (beneficence, non-maleficence, autonomy and justice) that we can all sign up to, whichever of these theories we may personally happen to endorse. Thus, the quarrels between philosophers of different persuasions need not hold up the real work of biomedical ethics: of applying the principles in health care contexts. In short, we need not dig any deeper than the values on which the four principles are based. In the applied field of biomedical ethics, we can use them as our basis for sorting out the issues and problems.

It is no wonder that the Beauchamp and Childress strategy has been popular. They rightly point up the unsatisfactory state of philosophical ethics. They doubt if it is even possible to construct a 'comprehensive' ethical theory. The good news, they tell us, is that whether it is possible and, if so, what the theory should be, simply does not matter – at least, it does not matter for the project of practical ethics. All the rival theories, they say, converge in agreement with the four principles that can provide the basis and framework for biomedical ethics.[3]

I, will argue (in chapter 4), however, that their own framework cannot, and does not, stand alone independently of one particular

(flawed) theory. Be that as it may, let us note that even if all prevailing theories are flawed, there is still no alternative but to persist with
theorizing, with philosophizing. We need not suppose, though, that
our theorizing has to involve us in constructing a moral theory, if by
this is meant some 'integrated body of principles'. That may not be
the best way to proceed. At least, it is not the only way. It will not be
our way.

A, if not *the*, central question in ethics is: how ought we to live our
lives? This may not be a clear or satisfactory question to ask. But
however unsatisfactory and contentious philosophers' responses to
that question have been, it does not look like a question that can be
shelved until they have sorted the matter out. In the meantime, we
have to live our lives. Decisions have to be made regarding whether or
not to ban or regulate practices such as physician-assisted suicide,
research on human embryos, and genetic modifications of human
embryos. Doctors and nurses have to decide whether they should
make it their rule never to lie on a serious matter to their patients or,
if that is too strict a rule to apply, what rule, if any, should take its
place. Should they, for example, adopt the policy advocated by Peter
Singer: privately, recognize that sometimes you ought to lie to your
patients; publicly, declare that lying is always wrong, 'for otherwise
patients will cease to believe what their doctors tell them'?[4]

The issues are here and now. So, like it or not, we have to try and
respond to them and to defend our responses to ourselves and to
others with reasons. When we do this, we are engaging in critical
reflection. Since this is what philosophical ethics (moral philosophy)
seeks to do, it stands to reason that we can be helped in doing it by
considering what philosophers have had to say – if only to avoid
repeating their many mistakes. The depressing fact that some, or
perhaps rather a lot of, illnesses result from medical treatment does
not mean that we should abandon medicine. Similarly, the fact that
some of the problems of medical ethics are caused by our muddled
philosophizing does not mean that we should abandon applying philosophical analysis to the problems of medical ethics.

The fifth and final misgiving to be addressed calls attention to the
difficulty of finding any common ground on moral matters. We are
interested here in extending agreement and understanding and in
resolving controversial issues. But extending agreement presupposes
that there is already some agreement, some common ground from
which to launch our discussion. Whereas Beauchamp and Childress
take as their starting point a set of 'norms' that they claim all 'morally
serious persons' agree upon, H. Tristram Engelhardt Jr. and Kevin

William Wildes argue that there is no such set of agreed 'norms' in our pluralist societies. The post-modern world, they say, is composed of 'moral strangers' who do not share a 'moral vision'. Hence, they argue, the whole project of establishing a 'content-full morality' to resolve contentious issues in medical ethics is doomed to failure.[5]

This claim about the lack of commonality in our views on moral matters has some truth in it, but is exaggerated. Engelhardt Jr. and Wildes are right to probe the complacent assumption that there is enough common ground among us for our project of establishing an agreed 'content-full morality' to succeed. After all, if ethics is about how we should live our lives, we should expect to find that religious believers and non-believers will come up with markedly different answers on some matters, at least. Is it not hugely relevant to how we should live our lives (and to how we should face our deaths) whether we believe that death marks the end of our life or, rather, a new beginning? If we discard the religious underpinnings of traditional teachings, what will remain from which to work out a new ethic? Maybe not as much as conservative-minded non-believers would like to think. Besides the division in society between those who are religious believers and those who are not, there are also, of course, many differences among believers. Some of these differences, too, may be relevant to what teachings seem appropriate.

Even so, the project of establishing an agreed 'content-full morality' may still be feasible, up to a point. Peter Geach remarks:

> people whose first practical premises, formulating their ultimate ends, are not only divergent but irreconcilable may nevertheless agree on bringing about some situation which is an indispensable condition of either end's being realized, or on avoiding some situation which would prevent the realization of either end. That is what compromise means, that is what diplomacy is in aid of.
>
> Consider the fact that people of different religions or of no religion can agree to build and run a hospital, and agree broadly on what should be done in the hospital. There will of course be marginal policy disagreements, e.g. about abortion operations and the limits of experimentation on human beings. But there can be agreement on fighting disease, because disease impedes men's efforts towards most goals.[6]

In short, even when we disagree in some of our aims and priorities, we may still be able to agree what is to be done here and now. Morality, it will be argued, has different parts. There is, and needs to be, agreement with regard to some of these, but not necessarily with regard to others. It matters which aspects we disagree over, not just the quantity of disagreement but the nature of it, and whether it pre-cludes our finding common ground from which to debate issues. So, we need to examine the parts of morality: its anatomy, so to speak. This I shall do (in chapters 1–4) through discussion, first, of the notion of virtues in general, and then, of two virtues in particular that are of key interest for our further enquiries.

I will attempt in this book to make something of a fresh start in how we draw on philosophy to help us in medical ethics. That said, my approach will follow a tradition, common since Aristotle, in seeking to ground ethical teachings in familiar, uncontroversial facts (home truths) about human needs and human aspirations, though *how* they are grounded in these will *not* always be familiar and uncontroversial. This approach will naturally lead us to attach central importance to the role of moral virtues and vices in what constitutes acting well or badly. My approach will not involve setting forth some systematic body of principles under the guise of 'virtues'. But nor will it exclude principles altogether from consideration. They naturally come within the ambit of the virtue of justice.

So-called virtue ethics has enjoyed a kind of renaissance in recent years, and others have sought to apply it in the field of medical ethics. But to my mind these treatments have sometimes been defective in two respects. My start will be 'fresh' if it manages to avoid these defects. One defect is that these treatments make the virtues out to be more homogeneous than they are. Let our approach, then, be 'virtues ethics' not 'virtue ethics'. Our attentiveness to the differences, the lack of homogeneity among the virtues, accords well with our appreciation of the wisdom of adopting a piecemeal approach. Some virtues we can expect to be more complex, more ramified – hence more challenging to give a good account of – than others.

The other defect is that many recent exponents of virtue ethics do not pay enough attention to the virtue of justice. The present-day neglect of justice no doubt partly arises from the modern tendency to focus exclusively on distributive justice. Justice used to be (from Plato to John Stuart Mill, at least) a broader notion, not simply concerned, let us say, with fair shares, but concerned generally with what we owe one another by way of helping or not hindering.

Very many, if not all, of the issues in medical ethics to which phi-losophy can contribute have to do with justice in this older, broader sense – with the rights, obligations and responsibilities of health pro-fessionals. For example, do nurses and doctors have a moral right to refuse to assist in any way in providing types of treatment that they personally consider to be unethical even if these are not illegal?

Do they have a duty to put the interests of the patient they are currently treating first, or to balance that patient's interests against those of other patients? And what if one patient's choice threatens the health of another: for example, if a mother refuses to breast-feed her baby, does the midwife have a duty to insist (given that 'breast is best') – to be (somewhat) coercive? Do doctors have a duty to rescue people from (repeated) suicide attempts? Are any of the duties of health professionals strictly binding in all circumstances? If not, how are they to tell when making an exception in a particular case is morally justified?

All these questions about rights and duties revolve around what justice requires or permits: what is 'owed' in the context of health care – because of either one's role, or one's contract, or quite generally. Justice has always featured on the short list of 'cardinal virtues'. As such, it has a central importance in the fields of medical and nursing practice, as elsewhere. But it also has a *distinctive* role, which sets it apart from the other cardinal virtues. It is not simply one important 'value' to be balanced against others. Compare how town councillors quite properly seek to balance some of their duties and to shuffle priorities, in line, perhaps, with the public mood: one year spending more on prettifying the town centre with spectacular flower beds, another year concentrating, rather, on keeping the streets clean and removing graffiti from public buildings or on installing new tramlines. It would be quite another matter if they adopted a similar attitude to certain other of their duties: those relating to people's basic rights. In times of acute hardship – for example, wartime – the councillors might decide to convert flower beds into vegetable plots, or to curtail the upkeep of public gardens. But they are not supposed to adopt a similar flexibility in respect of people's basic rights: as if they were to encourage the police to fabricate evidence against drivers accused of traffic offences as a handy way of raising revenue through fines. A kind of necessity tends to attach to what is owed as a matter of justice, having to do (partly, at least) with rights that *must* be respected.

Current philosophical accounts of justice (of what we owe one another) are inadequate. They do not make good sense of the kind of importance that justice has: for whom it is important and why. They do not explain well how it relates to the other virtues. Moreover, they tend to narrow the scope of justice unduly. It is often assumed that the starting point for examining what is just or unjust is the notion of 'having a right'. If all duties of justice were derived from rights, the assumption would be safe. It will be argued, though, that duties of justice have a broader scope – a matter of singular practical relevance, as we shall see, for the duties of doctors, nurses and of others who care for patients.

Finally, a note about terminology. I will use the term 'patients' to refer to those who receive advice, treatment or care from health professionals. So defined, 'patients' include people who are neither ill nor injured: for example, people seeking abortions or the enhancements of cosmetic surgery. I will use the term 'medical ethics' to refer to ethical issues concerning health care practices and policies. In settling for 'medical ethics' (rather than 'health care ethics') I do not mean to side-line the other health and health-related professions, apart from medicine, whose members also grapple with the issues to be addressed. In settling for 'medical ethics' (rather than 'bioethics' or 'biomedical ethics'), I do not mean, either, to exclude issues that have arisen only recently in the wake of developing novel technologies.

1

Virtues and Vices

In this and the next three chapters I will examine, first, the notion of virtues (and vices) generally, and then some puzzling aspects of two particular virtues, justice and benevolence, specifically. To some, this might seem a bad way to start a discussion of ethics in medicine. Why the broad introduction? Why not get right down to cases – or, at least, to discussing patients' rights, patients' duties, doctors' rights, doctors' duties, etc.? The reason is this: that without a perspective – indeed, without an appropriate perspective – the whole idea of 'morality' appears much more mysterious than it need be. And this unnecessary air of mystery is bad for our thinking. Problems, and even mystery, will doubtless remain, but these initial reflections on the virtues will reduce them to something more manageable.

How is one to live well?

As I have already said (p. 4), I take the question of how one is to live well to be a central question for moral philosophy. And this is the starting point of debate about ethics in Aristotle. He asks: 'what kind of life is to be thought of as fine, fortunate, enviable?' 'How would someone wise choose to live?' Aristotle supposes that we have enough in common to enable us to discuss in a general way how we should live our lives, whoever 'we' are. We might, of course, wonder whether there is a single answer. Might there not be a range of different but equally fortunate lives? But leaving that doubt aside, we may still agree that our shared needs and vulnerabilities do at least enable us to generalize about what is a bad (unfortunate) life.[1] The enterprise of spelling out what are human virtues or vices assumes that this is so: that (1) there are certain evils which can mar any human life, and that (2) to some extent, it is in our power to develop character traits that give us the best chance of avoiding these evils, or, where this is not possible, of minimizing the harm they do.

Virtues and vices

The Latin *virtus* (strength) is etymologically related to *vir* (man). By acquiring virtues, we fortify ourselves for life and for the challenges we face in life. Virtues and vices are dispositional traits: that is to say, they are relatively settled features that characterize how we behave over a range of situations.

How we fare in life depends, plainly, in many respects on factors beyond our own control – the times we live in, our genetic inheritance, the kind of family, if any, we are born into, the opportunities that come our way through life, and the accidents that befall us and those dear to us. Yet, however our personal histories unfold, the main influence or power we can each bring to bear on our fortunes is through developing virtues and avoiding vices. We do, of course, also influence our own fortunes through the skills we learn, the knowledge we acquire. Thinking of human virtues simply as strengths that fit us for living well, we might include on our list such features as physical fitness, health and mental skills – like having a good memory or being able to speak several languages. Indeed, Aristotle operates with a wider concept of virtue than we do nowadays. He divides human virtues into what are customarily called, in translation, 'moral' and 'intellectual'.[2] Aristotle by no means thought that ethics was concerned just with the moral virtues. Indeed, the key or master virtue, is classified by him as 'intellectual'.

In developing my ideas about virtues and vices, hereafter I will make much use of Philippa Foot's insightful writing on the subject. She suggests that the 'root notion' underlying what we have come to think of as (moral) virtues is connected with goodness of the will.[3] By the 'will' we must understand here whatever is presumed to fall directly or indirectly within the realm of the voluntary. That plainly includes what we intentionally choose to do or not do, but also what we wish for and sometimes even what we do or omit unintentionally. The surgeon who accidentally removes the healthy kidney rather than the diseased one is not intentionally harming the patient, but may still be at fault, culpably ignorant or careless. When do we blame surgeons for medical accidents? Only when we suppose that they were at fault:

that it was within their power to avoid them, that they should have and could have known better and acted differently. When is 'Sorry, I forgot!' an acceptable excuse? Not when, had you cared as you should have cared, you would not have allowed yourself to forget.

Teasing out how to understand the notion of a 'good will' here is difficult. I suggest that, we should understand by 'good will' simply a will that is not defective in any way. (Compare how we might understand 'being well' simply as not being ill.) Foot speaks of good, as opposed to defective, dispositions of the will (virtues, as opposed to vices). Foot's insight explains why we do not think of any and every advantageous feature in a person's make-up as a moral virtue:

> It is no part of the goodness that is goodness of the will that someone should be physically strong, should move well, should talk well, or see well. But he must act well, in a sense that is given primarily at least by his recognition of the force of particular considerations as reasons for acting: that and the influence that this has on what he does.[4]

Applying Foot's 'root notion', we can make a case for treating wisdom of a kind (prudence – in Aristotle, *phronēsis*) as a moral virtue – as a trait we are at fault for not cultivating. Indeed, Aristotle himself, while he classifies *phronēsis* as an intellectual virtue, still recognizes its special role in relation to virtues of character. He maintains that each moral virtue involves the exercise of *phronēsis* – the making of a sound judgement. And he distinguishes *phronēsis* from mere cleverness. You may be clever in the choices you make (being astute in finding appropriate means to achieve your goals) yet at the same time show disastrous lack of judgement (choosing goals which are of little worth). It might be thought that *judgement* is not involved in some virtues – say, in being honest or in being kind. And it is true that in many circumstances it is easy enough to know what is required if you mean to be honest or kind. But not always. Sometimes being honest requires a certain astuteness and finesse – as when you are trying to answer questions truthfully but without betraying important confidences. Likewise, your wish to be kind may explain why you respond to certain questions evasively. Yet your doing so may simply cause unnecessary distress, confusion and anxiety. Thus, lack of appropriate motivation is not the only thing that prevents people from being honest or kind. There is more to having a virtue than meaning well.

Foot observes that the kind of wisdom and understanding that *phronēsis* involves does not rely on high intelligence or special education: 'it implies no more knowledge and understanding than anyone of normal capacity can and should acquire in the course of an ordinary life'.[5] People who have this sort of wisdom, says Foot, 'make good decisions and they know, as we say, "what's what"'.[6] Hence, we can see how deficiencies in this matter manifest something blameable – it is a sort of wisdom that is 'available to anyone who really wants it'.[7] Not knowing some things suggests an indifference, a casualness, about matters we need to care about – for example, as car drivers, as fell walkers, as parents – if our lives are to go well.

Foot remarks on a difference between ancient moral philosophers and many moderns:

> of the four ancient cardinal virtues of justice, courage, temperance and wisdom, only the first now seems to belong wholly to 'morality'. The other three virtues are recognised as necessary for the practice of 'morality' but are now thought of as having part of their exercise 'outside morality' in 'self-regarding' pursuits, 'moral' and 'prudential' considerations being contrasted in a way that was alien to Plato and Aristotle.[8]

This might reflect a mere variation of usage of 'moral'. But Foot suggests that it reflects a substantial alteration of understanding – for the worse. 'That we tend to speak in moral philosophy only of volitional faults that impinge particularly on others gives the whole subject an objectionably rigoristic, prissy, moralistic tone that we would hardly take up in everyday life.'[9]

The value of acquiring virtues

Of course, the very project of distinguishing human virtues and vices cannot get off the ground unless it makes sense to generalize about what characteristics are advantageous in life and what are disadvantageous. But we can generalize in just this way about some traits. Individuals who are trustworthy, fair, courageous, wise, humane and industrious can be expected to fare better in the hurly-burly of day-to-day living than do those who are shiftless, cowardly, foolish, mean or lazy. Isn't this true whether the individuals we are speaking of happen to be young or old, male or female, rich or poor, in robust health or invalids, contemporary Britons or those to whom Aristotle gave his lectures in the Lyceum around 347BC?

While identifying certain traits as virtues or vices does imply that we can generalize about what are volitional strengths and defects of character, it does not imply that those who have virtues are bound to fare well in life, or that those who have vices are bound to fare ill. Aristotle makes no such claim. The idea is simply that certain traits, the virtues, are, as Rosalind Hursthouse puts it, 'the only reliable bet' for faring well.[10]

Don't we all, for instance, need to learn, if we can, to handle fear? If we understand by 'courage' a disposition to face the fearful things we need to face, acquiring it will involve developing both judgement and will-power. Having sound judgement and the resolve to act on it is obviously a strength of character, and is so whoever we are. It is not merely a virtue in communities where we are expected to do our turn of military service. There are all sorts of fearful situations that people have to learn how to handle – not just physical threats, such as are faced on battlefields, but threats of ridicule and humiliation such as may be faced by children in playgrounds or by medical and nursing students on ward rounds.

Just as everyone is subject to fear and needs to learn how to handle it, so too everyone is subject to anger and needs to learn how to handle that. Again, the virtue – let us call it 'well-temperedness' – which enables us to handle anger will involve both resolution and judgement: so that we are angry about the right things and in the right way – and for the right reasons.

While we have to assume that the qualities we define as moral virtues or vices are such that it is in our power (at least for a while, if not throughout our lives) to develop or avoid (otherwise, blame for failing to develop virtues would be out of order), we need not suppose that it is equally easy or difficult for all of us to do so. Nor need we suppose that acquiring these traits is a once and for all event. Acquiring a virtue may be a process that takes time, and losing it likewise. And although we do not count a trait as a moral virtue unless it seems to be pervasively relevant, that is not to say that some virtues are not more prominently tested in some roles and contexts than in others.

The philosopher G. E. Moore belittled his own honesty as something easy and unmeritorious. He was *never* tempted to act dishonestly, he said. But when he said this, it seems that he was thinking of honesty somewhat narrowly, as to do with not stealing. He, a Cambridge don, Fellow of Trinity College, being tolerably well-off and content with his material possessions, did not have to battle with covetousness or avarice. If honesty had to do only with temptations of that kind, it might seem to be a minor virtue, at best. But if we think of it as a more significant virtue, one that is pervasively relevant, we will think of how even well-healed and comfortably circumstanced academics must face situations where truthfulness (honesty in communication) is tested – where, for example, they may be tempted to lie to protect a colleague's feelings or to cover up their own embarrassing ignorance or forgetfulness.

Two problematic virtues

Come to that, though, by what right do we assume that honesty or truthfulness *is* a virtue in the first place? Is there not a difficulty in treating it alongside the virtues we have initially been looking at – courage and well-temperedness? Plato and Aristotle would both locate honesty under the heading of justice. Justice (*dikaiosunē*), as they understand it, also includes fairness and much else besides. Roughly speaking, it seems to cover what nowadays we would refer to as respecting one another's rights – what we owe one another by way of help or forbearance. It would include various general duties – like the duty not to murder and not to torture. Now is such a disposition (or set of dispositions) a strength of character that it is *personally* advantageous to acquire? The moral virtues are defined as traits that we each of us need for our own lives to go well. It is readily understandable how courage, patience and well-temperedness are generally advantageous in this way to those who have such traits – and how, conversely, being of a cowardly, impatient or ill-tempered disposition is an impediment to doing well in life. But justice?

And what about benevolence? Neither Plato nor Aristotle makes room for it (though Aristotle does rank friendship among the most important elements of a life worth living and does also include liberality in his list of virtues). But Christian ethics treats benevolence (charity) as of central importance, and though Aquinas treats it as a theological virtue (a trait, that is, which makes sense as a virtue only within the context of certain theological beliefs), contemporary philosophers seem confident that it belongs firmly on the list of virtues within their secular account of morality. Rosalind Hursthouse observes: 'Charity or benevolence . . . is not an Aristotelian virtue, but all virtue ethicists assume it is on the list now.'[11]

I will explore over the next two chapters some of the difficulties of incorporating justice and benevolence within the account of virtues so far sketched. Certainly, it bodes ill for our project of making sense of morality if we cannot accommodate these virtues. They seem pretty basic and central to most people's understanding of what morality is about: be kind to your neighbours, don't pull the cat's tail, don't rob the bank. An account of morality can hardly be taken seriously if it does not accommodate such judgements. Both virtues, moreover, seem pretty central to the issues of medical ethics. Isn't the ultimate aim of medical treatment to benefit people by attending to their health needs? And aren't many of the issues in medical ethics about how to further that benevolent aim while respecting people's rights?

2

Justice – A Problematic Virtue?

The virtues are strengths, the vices are weaknesses. Strength does not guarantee success, nor weakness failure. But anyone has reason to choose to be strong. The virtues are enabling, the vices are disabling. This, at any rate, seems a very intelligible account of the virtues. At least, so it appears if we think of three of the four cardinal virtues: prudence, courage and temperance. Plainly, these traits are characteristically advantageous to their possessor, as Aristotle's account makes clear. Anyone is better off being prudent if we mean by this, as does Aristotle, not some narrowly self-regarding circumspection but general sagaciousness in practical matters; better off being courageous, if by this we mean, as does Aristotle, not simply controlling fear but showing sound judgement in how we react to fearful situations: standing our ground just when that is necessary. Thus, Aristotle distinguishes courage not only from cowardice, but also from recklessness. Likewise, we are all personally better off being able to control our appetites in a well-judged way – hence, being temperate. It is very evident that these traits are enabling. Virtues, so understood, make the will good, in that they bestow beneficial strengths on the will.

So far, so good. Yet what about the other cardinal virtue, justice? We can hardly leave it out of account, especially as we are addressing issues in medical ethics: for it is going to be the virtue that concerns us most. Is *it* a strength? Is it a strength *in the same way* as are the other three? Plato writes as if this is indeed the case – in the following passage from his dialogue, *Crito* (47d) (my translation):

> Socrates: There is a part of us which is improved by healthy actions and ruined by unhealthy ones. If we spoil it by taking the advice of the

ignorant, will life be worth living when this part is once ruined? And that part is the body is it not?
Crito: Yes.
Socrates: Well, is life worth living with a body which is worn out and ruined in health?
Crito: Certainly not.
Socrates: What about that part of us which is injured by unjust actions and benefited by just actions? Is life worth living if this part is ruined? Or do we believe that this part of us, whatever it may be, which is concerned with the just and the unjust, is less important than the body?'
Crito: Certainly not.
Socrates: Is it really more important?
Crito: Much more.

What is going on in this passage is, perhaps, not altogether clear. But for us what is particularly interesting is the analogy implied between the harm we do ourselves if we neglect our bodily health and the harm we do ourselves if we neglect to act justly. Is the analogy sound?

As I have already suggested, justice has traditionally been thought to cover what we *owe* one another. This is what we get in Plato. Later, following in the same tradition when Roman law was formulated, the *Institutes of Justinian* sums up the precepts of justice, as 'to live honestly, to injure no one, and to give every man his due'.[1] To be of just character, then, will be to have that trait (or set of traits) that disposes and enables us to observe those rather general precepts. In our own time, Philippa Foot, following in this tradition, formulates justice as having 'to do with that to which someone has a right – that which he is owed in respect of non-interference and positive service'.[2] It is justice in this broad sense that is our subject here.

Being just, then, involves forgoing advantages – out of respect for others' rights, as we might nowadays say. It involves exercising self-restraint (for example, not using force or fraud to get what we want). Yet, on the face of it, restraints *reduce* our freedom; they inhibit us from using our strength. Virtues, as we have said, are supposed to be enabling. Justice, however, appears to be disabling. Philippa Foot points out the problem that seems to arise if we suppose justice to be a virtue on all fours with others. How are we to show that 'any man whatsoever must need to be just' in the same way as 'he needs the use of his hands and eyes, or needs prudence, courage and temperance'.[3] Of course, we see well enough that we are better off generally when people take care not to treat *us* unjustly: who wants to be robbed or raped? It is much less obvious, if it is even true, that we can expect to reap benefits ourselves by taking care that we do not treat others unjustly.

Notwithstanding the passage quoted above from the *Crito*, Plato shows elsewhere that he is alive to the difficulty of portraying justice as a strength to its possessor in the way that we are supposing the other virtues to be. As Thrasymachus, one of the parties to the discussion about justice in Plato's *Republic*, puts it: justice seems to be 'another man's good'.[4] That is to say, its status as a moral virtue of a piece with other virtues, such as, courage, patience and well-temperedness, is problematic.

Glaucon's challenge

Another party to the discussion, Glaucon, clarifies the thought behind Thrasymachus's observation, telling the story of a shepherd, Gyges, who happens to discover a ring with the magical property that enables the wearer of it to make himself invisible at will. The shepherd uses this ring to get himself included in a group of messengers sent to report to the royal palace. There he seduces the queen, and together they plot the murder of the king. Gyges then seizes the throne.

Glaucon invites Socrates to show, if he can, what mistake we are making, how we are being unwise, if, like Gyges, we act unjustly but secretly. Often the ill effects of our conduct are inescapable: we drink too much, we feel bad. The ill effects of acting unjustly, on the other hand, may sometimes seem to be easy enough to escape so long as we use cunning. If, for example, nobody knows that what we are divulging is a secret that we solemnly promised *never* to divulge, what danger or disadvantage do *we* suffer? Hence, the common thought: 'If God does not exist, everything is permitted'.

Glaucon suggests that justice, *as it is popularly conceived*, is not the sort of thing that it makes sense to pursue except under a kind of (externally imposed) necessity. In that case, nobody of sense should care about justice *for itself*. Glaucon compares how we value 'exercise and medical treatment and earning one's living as a doctor or otherwise. All these we should regard as painful but good for us; we should not choose them for their own sakes but for what we get out of them, wages or what not.'[5] Whereas it would be simply foolish not to take the medicines that restore or preserve our health, even if we could hide our non-compliance from our doctors and nurses, it is not at all obvious that Gyges is making some *mistake* if he supposes that he no longer has any reason to be just, since no one is going to find *him* out – except, of course, his new wife, who is now his willing accomplice.

Glaucon wants Socrates to show that, appearances notwithstanding, justice is a virtue, and character strengthening, no less than is courage. He would like Socrates to show that Gyges is in fact not acting smart at all; indeed, that he is being quite as foolish as we would think a person who only wanted to seem wise and not to be wise, or to seem healthy and not to be healthy. Thus, Glaucon believes that the common opinion fails to attach the right kind of importance to this virtue. He wants Socrates to give an account of justice that shows it to be needful for Gyges to possess, in the same way that courage remains needful, ring or no ring.

There are two ways in which Glaucon's challenge might be met. One way is to meet it head-on – which is what Socrates attempts in the *Republic*, arguing that being of unjust character is personally incapacitating; that it is a kind of weakness of character, of a piece with the weakness of those who lack control and judgement in regard to things fearful. The passage in the *Crito* seems to be conveying a message of this kind. The other way is to defend the common opinion about justice against Glaucon (and Socrates) at least in so far as it reveals that justice is *not* of a piece with virtues like courage. If we take the second way (as we shall), but still want to portray justice as a virtue, we have to loosen up our account of moral virtues to accommodate traits that are importantly different, though not so very different as to sever all connections with virtues like courage.

To my mind, the answer Socrates gives Glaucon is unpersuasive. Socrates appears to assume that people act unjustly only because they are *driven* to do so against their better judgement – hence, acting unjustly is a sign of weakness. And he further assumes that what drive people to act unjustly are exclusively lowly and worldly desires. Neither assumption is safe. People may choose to act unjustly in a cool hour when they are very much in command of themselves, and sometimes their motives are disinterested and high-minded.

Medical wrongdoings easily afford us examples of each. A team of clinical researchers may be tempted to 'improve' (falsify) their results, in order to secure further funding, not out of personal acquisitiveness, but merely out of concern to find a cure for a devastating illness. What tempts a nurse to falsify notes to cover up a colleague's error may be sympathy for the colleague who has acted untypically after an exceptionally long and stressful stint on duty. The nurse may realize that what she is up to, falsifying the notes, is a very risky undertaking, and not at all advantageous to her even if she is not found out. It is implausible to imagine in such a case that the nurse would be driven to do this – would not be able to help herself doing so.

Let us then consider how we might counter Glaucon's challenge the other way: by defending the common opinion – up to a point, anyway. We need, then, to explain how justice, though it is not important and necessary in quite the same way as other virtues, is nevertheless important and necessary in its own distinctive way, and is no less a virtue than they are.

Making sense of justice as a virtue

The clue to how justice is a virtue, even though it is not personally advantageous in the direct way we suppose other virtues to be, is to be found in another of Plato's dialogues, *Protagoras*, where we are given a whimsical account of the origin of justice. In this dialogue, Plato has Protagoras tell how when the gods created living creatures, they initially botched their fashioning of humans, leaving them so ill-equipped to fend for themselves that the species was in danger of becoming extinct. To remedy this, the gods first bestowed on humans intelligence, so that they could work out how to provide for themselves. That, however, proved to be inadequate. People could only defend themselves against beasts if they banded together into communities. But this they were unable to do; they were too quarrelsome. The gods, therefore, bestowed a further gift: 'respect for others and a sense of justice'.[6]

This fanciful story contains valuable insight into the kind of importance that justice has for us, collectively and individually. From the collective standpoint, it calls attention to how much social co-operation depends on people generally being committed to act as justice requires. From the individual standpoint, it calls attention to how each of us has a stake in social co-operation and, hence, in sustaining just practices.

David Hume's later, more prosaic explanation of how people would have come to see justice as a virtue seems in its essentials to be patterned on the Protagorean account.[7] And it is hard not to see something similar at work in what John Stuart Mill has to say about justice in chapter 5 of *Utilitarianism*.[8] These later accounts capture the insight in *Protagoras*: both how the social co-operation that is needed if we are to live together in peace and security rests on there being a general commitment to just ways of acting and how, individually, our living tolerably depends on there being conditions of peace and security.

Now the Protagorean account may explain clearly the usefulness of justice, but that is not by itself enough to answer the charge put by Thrasymachus: that justice is *merely* 'another man's good'. If justice were useful merely in *this* way, it would not be a human virtue. A gardener may see it is a virtue in the weeds that he is about to dig up that they have shallow roots. A thief may see it as a virtue in the lock he is about to pick that it is rusty. But human virtues, on our account, have to be strengths or excellences *for* their possessors. Does the Protagorean account of justice cast light on the way in which we personally are stronger if we keep to just ways?

David Hume claims that each individual who is committed to just ways of acting must 'find himself a gainer, on balancing the account; since, without justice, society must immediately dissolve, and every one must fall into that savage and solitary condition, which is infinitely worse than the worst situation that can possibly be supposed in society'.[9]

Recollecting the Gyges story, we might wonder, though, whether Hume is right to say that the individual *must* find himself 'the gainer' on balancing the account. We can hardly pretend that society is bound to dissolve if some people in it act unjustly. Nor is it obvious that those individuals who are prepared to seize opportunities to act unjustly are bound to lose more than they gain as a result. Harold Shipman, the Lancashire GP who quietly did away with a number of his elderly patients (at least 250, it is estimated[10]) who were in no way wanting to be 'helped' to die, did get caught, eventually, but who knows how many doctors and nurses have repeatedly abused their positions and escaped detection? Maybe Dr John Bodkin Adams was a case in point. Adams, a GP in Eastbourne in the 1940s, was arrested on suspicion of killing off a number of his elderly female patients who had left him something in their wills, e.g. canteens of silver, Rolls-Royces. Though he was eventually acquitted for lack of evidence, the suspicions persisted.[11] It has been mooted that Adams may have been a role model for Shipman: they did have a colleague in common.[12]

In other words, however indispensable and beneficial justice is to us collectively, being just is not necessarily always indispensable and beneficial to us individually. There is a striking difference to note between a virtue such as courage and the virtue of justice. With the latter, but not the former, there may be advantage in merely pretending to have the virtue. In that way you may enjoy the same benefits as do those who really are just, without paying the costs. There is, let us note, no similar gap to be marked between courage and the pretence to courage. What you need to cope with things fearful in life is the virtue, not the mere pretence to it. If you discover blood in your urine and know that you should have this investigated but are too scared to tell anyone, no one will realize you are a coward, but the consequence may be no less grim for you on that account. If, though, you have got your job or your research grant by lying about your qualifications and no one ever finds out, the consequences for you may be altogether agreeable.

All the same, while it is easy enough to call up examples of real-life Gyges types who act unjustly and prosper, what does that prove? Virtues and vices are dispositional traits, and in weighing up whether we do someone a benefit by encouraging them to acquire a certain character trait, we need to reflect on what traits are likely to be advantageous or disadvantageous to them, bearing in mind the uncertainties of life. Compare how someone goaded to give up smoking might protest: 'What about Bertrand Russell? He smoked continuously and he lived a vigorous life to the age of 98!' In providing moral education to the young, we need to consider *ex ante* what kind of characteristics a child needs to acquire in order to live well – what traits are the *best bet* for faring well in life. From that standpoint the Protagorean account of justice does support the idea that acquiring just ways is personally advantageous.

We have also to bear in mind that character traits cannot be put on and off to fit the circumstances of the day. It is not like deciding whether or not to take an umbrella when you go out – when you can accommodate yourself to the latest weather forecast. Thus, we can acknowledge *both* that acquiring just ways is personally advantageous in general *and* that there are situations where someone who has not acquired just ways is better off, is not acting irrationally, in acting unjustly. Suppose, for example, that you discover that you are terminally ill and have probably only a few months to live. In that case, you might, like Gyges with his ring, seize on the opportunity to act unjustly with impunity. And this you might do with high aims in view or with low: stealing money in order to 'redistribute' it or, rather, to hire a gun-man to kill someone you have always envied.

What may be gleaned from these considerations about the difference between justice and other virtues? There is a connection between being just and being personally better off. But it is not so tight and uniform a connection as that between being courageous or patient and being better off. We should, nevertheless, regard justice as a virtue, for the following reasons:

1 Each individual called on to be just has a personal stake in the success of the social teaching. The individual is not simply being exploited for the good of others.
2 Teaching children to be just *is* like teaching them to be courageous in so far as both teachings genuinely are in part for their *own* good.

Were that not so, it would simply be a cheat to describe justice as a virtue.

The central importance of justice

Given that human nature and circumstances are (always have been and surely always will be), as Hume says, deficient in certain ways that can only be remedied by the introduction of precepts of justice, justice is a universal human virtue. But notice that justice is, as so far defined, simply a device we need to govern our dealings with *one another*. The Protagorean account picks out our need to join together to defend ourselves from threats to our security and survival. This consideration may, though, be too narrow. Only think how immeasurably difficult life would be if there were no possibility of being able to rely on promises or the like in getting others to do as we want. Elizabeth Anscombe asks:

> What ways are there of getting human beings to do things? You can make a man fall over by pushing him; you cannot usefully make his hand write a letter or mix concrete by pushing . . . . You can order him to do what you want, and if you have authority he will perhaps obey you. Again if you have power to hurt him or help him according as he disregards or obeys your orders, or if he loves you so as to accord with your requests, you have a way of getting him to do things. However, few people have authority over everyone they need to get to do things, and few people either have power to hurt or help others without damage to themselves or command affection from others to such an extent as to be able to get them to do the things they need others to do.[13]

Maybe the standing needs, the interests, to which this passage calls our attention could be summed up as: our interests in being able to trust and be trusted. The Protagorean account should be modified, as it easily can be, to accommodate these wider needs beyond our basic need for security. I will, though, hereafter refer to the Protagorean-type account as the 'securitarian account', not meaning thereby to denigrate the relevance of the other needs that Anscombe describes.

A disturbing implication of the securitarian account

The need for security, together with the other needs mentioned in the passage above, all help to explain the kind of restraint we need to exercise towards one another in our daily dealings. The virtue protects us where we are vulnerable – where we need to have co-operation from others and cannot get it in some other way. In that case, then, is the virtue something that *only* arises among people who are relatively equal and who thus stand to benefit by being just with one another? Do duties of justice make sense only among those able to inflict harm on each other and able to benefit by agreeing not to do so? Do duties of justice arise only *within* a community – which, of course, may not be coextensive with the society or state in which it is located? The strength of our own community may even be menaced by the wider community, by the latter's laws and law-enforcers.

It seems that Hume does notice this implication. He writes:

> Were there a species of creatures intermingled with men, which, though rational, were possessed of such inferior strength, both of body and mind, that they were incapable of all resistance, and could never, upon the highest provocation, make us feel the effects of their resentment; the necessary consequence, I think, is that we should be bound by the laws of humanity to give gentle usage to these creatures, but should not, properly speaking, lie under any constraint of justice with regard to them, nor could they possess any right or property, exclusive of such arbitrary lords. Our intercourse with them could not be called society, which presupposes a degree of equality; but absolute command on the one side, and servile obedience on the other.[14]

This passage in Hume is reminiscent of the memorable declaration of Thomas Hobbes: 'Power irresistible justifieth all actions really and properly in whomsoever it be found. Lesser power does not.'[15] Imagine a being with absolute power. What reason could such a being have to forgo anything, to modify its actions, out of a concern for justice? That would be like someone using a crutch who does not need one. It would simply be irrational – a weakness of character, not a strength. Hume illustrates his point, about justice applying only among rough equals, with a comparison between ourselves and inferior beings. But the point would apply likewise if we were to compare ourselves with superior beings. If, for example, Martians were to visit our planet, would they have any reason to pay attention to justice in how they treated us? If they were not in the least vulnerable to us, how could it be a virtue, a strength, in them to act within the constraints of justice?[16]

Consider some of the implications of the securitarian account for issues in medical ethics. It would appear that certain categories of patients, such as infant patients, cannot be wronged. To be sure, doctors and nurses may still have *duties* regarding their welfare. Compare how you may have a duty to attend to the welfare of your neighbours' vegetable plants while they are away on holiday – because you have promised to do so. The duty is owed not to the plants, but to the neighbours. Yet this implication of the securitarian account contradicts something that is widely accepted as axiomatic about justice: the idea that there are certain general duties of justice that bind us no less towards the powerless than towards the powerful. No one supposes that raping and robbing are objectionable only if perpetrated against our rough equals. On the contrary, if the victim is very young or very old or a prisoner, the wrongfulness of the deed is magnified.[17]

The idea that all human beings are owed a kind of reverence, and that each owes this alike to each, regardless of their relative power, seems important and central to our understanding of justice. Yet the securitarian account does not explain it. If anything, it undermines it. And this is not just in theory. Theorizings about what we owe one another influence our practices – and especially in medical ethics, where the notion of justice plays such an important part. The idea that justice arises only among rough equals underlies some justifications of elective abortion, and indeed infanticide. We will explore further the idea that these kinds of killing are not essentially unjust in chapter 10.

The securitarian account of justice, then, helps us to makes some sense of how justice is a virtue. There must be something right about it. But it fails to explain what we take to be the scope of these duties. It fails to explain how we can have such duties towards people who are far away, people whose co-operation we do not need. It fails to explain why we have duties to people near at hand if we can get what we want from or with them without gaining their consent. This failure indicates that our understanding of justice is seriously deficient. Here, as elsewhere, it seems that we know more than we understand. While we strive for better understanding, we meanwhile need to be cautious in how we apply our limited understanding in debating the issues in medical ethics.

Virtues, rules and duties

Contemporary discussions of 'virtue ethics' quite often claim that this approach does not tell us what we *must* do (what is obligatory), but rather only what it is *fine* or *good* to do. This complaint invites us to draw a false dichotomy. An account of virtues will cover both attention to what is fine and attention to what is obligatory. How else can we begin to give an account of the virtue of justice without spelling out rules that must be observed – typically, rules that lay down what we must *not* do? Those who are honest do not lie. They deal fairly. Their word can be trusted. They are mindful of what they owe others. We are not here assuming that the rules of justice do not incorporate exceptions. Maybe some of them do, and some of them do not. Being just, in short, involves a commitment to rules; though it does not involve only that; for it is part of the virtue that you not only care to be just but also care in some degree that others are treated justly. Contrast what is involved in being courageous, temperate or generous. Those who have these traits also behave in predictable ways – but not by being mindful of certain rules. This is one way in which justice stands apart from these other virtues.

It is useful to label virtues that are characteristically more obviously and prominently strengths to oneself (like patience or well-temperedness) as *personal* and those that are characteristically more obviously and prominently strengths to one's community (like justice) as *social*. The categories are overlapping. But suppose that a particular character trait turned out to be merely social – advantageous *only* to the community, and not, except maybe incidentally, advantageous to its possessor. In that case it would not *be* a human virtue. This seems to be the gist of Glaucon's worry about the usual accounts of justice. He sees that these render its status as a (personal) virtue on all fours with the other cardinal (human) virtues problematic.

We need to be attentive to the differences among the virtues: each human virtue, by definition, must be a trait that is valuable for our personal living well and faring well. But they may be valuable in quite different ways. Justice considered alongside courage or temperateness looks problematic as a human virtue, though less so when we consider its distinctive role as a social virtue *in which we each individually may have a personal stake*. In the next chapter we will consider another candidate for the category of social virtues: benevolence. Is it merely a social virtue?

3

Benevolence – A Problematic Virtue?

Nowadays, benevolence is generally agreed to be at least one of the moral virtues, if not, the most important of them.[1] Yet, as we have already remarked in chapter 1, while benevolence does *not* seem to feature among the virtues mentioned by Plato or Aristotle, charity is a Christian virtue – famously given pre-eminence by St Paul: 'For now abideth faith, hope and charity, these three; but the greatest of these is charity' (1 Corinthians 13: 11), and he adds that, if I 'have not charity, I am nothing' (13: 2). Maybe, though, what St Paul had in mind by 'charity' is not quite what people nowadays would take it to mean. According to the *Oxford Dictionary of the Christian Church*, charity is a 'theological virtue': 'it is directed primarily towards God; but is also owed to ourselves and our neighbours as the objects of God's love'. But can it be made sense of as a secular virtue? Peter Geach thinks not: 'love of men that does not flow from love of God may be an agreeable thing enough, but it is only part of the fashion of this world that passes away, and we should not overvalue it'.[2]

Hume, on the other hand, seems to see no difficulty in making a case for benevolence as a secular virtue. He portrays it as a trait that is agreeable and useful both to its possessor and to others – which is to say, that it is to be counted as both a personal and a social virtue. Benevolence and its kindred virtues, says Hume, 'keep us in humour with ourselves as well as others'.[3] 'What other passion is there', he asks, 'where we shall find so many advantages united: an agreeable sentiment, a pleasing consciousness, a good reputation?'[4]

But perhaps what Hume has in mind here as 'benevolence' is not quite the same trait as that to which St Paul is alluding. For sure, there is a trait (or cluster of traits) that is undeniably useful and agreeable from a wholly secular standpoint and that one might have in mind in commending amiability as a trait worth acquiring. To be the sort of person who is empathetic, companionable, affable, friendly – a good mixer – is obviously advantageous in all sorts of ways. Maybe this is what Geach has in mind as 'the love of men that does not flow from love of God'. At any rate, it does not seem tied necessarily to the kinds of concern commonly associated nowadays with Christian charity – concerns for the world's poor. You might be an excellent mixer, good at putting people at their ease, a good listener, responsive, affable (that sort of thing), yet not be much exercised about the plight of the (materially or spiritually) poor in the world at large. You might teach your children the importance of being friendly and considerate – learning the companionable traits, the social graces – without bringing the world's poor into the picture at all.

If being affable, clubbable, etc. is the sort of thing that Peter Geach has in mind as the secular analogue to charity, it is not so startling that he dismisses such a trait as merely 'an agreeable thing'. It might be a minor virtue at best – overlapping perhaps at some points a virtue that Aristotle does make room for: liberality (being generous with one's wealth, not being mean or tight-fisted).[5] We might even question whether it is any virtue and not rather a matter of social skills – 'people skills'. Iago was not lacking in such skills – but he was utterly heartless. We would hardly count these skills of his as morally redeeming aspects of his character. Nor would we in the case of the aforementioned serial killer, Dr Harold Shipman, who was said to have an excellent bedside manner.

Benevolence as kindness

Maybe, though, it is not so much 'amiability' that Hume has in mind, as 'kindness'. Kindness is surely something apart from mere amiability. And shouldn't it not only be ranked among the virtues but be singled out as among the most important? 'It is the history of our kindness that alone makes this world tolerable', wrote Robert Louis Stevenson. If what Stevenson meant was that without kindness the world would be intolerable, that may well be true. If, though, he meant, more extravagantly, that provided there was kindness, nothing else was needed to make the world tolerable, we should not agree with him. Have we not already established that justice is needed? And justice sometimes imposes limits on kindly acts.[6]

Hume points out that not only can the act that justice requires of us on occasion stand in the way of our doing some good, the act may predictably be of no benefit to anyone – even do some harm. He instances being obliged to restore a 'great fortune to a miser, or a seditious bigot'.[7] Yet, he claims, unless people are generally prepared to keep to just ways without calculating on each particular occasion what they or others stand to gain by it, the overall benefits of justice cannot be had: 'But however a single act of justice may be contrary, either to public or private interest, 'tis certain, that the whole plan or scheme is highly conducive, or indeed absolutely requisite, both to the support of society, and the well-being of every individual. 'Tis impossible to separate the good from the ill.'[8] Kindness, then, seems not to be the only virtue. It is sometimes kept in check by another. But we will revisit the possibility that it is, after all, the only virtue in the next chapter.

Meanwhile, how might we establish that kindness is at least *a* virtue, one of the traits we need, though by no means the only one? I have already argued that justice is a virtue – that we need to be just, to live co-operatively and in peace. But is justice a virtue that could survive on its own, unsupplemented by kindness? Kindness implies an empathy with others, sharing in their joys and sorrows. Those who acquire this trait show it not only by their deeds but also by their sentiments: for example, their 'generosity in judging the motives and meanings of other men', which, as Geach says, 'pays off in increased mutual understanding' between neighbours.[9]

Imagine a world in which everyone acts as justice requires – never murdering, never lying or cheating: is such a world possible in the absence of cordiality, friendship and affection? Gratitude seems to be something that is owed as part of justice *and* that involves recognizing, appreciating and responding to kindness. But how are we to learn to give or receive affection if we are devoid of kindness? In short, if justice is a virtue, and if acquiring and sustaining this trait is difficult, maybe not even possible, without also acquiring some kindness, then kindness too is a virtue.

Admittedly, in particular situations kindness may *seem* to tug us in the opposite direction from that which justice dictates. Only 'seems', though, since if kindness is a virtue, it will *not* require us to act unjustly. Kindness does not require that I lie optimistically to my students who come seeking advice and support about their prospects. However, if I am a kindly person, I may regret that sometimes I cannot truthfully respond more encouragingly. Sometimes, to be sure, we may rightly break our promises from some kindly motive. But this is not to say that we must, then, be putting kindness before justice (acting unjustly from a kindly motive). Promises are not always binding. A kindly concern could well justify the breaking of a particular promise, rendering our doing so not unjust.

The basis just offered for counting benevolence among the virtues – viz. that it is supportive of the virtue of justice – only renders benevolence unproblematic in so far as justice is. As I have noted, the securitarian account of justice, on which I have drawn, limits our duties of justice to members of our own community (or anyway to those with whom we need to have dealings). Consequently, this justification for counting benevolence among the virtues, as supportive of justice, may be similarly limited in its scope. It might less misleadingly be described as a virtue of neighbourliness.

Beyond duty

There is, however, another way in which we may see benevolence as a virtue which stands on its own and is not merely a necessary prop to justice. Those who have this trait are ready on occasion to go beyond duty. That kind of readiness is something on which much social good hangs. It also seems in some way of benefit to those who are so minded. We admire those who go beyond duty. We do not suppose they lack good sense or are weak-willed.

How, though, should we distinguish what we are duty-bound to do from what is praiseworthy but beyond duty (supererogatory)? Can it be reasonable to *require* people to face great risks to themselves above and beyond the normal call of duty? If people have acted heroically, and then say that they were only doing their duty, must they be mistaken? Let us consider how to answer these questions in the light of the following two cases.

Dr Matthew Lukwiya was a young and very able doctor who could have had a lucrative practice abroad but chose instead to settle in Gulu in northern Uganda and to stay on there to care for patients when an epidemic of Ebola broke out. The risks of so doing were extreme, as he very well knew, since the disease is highly infectious, particularly for those attempting hands-on care of the afflicted. Dr Lukwiya became the 156th recorded victim of Ebola after becoming infected while tending a dying colleague. But without his presence in the hospital and the protective measures he introduced to try to prevent staff from becoming infected, many more people would have died.

His widow said: 'I don't think he would regret this. He knew the risk. He saw what was needed for his patients and he did it. That was him.'

Dr Carlo Urbani was an infectious disease specialist in the World Health Organisation. While he was based in Hanoi, he was asked to advise on a case of suspected atypical pneumonia in an American businessman who had been admitted to hospital there. He realized the severity of the symptoms and the threat of epidemic. He advised hospital staff about protective measures (patient isolation, high-filter masks, double-gowning) that were not routine measures in Vietnam. Thanks to his action, the epidemic was contained in Vietnam, and the World Health Organisation was alerted to the problem of SARS. He, though, having been in daily close contact with SARS patients, caught the infection and died.

A few days before he fell ill, his wife remonstrated with him over the risks he was taking. He said: 'If I cannot work in such situations, what am I here for – answering emails, going to cocktail parties and pushing paper?' He was 47.

Were these two doctors doing no more than their duty, or did they go beyond duty? It is, of course, quite usual for people who act heroically and survive to *say*, self-depreciatingly, that 'they were only doing their duty' – what they 'had' to do. But we don't have to agree that they were merely doing their duty. It would, after all, have been quite easy for either doctor to have retreated from the extreme dangers that developed, without breach of duty. This seems especially obvious in the case of Urbani, who was not himself even on the staff of the hospital where the epidemic occurred. He went in to advise on a particular case. When he realized the dangers, he need not have returned to the scene, day after day.

While these two examples of going beyond duty involve heroism, there are many instances of going beyond duty that do not. Heroism suggests facing peril. It requires courage. Some people, however, give a service or pursue a cause in a way that is beyond duty. They show remarkable commitment, selflessness and humanity in how they pursue their work. But what they do may not particularly call for courage. Their work may not expose them to dangers above and beyond the usual. Many people who do voluntary work of one kind or another show this sort of dedication.

Is heroism, by definition, beyond duty? How, after all, can it be reasonable to *require* people to show exceptional courage? Isn't exceptional courage exactly what we mean by 'heroic'? Yet we traditionally honour war heroes who died 'doing their duty' – which goes to show that in some circumstances people are, after all, expected and required to act heroically. Indeed, even the minimal demands of justice may on occasion require heroic sacrifice. At least, this will be so if there are some types of actions (for example, assisting in a massacre, torturing a prisoner) that it would be wrong (unjust) to do no matter what threat or inducement is presented.

4

Benevolence – The Only Virtue?

Let us return now to the idea that, contrary to what Hume and others suppose, benevolence (kindness) might, after all, be the whole of morality. John Stuart Mill singles out benevolence as the most important virtue: 'In the golden rule of Jesus of Nazareth, we read the complete spirit of the ethics of utility. To do as one would be done by, and to love one's neighbour as oneself, constitute the ideal perfection of utilitarian morality.'[1] Evidently Mill himself takes 'neighbour' to mean everyone – perhaps, as people nowadays say, 'all sentient beings'. Arguably, its intended scope as it occurs in the parable of the Good Samaritan, is more modest. That parable might be construed to suggest no more than that we ought to come to the aid of anyone in our proximity in need of succour – not that we ought to actively scour the world for individuals in need of succour, let alone that we ought to bestow kindnesses upon others who are not even in need of succour, who are already doing nicely, though we might be able to improve their situations still more.

The very aim of morality, according to utilitarianism (in its classical form) is to produce the best state of affairs one can: 'the best' being that which contains the greatest net aggregate of happiness or pleasure or satisfaction of desires.[2] On this view, benevolence, which directly motivates us to alleviate suffering and promote happiness, would appear to be the fundamental virtue. Other dispositions may count as derivative (not basic) virtues just in so far as they equip us to exercise our benevolence more effectively: if we are to do good – that is, make others happy – we need to learn how to control our tempers, our fears, our lethargy and so on.

If there is ultimately just one basic virtue, benevolence, from which all other virtues derive, the problem of reconciling one virtue with another does not arise. If morality is all about 'doing good', maximizing utility, then we would seem to have a common measure to apply when choosing what to do. From the standpoint of ethics, the right (required) choice will always be that which promises to yield the best consequences – the most beneficent.

There are many thoughtful and sophisticated defences of utilitarianism in its different versions. It is not to my purpose here to delve into these. I will just mention briefly three of the most common objections, and then pass on to discuss one further objection which seems to me to tell against all versions.

Three common objections to utilitarianism

First, in so far as utilitarianism is concerned with bringing about the greatest net aggregate of happiness, *how* that is distributed among individuals is of no direct concern. Applying the utility test to options available to us, it might turn out that morality requires that we do awful things to a few in order to benefit the many. For example, by selecting a few people and forcing them to serve as human guinea pigs, we might discover cures for cancers and thus prevent many people falling victim to these diseases. And subjecting the few to something awful would be obligatory even if the net benefit was modest. For example, producing a slightly better cosmetic might please a million people just a little and be judged 'worth' the loss of someone's life. From a utilitarian standpoint, whether sacrificing the few to benefit the many is not only permissible, but may be morally obligatory, is *simply* a matter of doing the sums: weighing the benefits (how much to how many) against the harms, and comparing the results with any alternative strategies that are available.

Second, utilitarianism requires that we do *whatever* will yield the best outcome. The 'whatever' could mean doing something quite vile if that is the only way to prevent others doing more equally vile things. Suppose, for example, we have captured a terrorist and know that he (or, of course, could be a she nowadays) is involved in a murderous plot. In order to extract information in time to foil this plot, we might find it 'necessary' to torture the terrorist's innocent child in front of him. A utilitarian would not rule out such a strategy as unconscionable. Indeed, is there any room in the utilitarian understanding of morality for the notion of some kinds of deeds being unconscionable?

Third, utilitarianism seems to be demanding in a way that is not just excessive but absurd, even risible. Admittedly, there is no reason to assume that morality does not sometimes make heavy demands on people. It surely does. If your child suffers a devastating illness or injury, you may have to give up many things dear to you – maybe for good. But utilitarianism seems to assume that *everything* you do or omit to do demands a justification: whether it is the best thing you can do, the most productive of good.

If the duty to do what is best for their patients dogs every step of doctors and nurses, choices that are widely presumed to be innocent turn out to be morally dubious. Consider, for example, those health professionals who choose to work part-time or to take early retirement. Of course, they might have impeccable excuses: the nurse who works part-time so that she can look after a frail elderly parent; the doctor who takes early retirement in order to have more time for political campaigning to improve the public health service. But are excuses needed? Suppose that a consultant chooses to work part-time in order to have more time for his fishing. Does this require an excusing reason? If you are a doctor or a nurse, do you have to defend any choice that makes inroads on your availability to patients (like the choice to marry or have children) by appeal to some other overriding duty?

Now those who think of morality as something that sets forth mandatory open-ended aims may seek to accommodate this point about our liberty to pursue our own personal aims and projects by making this out to be just another duty (a duty of self-development?) that can compete with and sometimes override our professional or other duties. We might 'justify' our being idle, saying that everyone needs to *rest* sometimes. But why suppose that any justification is called for – that every moment of our life is to be accounted for in relation to the aim of morality? Why suppose that 'morality' has an aim? If it does have an aim, how are we to explain its importance – why we have good, even decisive, reason to further it?

Does moral teaching, properly understood, have some unitary goal?

This suggestion that morality is to be seen as aiming to achieve some overarching goal brings us to another objection that has been levied against utilitarianism – by Philippa Foot.[3] As we have said, the three objections to utilitarianism listed above have been in circulation for a long time, and defenders of utilitarianism have contrived to answer them by developing ever more sophisticated versions of the theory. Foot's more recent objection both casts light on why the theory seems 'uniquely rational and therefore irresistible' and why, all the same, it is mistaken.

Foot introduces this objection, saying: 'I want to suggest that what is most radically wrong with utilitarianism is its consequentialism. But I also want to suggest that its consequentialist element is one of the main reasons why utilitarianism seems so compelling.'[4] She proceeds to explain how she is using the term 'consequentialist':

> Consequentialism in its most general form says simply it is by its 'total outcome', that is, by the whole formed by an action and its consequences, that what is done is judged right or wrong. A consequentialist theory of ethics is one which identifies certain states of affairs as good states of affairs and says that the rightness or goodness of actions (or other subjects of moral judgement) consists in their positive productive relationship to these states of affairs.[5]

The (only) 'right action' is that which answers to the (alleged) aim of morality, the action which will yield the best outcome – the best state of affairs. Utilitarianism is a form of consequentialism. As usually defined, it consists of consequentialism together with the identification of the best state as that which yields the most happiness, pleasure or satisfaction of desires.

What makes consequentialism so compelling, what beguiles us into thinking that it is the only rational morality is, in the words of Samuel Scheffler, its very 'simple and seductive idea: namely that so far as morality is concerned, what people ought to do is to minimize evil and maximize good, to try in other words to make the world as good a place as possible'.[6] As he goes on to observe, 'this idea, which lies at the heart of consequentialism, seems hard to resist'. Those who do resist appear to be 'committed to the claim that morality tells us to do less good than we are in a position to do, and to prevent less evil than we are in a position to prevent'.[7] This is precisely the cause that Foot has identified to account for the 'spell' cast by consequentialism. It is tied up, she says, with the 'rather simple thought that it can never be right to prefer a worse state of affairs to a better'.[8]

Foot proceeds to argue that the notions of 'good (or "best") outcome' and 'good (or "best") state of affairs' are problematic *as used by consequentialists*. Comparing human actions, and asking if this action is better or worse than that, does not make sense unless we locate our question within some sub-variety of good. As Judith Jarvis Thomson has, later, put this thought: goodness is always 'goodness in a way. When it is asked whether a thing is good – whether the thing is a book or a pie tin, or a person or an event – the context, or the speaker, needs to let us in on what the relevant way of being good is, or we not only can't answer the question, we don't even know what question was asked.'[9] Thus, for example, an amputation of a leg might be well done from a technical standpoint, but ill done from the standpoint of what is beneficial (as, for example, if the surgeon accidentally cuts off the wrong leg). Generally, when we speak of good or bad states of affairs, the context indicates the relevant sub-variety or standpoint from which we are judging: hence, what sort of interests or whose interests are relevant. Is a good casualty officer a wall or a sieve? Minus any reference to a sub-variety, or to what is in some party's interests, or what some party is interested in, how can a judgement of good or bad, better or worse, be made? It is like being hailed by a motorist at a roundabout and being asked which is the best road to take. Don't we need to know first where the enquirer is trying to get to?

Now it is common ground between consequentialists and many of their critics that doing good to others in the sense of serving their welfare is part of morality, is the aim of one of the virtues. But 'the fact that benevolence is a virtue which dictates attachment to the good of others, does not . . . give morality a universal end or goal'.[10] There is a danger here, Foot points out, that the critics of consequentialism will 'unwittingly accept its key idea', falling in with the notion that morality is nothing other than 'a device for achieving a shared end' – the general good. If, when consequentialists speak of 'the general good', they mean by this simply the general welfare which is the aim of benevolence, what they postulate is an intelligible goal. But what does it mean to say that it is the goal of morality itself? Those who believe that morality has also to do with other ends *and concerns* should not go along with the assumption that 'the general good' is the aim of morality itself. Nor should they seek some other more comprehensive aim to put in its stead – as if there has to be *some* end to which all defensible action must aspire.[11]

The very idea that it makes sense to speak of what is 'good from a moral point of view', that there is any such viewpoint, is what needs challenging here. Foot compares the oddity of asking what is 'good from a legal point of view' or what is 'good from the point of view of etiquette'. Doubting that there are these goal-focused viewpoints does not imply that law and etiquette are not useful and important. But it somehow shows incomprehension of how they are useful and important, the part they play in our affairs, to ask such questions. If morality were some kind of goal-directed pursuit, then it would make sense to ask what are the right (appropriate) courses to follow in relation to its aim. But while there are aims within morality (attaching to some virtues), there is no reason to suppose that these are all united in some shared goal.[12]

Beauchamp and Childress on beneficence

Part of the appeal of Beauchamp and Childress's 'principles' approach to biomedical ethics, as was mentioned in the Introduction (pp. 3–4), is that it appears to spare us the need to get involved in theoretical wranglings between utilitarians and their critics. The principles are supposed to be common ground – ground we would reach whatever theory we might happen to favour as our starting point. But is their principles approach as neutral as they suppose? Does it not succumb to what Foot calls the 'key idea' of consequentialism?

This is not immediately obvious, since Beauchamp and Childress do not rank the principle of beneficence above the other principles they single out as collectively providing a framework for ethical decision making in the context of health care issues. Alongside beneficence, they identify other aims of morality: not to set back interests, to respect autonomy, and to be fair. The duties relating to each of the principles which underpin these aims, they say, are *prima facie* binding. That is to say: you are obliged to act in accordance with all four unless there is a conflict that forces you to make a choice – in which case you must decide which principle in the particular circumstances has more weight and should override the other. Thus, for example, the principle of beneficence obliges you to do what is best for your patient's health-related interests unless you are prevented by another of the principles which turns out to be overriding in the particular circumstances.

But in terms of *what* is the weighing of conflicting, independent principles to be done? In terms of what good or value? Moral good or value, presumably. But what is *that*, and how do the distinct principles (or duties to which they relate) contribute to it? Why even suppose that there is such a thing as 'the good' to which respecting autonomy, being fair, and promoting welfare each in its different way contributes? Doesn't this supposition make out morality to be some kind of goal-directed pursuit – a pursuit aimed at maximizing 'the general good'? In other words, it is the consequentialist's picture of morality. Beauchamp and Childress introduce their discussion of utilitarianism, remarking how 'At first sight, utilitarianism seems entirely compelling. Who would deny that agents should minimize evil and increase positive value?'[13] Their own proposal that *prima facie* duties are to be weighed and balanced falls in with the idea that all these duties are somehow commensurable – are part of the fundamental duty of morality: to increase 'positive value'. But just what is this 'positive value'?

Are there, though, versions of consequentialism that do not assume that all goods can be ranked on some common scale? Am I perhaps foisting on Beauchamp and Childress too literal a view of what their 'weighing' of duties amounts to? Martha Nussbaum singles out certain contemporary consequentialists whom she dubs the 'sensible consequentialists'.[14] They are not committed to the idea that all goods are commensurable. They do not treat goodness as some common property shared by all things we call good. They maintain that different goods may be comparable, though they are not measurable in terms of any single standard. A consequentialist of this stamp does not say: 'Select from the choices open to you that than which there is none better!', but 'Select from the choices open to you any one that is not worse!' The thought here is that it may be evident to you that some choices would be worse, but not the case that you suppose that among those left over one is uniquely better, or indeed that any kind of ranking of these makes sense.

Nussbaum illustrates how this might work with the following example. 'Let us say that I have a hundred dollars. I can (a) give it to a needy friend; or (b) give it to Oxfam; or (c) flush it down the toilet; or (d) buy myself a luxurious dinner.'[15] She maintains that the sensible consequentialist might well argue in such a case that while it is not possible to rank (a) against (b), both options are 'clearly superior to (c) and almost certainly to (d) as well'. Sensible consequentialists in this case need not think that (a) and (b) tie in being equally good. Rather, they may regard these options as too different in kind for it to make sense to attempt to rank one against the other.

How, though, asks Judith Jarvis Thomson,[16] is the sensible consequentialist to do the ranking of (a) and (b) over (c) and (d) except by singling out some *way* in which the former options are better than the latter? If the former are better, hasn't that got to be better *in some way*? In other words, it just does not make sense to make evaluative comparisons, to rank options, for example, except *in respect of* some feature or other.

There is something else to notice about the Beauchamp and Childress account of duties of beneficence as *prima facie* duties. On this account, doctors are obligated to act beneficently whenever opportunity arises, except where another duty overrides this one. Suppose that after you have finished your surgery for the day, you stop off on your way home to call on an elderly, recently widowed patient.

The patient has not requested a visit, and you have no reason to suppose that there is a medical need for it. But you know this patient is lonely and would welcome your call. So described, your call is a kindly act. But is it also a duty? Is it morally required that you pay this call unless you have some other overriding duty to attend to? Or suppose that after finishing your surgery for the day, you relax over a beer. On the Beauchamp and Childress account you need an excuse for doing this – indeed, the excuse that you have an overriding duty to have the beer. Otherwise, you would be obliged to get busy benevolently sweeping the pub floor, or something of the kind. People who have not been got at by philosophers do not think of morality as ubiquitously demanding in this way. They do not assume that morality has some unitary objective towards which all moral choices are journeying, so that any pause *en route* calls for an explanation. Yet Beauchamp and Childress claim 'common morality' (morality, we may presume, untainted by philosophy) to be their touchstone.

If benevolence (or at any rate, neighbourliness) is a virtue, everyone ought to be benevolent. It does not follow, though, that benevolence imposes or 'dictates' duties anymore than courage or generosity do. Not every 'ought' implies a duty. If you discover blood in your urine, you ought to have the courage to go to the doctor. It does not follow that you have a duty to do so. Where your failure to help someone in need *is* a failure of duty is precisely where help is owed as a matter of justice, maybe because of specific undertakings you have made or because of a special relationship in which you happen to stand to the one needing help (it is your own grandmother; you are the only witness), or because you are in some way responsible for the predicament of the one needing help. In each case, the duty is owed as a matter of justice, not benevolence.

How to proceed?

I said at the outset that it would be worth our while to reflect initially on virtues and vices before launching into discussion of ethics in medicine. Already we should see some pay-off. Many discussions of ethics in medicine begin badly. They start out as if it makes sense to be asking, 'What is the right thing to do?' It is assumed that ethical theory does or should provide the answer. Our reflections on the virtues should help us to see that this way of thinking is unsound. It no more makes sense to assume that there is always or even generally a morally right thing to do than it does to assume that there is always or even generally a legally right thing to do. Let us suppose that at this moment you are alone, sitting by your fire, drinking a cup of tea and reading this book. Ask yourself: is this what the law requires you to be doing at this moment? Isn't that a strange question? Why suppose that the law has anything to say to you just now? And if it does not, we do not suppose the law to be somehow deficient or incomplete. So too, we should not assume that it always makes sense to be asking what is the morally right thing for us to be doing.

In regard to virtues and vices, the question 'What is the right thing to do?' does not arise. Acting justly is not 'doing the right thing' but simply not doing what is wrong – which characteristically allows us a range of choices – whatever is permissible. We may presume that your sitting by the fire drinking tea and reading this book is a permissible choice. For sure, there is more to being just than avoiding acting wrongly. There is also, as I have mentioned, the concern that people are not treated unjustly by others. It is a mistake to suppose, though, that you do not have this concern unless you suppose yourself obliged to prevent injustice wherever possible.

Having rejected utilitarianism in its various guises, then, we are not going to be seeking out some alternative device, some theory or big idea to enable us *to find out what to do*. We shall instead be asking whether this or that practice or policy is right or wrong – 'right' here meaning not 'the right practice' or 'the right policy', but a practice or policy that is *all* right (permissible). That is to say, our focus hereafter will be pretty much fixed on one virtue – justice. If we can shed light on what is and what is not wrongful treatment in the context of health care, we will have achieved something useful. But the way ahead will not be easy. Justice is no easy virtue to handle. It is many-faceted, and even in our brief discussion of it in chapter 2 we ran into big difficulties over how to explain the scope we suppose it has – difficulties we could not entirely resolve.

Is it not, though, outrageously *narrow* to suggest that we can usefully explore the issues of medical ethics with our focus mainly on justice? I think not, bearing in mind, of course, what I have taken justice to be – that I am by no means taking it to be merely a matter of fair shares, or of obeying the law, or of keeping to the terms of contracts. Justice in my sense is not a narrow notion at all.

Even so, it may be said that something is missing if we focus only on justice – because there is more to being a good doctor or nurse than simply avoiding doing wrong. That is most certainly true. Anyone who has been a patient or has been close to someone who has been seriously ill, is well aware of how many other important qualities play a part in being a good doctor or nurse – such as having sensitivity, friendliness, communication skills, a sense of humour, as well, of course, as having good sense and medical or nursing competence.

All the same, precious as *all* these qualities are, people are not going to gain insights into how to acquire them or apply them from books written by philosophers – maybe not from *any* books, aside possibly from works of fiction. They will certainly not get them from *this* book. Presumably, medical and nursing competencies can only be taught by those who have them. As for the other items in our list, these valuable qualities are perhaps not so much taught as absorbed, and largely from example – from meeting and working alongside experienced doctors and nurses who have unusual flair and humanity in all sorts of different ways. In any case, appreciating the importance of these and other such qualities should not distract us from paying attention to the singular importance of justice. In a way, what justice requires of us is minimal, but it is also indispensable. Justice is the essential core of ethics in medicine. A good doctor or nurse will not wrong anyone.

5

The Dictates of Conscience

It is widely assumed to be a hallmark of civilized society that we exercise tolerance towards people with whom we disagree deeply on moral or religious matters. And it might seem to be a minimal and entirely reasonable exercise of this tolerance that we find ways to avoid forcing people to disobey the dictates of their consciences. It is in this spirit that some provision has been made for conscientious objectors in times of war. Since deep disagreements on moral matters can arise elsewhere, it stands to reason that other kinds of conscientious objectors may need accommodating too. A case in point is the medical profession. If a controversial medical procedure becomes lawful, provision may be made for conscientious objectors within the profession. The usual accommodating solution that is adopted here is 'referral': the doctor who has an objection to a practice is supposed to refer the patient to a colleague who does not share it.

This gives rise to various questions. Is referral a suitable form of accommodation; a fair and honourable compromise on both sides? And if doctors who have a conscientious objection to a treatment that is available should be allowed to decline to assist on conscientious grounds, what about other people who may be called upon to assist in one way or another? Should not only nurses, but also anaesthetists, pharmacists, doctors' secretaries, and hospital porters, etc., be allowed to refuse to assist? Or, should neither doctors nor any of these others be allowed to refer? Is referral unfair to those who do not use this escape route from providing treatments which, however necessary and proper, no one likes being involved in carrying out?

More generally, do people have a right to act as their consciences permit or dictate? Are there times when we ought to try to persuade someone that their conscience is mistaken? Are there times when we should try to coax someone out of acting as their conscience dictates? Why, anyway, is any 'respect' owed to beliefs, however sincere, if they are based on ignorance, prejudice or muddled thinking? Does 'respecting people's beliefs' in this context mean, not that the beliefs themselves deserve respect, but that those who hold them should be allowed to make treatment choices in the light of them none the less? We may even raise a doubt as to the admirability of tolerance. Whether being tolerant is, after all, such a hallmark of civilization might rather depend on what the moral or religious views we see fit to tolerate are, and on what our being 'tolerant' implies.

I will try to go some way towards addressing this doubt and answering these questions, though there are bound to be loose ends and problems touched on that remain unresolved.

What is a 'judgement of conscience'?

Let us here understand 'judgements of conscience' to consist of our judgements as to 'right and wrong' – that is, as to what is just (morally permissible) and what is unjust. People talk of conscience as if it were an independent agent – a guardian angel, as it were, sitting on our shoulders, who speaks to us, issues orders, and scolds and punishes us when we disobey. This not-too-serious manner of speaking does not necessarily derive from theistic beliefs. The idea that the soul has parts, and that one of them is 'commanding' and is not always obeyed, though it should be, is as old as Plato. And in everyday life, we talk of ourselves as acting 'against our better judgement'. Or we say that our head says this and our heart says that. Still, these fancies aside, we shall take the agent which makes judgements of conscience to be simply ourselves.

People often suppose that judgements of conscience are based on 'feeling': the feeling, perhaps gut feeling, let us say, that sex outside marriage or physician-assisted suicide or drinking beer is wrong. But clearly people who talk this way are not really reporting feelings. If someone says, 'I feel that X-ing is wrong', it would just be a joke to ask, 'Where do you feel it?' And if saying that drinking beer is wrong really was reporting a feeling, wouldn't we have to suppose that saying that drinking beer is *not* wrong would be reporting an *absence* of feeling? Maybe people resort to this language of feeling because they are at a loss as to how they might back up their judgements with a satisfactory story or justification. But this is true with regard to judgement in general, and tells us nothing about judgements of conscience in particular.

Judgements of conscience can be judgements about the wrongness of particular actions, or of types of actions or practices. And the judgement may apply to actions or practices of our own only or of anyone. You may believe that it is wrong for *you* to stay at home pottering about in the garden today because you solemnly promised to be elsewhere. You may believe it is wrong for *anyone* to molest a child. Thus, some judgements of conscience are private and personal in their implications in a way that others are not. Staying at home is not a wrong type of action, though it may happen to be wrong for you to do so today, whereas child molestation is wrong for anyone to engage in any day. This is worth mentioning, though it is very evident, since there is a tendency to suppose that judgements of conscience must always somehow be private.

Are the judgements of conscience infallible?

Conscience delivers judgements, but can it be mistaken? Might its deliverances be infallible? We surely know very well that they are not. This may be too obvious to need showing. But in case it is not obvious, consider the following.

First, people do the vilest things 'with a clear conscience'. The 69-year-old Pol Pot was reported in the *Guardian* (23 October, 1997) as saying, 'My conscience is clear'. He did admit to making mistakes: 'You know, for the other people, for the babies, the young ones, I did not order them to be killed . . . I feel sorry for that. That was a mistake of when we put our plan into practice.' (The babies and children in question were killed by a lorry which was carefully driven over their heads.) No doubt, the terrorists who took part in the September 11 killing were acting with clear consciences.

Second, and furthermore, one person's conscience disagrees with another's. Some people think that suicide is wrong, and others think it is not. They cannot all be right. To be sure, there are some kinds of 'disagreement' where both parties may be right. Thus, if you fast during Ramadan and I do not, this may be because our consciences direct us differently. But this is only superficially a 'disagreement'. Muslims who fast during Ramadan do not believe that non-Muslims do wrong in not fasting. By contrast, where we disagree about the wrongness of, say, capital punishment or of being prepared to use nuclear weapons or of child molesting, the disagreement is real. In these cases the judgements on one side or the other must be mistaken.

Third, people change their minds as to right and wrong, as with other matters. Suppose, then, I judge truly today that my judgement yesterday was mistaken, then it is clear that conscience can err. If I judge falsely today that my judgement yesterday was mistaken, then once again, conscience can err.

So we must admit the possibility of an erring conscience. Perhaps this seems so obvious that it may be wondered why anyone should have thought otherwise. No doubt it has to do with the idea that God has promulgated the law to everyone. St Paul writes in Romans 2: 15 of 'the law written in men's hearts' and the Authorized Version makes use of the word 'conscience' in this connection.

Since, however, judgements of conscience are evidently quite often mistaken, it might more plausibly be claimed that it is judgements 'in good faith' that cannot be mistaken – where people might interpret 'good faith' here to mean what people call 'sincerity'. But even this restricted thesis seems most implausible. What people believe is deeply bound up with what they are taught – and with what goes unquestioned among those they encounter and have reason to rely on.[1]

How acting with a mistaken conscience affects the moral character of what we do

Aquinas makes a key distinction here,[2] discussing separately two questions:

1. Does an erring conscience bind?

That is to say, if you think, mistakenly, that an action is bad, is it bad for you to do it? Clearly, the answer is yes. You show yourself willing to do wrong. In such a case, you must be culpable – very much so if you think that what you are doing is very wrong. This is fairly straightforward. The virtue of justice at least requires our having a settled will not to act unjustly.

2. Does an erring conscience excuse?

That is to say, if you mistakenly think that an action is all right, is it all right for you to do it? Well, what you do is still wrong. Your thinking it all right does not change this, any more than your thinking what you are doing is sensible or is legal is so simply because that is what you sincerely and firmly believe. But there is another question. Are you necessarily blameworthy if you err? That might depend. Certainly, you *may* be at fault. There is such a thing as culpable ignorance. Thus you cannot simply fend off criticism by protesting truthfully that your conscience was clear. There is the Scottish story about damnation. The respectably wicked say on the Day of Judgement, 'Lord, we didna ken!' To which the Lord grimly replies, 'Ye ken the noo!'

An interesting corollary: an asymmetry between acting well and acting badly

We have noted that if you do what you think is wrong, then you act badly (culpably), yet if you do what you think is not wrong, but all right, you are not necessarily in the clear, but may still be at fault. That may sound harsh, but it is simply a matter of understanding the concepts. Here is a medical analogy: you always act badly if you give a patient what you believe is the wrong dose, even if, as it so happens, it is actually the right dose. But if you give the wrong dose believing it is the right dose, you may also be at fault for all that you *mean* no harm – because maybe you *should* have checked or found out.

This suggests a more general asymmetry, which Aquinas points out, in the concepts of goodness and badness – hence, in the concepts of acting well and acting badly.[3] If your action is bad in any *one* respect, as, for example, if it is done from a bad motive, or if it is a bad type of action, or if, though it is not a bad kind of action, it is bad in the circumstances, or if you happen to *think* it is bad, you are on that account acting badly whatever else is true. If, on the other hand, your action is good in some one respect, as for example, if done from a good motive, or if it is a good kind of action . . . that never by itself suffices to ensure that you act well in doing it. You act well only if there are none of these defects. Again, this is simply a conceptual matter, not a stern teaching. Compare how, to be healthy, you need a healthy heart *and* a healthy liver *and* healthy lungs. One defect spoils the whole.

The Jehovah's Witness dilemma

Suppose you have a patient who needs a blood transfusion to survive, but the patient refuses, believing it is seriously wrong to receive blood. Let us suppose that the patient is a young woman in her twenties. If only she would consent to the transfusion, you have every reason to expect her to have a full and healthy life thereafter. What are you justified in doing? Let us compare two different tactics. First, you might warn her of the consequences if she persists in her refusal and spell out how much better it will be for her and those dear to her if she complies. Let us call this the *persuasion* tactic. Second, you might seek to change her mind about the wrongfulness of undergoing a transfusion. Perhaps you show her an article by an authority from her own sect who reinterprets certain biblical texts in a way that allows members of the sect to receive blood. Let us call this the *conversion* tactic.

Suppose you adopt the first tactic: persuasion. You do not bully with threats. You simply point out truths: that treated, she stands a very good chance of full recovery and a long life; untreated, her chances of survival are nill. You dwell on the good things she will miss out on if she dies now. She will miss seeing her children grow up, not to mention leave them motherless. She is just on the threshold of such a promising career – and to think how hard she has worked to get to this point.

Here you are pointing out truths merely in order to lure her away from the dictates of her conscience. If you succeed, she will have yielded to temptation. You will have deliberately corrupted her. It is bad for her to do what she believes is bad, and it is bad for you to tempt her to do what it is bad for her to do.

Suppose, instead, you adopt the conversion tactic. If it works, it resolves the problem. If she is converted and consents to the transfusion, she is not, in submitting, acting against her own conscience. This tactic seems in itself morally defensible – assuming that you do not resort to lies or trickery to bring her round. You have not corrupted her. And she does not comply out of weakness.

Which of these tactics, then, comes out as easier to justify? If you use persuasion in such a case, you are aiming to corrupt your patient, which seems plainly wrong. If you use the conversion tactic, you are not aiming to corrupt. On the other hand, this tactic, unlike the other, involves your 'interfering' with the patient's religious beliefs which, as a doctor, it might be said, you have no business doing. Yet interfering in this way seems less harmful and more respectful of the patient's beliefs in such a case as this.

There is, obviously, another way of resolving the dilemma. A doctor might simply *compel* the patient to undergo the treatment. These days, this way, to be sure, would be widely denounced as a gross violation of the patient's moral and legal right of self-determination, assuming that the patient's competence was not in question. But which shows more 'respect' for a person's conscience: forcing them to do what they believe is wrong or coaxing (tempting) them to do so? I suggest the latter may be the grosser interference.

Conscience clauses

It has been customary when seeking to introduce legislation decrim-inalizing a morally controversial medical practice to provide a 'con-science clause' so that no one is obliged to participate in the newly permitted practice if they still believe it wrong. Thus a conscience clause was included in the UK 1967 Abortion Act, and the US Congress enacted a similar conscience clause after *Roe* v. *Wade* (1973), since when forty-seven states have passed clauses allowing health care providers to opt out of performing abortions or sterilizations.[4] The UK Human Fertilisation and Embryology Act (1990) also has such a clause, permitting people to refuse to participate in technical proced-ures relating to contraception or pregnancy. More recently, in coun-tries or states where physician-assisted suicide has been legalized, provision has been made for opting out from that too – for example, with the enactment of the Death with Dignity Act in Oregon, 1997.

We need not suppose that the legislative acceptance of 'conscience clauses' reflects some sensitivity on the part of legislators regarding the importance of not forcing people to act against their own con-sciences. The likelihood is that all it reflects is the need to swing votes in contentious legislation by including such a clause. It is interesting to note in this regard that once the legislation to permit induced abor-tions went through in the UK, the law resisted extending the protec-tion of the conscience clause to anyone other than doctors and nurses. In *Janaway* v. *Salford Area Health Authority* [1988] All E.R. 1079, Mrs Janaway, a doctor's receptionist who refused to type a letter of referral for abortion on the grounds of conscientious objection and was dismissed from her job, sought by way of judicial review to get a declaration that she was not obliged to type the letter. She pursued her contention all the way to the House of Lords, but did not succeed.[5] This judgement invites the question I raised before: is it not arbitrary to allow doctors and nurses to refuse to assist on conscien-tious grounds, but not to allow doctors' receptionists, pharmacists or others to refuse? Imagine a personal secretary of Josef Mengele fending off criticism of her role in arranging for more concentration camp prisoners to be delivered for use in lethal experiments, protest-ing: 'You can't criticize me, I merely typed the letters'.

Wherever a policy is imposed (whether by new legislation or by a regulatory body or by the institution in which you work), there is the possibility that you may be required to act in ways that you believe to be seriously wrong. Obviously, it need not be to do with abortion or physician-assisted suicide. It might, for example, be a policy requiring you to apply cardiopulmonary resuscitation (CPR) to any patient who has a cardiac arrest in hospital unless they or their relatives have given prior consent to its being withheld – a policy which you might consider both futile and unacceptably burdensome for some patients.[6] To be sure, with regard to this particular policy you might object but not think it downright wrong. You might, for example, consider it 'not ideal' or even think it 'inappropriate' or 'ill-chosen'. Only if you think it wrong, unjust, does occasion for conscientious objection arise – as, for example, if you thought that applying this policy to some of your patients, such as the very frail and elderly, would offend against your duty to do no harm.

The conscience clause protects those who disagree with the practice from being made to engage in it. But objectors are, of course, expected to refer any patients they are unwilling to treat to others who are willing, and to disclose their objection in advance so that alternative arrangements can be made for the provision of the service to patients. Is this response to those who have conscientious objections reasonable? Not so, according to Ian Kennedy. Commenting on the conscience clause which was attached to the 1967 Abortion Act, he observes that the Act might not have passed without it, but argues that objectors have no business opting out – at least they have no business doing so if they are working within the National Health Service: 'To the doctor who complains that he wants to practise medicine without abortions, the answer must be that he can choose to engage in private practice, and thereby arrange his affairs by agreement with his patients. If he joins the NHS, he should remember the last word of the three, "service", and serve. Membership of the profession would seem to demand this.'[7]

There are, though, two reasons at least for providing conscience clauses (aside from the above-mentioned tactical concession): a pragmatic reason and a reason of principle. We will consider these in turn.

The pragmatic reason is that the professions may have problems recruiting and retaining talented members in certain specialties if they do not find a way to accommodate those with divergent views. The reason of principle is that it is wrong to compel or even tempt people to do what they believe is seriously wrong. We can see this in the light of our previous discussion about how an erring conscience binds. If you think that X-ing is wrong (whether or not you are mistaken in your view), you act unjustly if you go ahead and X. Thus getting people to do what *they* think is wrong is getting them to act unjustly, which is unjust.

There are, then, these two kinds of reasons for seeking some way to accommodate conscientious objectors. But is the *kind* of accommodation that conscience clauses offer appropriate? This kind of accommodation imposes certain obligations on objectors. GP objectors are obliged to refer. Nurse objectors are obliged to disclose. Any objectors are obliged to provide or assist in providing in an emergency, if no one is available to take their place.

Now this kind of accommodation would make perfect sense if we were to suppose that conscientious objectors did not consider the type of action or practice in question to be wrong for *anyone* to perform, but merely wrong for them *personally* to perform. We can imagine how this might arise as a matter of discipline internal to a religion. Suppose you are Jewish and on holy days consider it wrong for you to go to work. In such a case, assuming that you have colleagues who are not Jewish, the accommodation of referral (and disclosure) makes excellent sense. You do not think ill of non-Jews that they do not observe your holy days, any more than you mind in the slightest being asked the way to a pork-butcher shop by a non-Jew, even if you consider it wrong for you to eat pork. Furthermore, it could well be that though you believe it is wrong for you to work on your holy days, you do not think it is wrong for you to do so in an emergency situation. In that case, there is no problem at all for you in agreeing to work under the terms of the conscience clause provisions. It is altogether reasonable.

But conscientious objectors to abortion, physician-assisted suicide, etc., do not see the practices they object to as simply wrong for *them*. They consider the practices they object to as wrong for *anyone* to engage in. Bearing that in mind, does the accommodation involved in requiring objectors to refer, and to stand in occasionally in an emergency, make any sense? It does not.

Why referral is not a neat solution

Referral involves only semi-withdrawal. Suppose, for example, you believe that physician-assisted suicide or female circumcision is seriously wrong, how then can you suppose that you are justified in helping a patient get this 'service' by arranging for someone who thinks differently to provide it? If doing X is wrong for anyone to do, so too is fixing for someone else to do X.

Referral involves only conditional withdrawal, withdrawal on condition that someone else is available to act in your stead. Yet, if you believe that it is wrong for anyone to do X, let us say, to perform female circumcision, you cannot think it is permissible for you to do X if on occasion, however rarely, there is no one else available to do it. If it is seriously wrong in the way we all presumably think that rape or child molestation is wrong, it is simply unthinkable to be willing to do it at all – even if we know that there are some who evidently do not share our view.

It may be argued that referral is not so obviously unreasonable as I have just made out. Are doctors who refer sufficiently distant from the practices they object to, that they are not rightly portrayed as collaborators or accessories? Or, should we say, on the contrary, that any doctors who are willing to 'pass the patient on' demonstrate a lack of sincerity – or else, are not thinking clearly? Just how paradoxical it is to be willing to pass the patient on is perhaps made more obvious if we imagine a case in which doing so requires some effort – having to phone around all morning to find someone to whom to refer your patient.

How, then, are we to decide what counts as being an accessory? Recall the Janaway case, where a receptionist refused to type a letter of referral for an abortion. In that case the court ruled that her involvement was too remote to count as 'participating' in the administering of the treatment. Yet again, we must wonder why if a GP is allowed to decline to sign a certificate on conscientious grounds, the same kind of right is not accorded to the secretary who declines to type a letter of referral. As for pharmacists, their involvement in procedures to which they may have moral objections may be quite close – as, for example, when pharmacists who object to elective abortion are still expected to provide RU-486.

Helen Watt suggests a possible way of drawing a line between co-operating in a manner that is bound to be wrongful and doing so in a manner that may not be. She distinguishes what she calls formal co-operation from material co-operation.[8] Your co-operation is *formal* if you share the aim, the intention, of those who carry out a treatment. Your co-operation is *material*, rather than formal, if you do *not* share the intention although you foresee that the treatment in question will be carried out in consequence of what you do. Formal co-operation is bound to be bad; material co-operation is not necessarily bad.

What Watt says here makes sense when we recall that there are two components to the virtue of justice. The first is this: if you have this virtue, you do not mean yourself to act unjustly. That being so, you must reject formal co-operation which involves you in intentional wrongdoing. The second component is this: that you have *some* concern that others are not treated unjustly. Having the concern is in a way secondary, but if you were not in the least concerned, you could hardly be said to have the virtue. Material co-operation in some cases might belie your concern, and in other cases not do so, depending on the particular circumstances of the case. There is bound to be indeterminacy here. There is, after all, no definite answer to the question of how much concern is 'enough'.

It is worth noting here that while we say that the primary focus of the virtue is on not acting unjustly, this should not be taken to imply that you must have some narcissistic preoccupation with your own conduct – with your 'integrity'. That would suggest a kind of perversion. We should explain this primary focus by putting the emphasis in the right place – stressing the importance of not ourselves *wronging*, as distinct from the importance of not *ourselves* wronging.

Helen Watt's distinction goes some way to settling things. Some cases of material co-operation must be innocent. It would be ridiculous to suppose that you act unjustly whenever you do something that you know will facilitate wrongdoing. Driving a train, selling cameras or maps, and building bridges are all activities that we know will facilitate wrongdoing in some way. But inevitably, as we have said, there will be much indeterminacy in regard to material co-operation. It may be close or remote. And we can imagine a spectrum of cases. Compare the role of a nurse who hands the instruments to the consultant who is carrying out female circumcision, to that of the nurse who has prepared the tray of instruments, to that of the nurse who has admitted the patient to the ward, to that of the postman who merely delivers mail to the clinic. Cases at either end of such a spectrum may be unproblematic. If you are handing the instruments to the consultant, you are too closely involved to claim that you do not share responsibility for what the principal agents are doing. If you are merely the postman delivering mail, you are sufficiently remote not to count as a collaborator. But there will be many problematic cases, more to the middle of the range – like, perhaps, the taxi man who conveys people taking a protesting child to the clinic and who knows exactly what is up, but says, 'It's none of *my* business – it's just a fare'.

'Imposing our values'

It is often said that conscientious objectors should be accommodated, but not in a way that allows them to 'impose their values' on others. That is why conscience clause arrangements are devised in such a way that the service to which some have objection is not disrupted. After all, it is said, the same right that objectors are accorded to be free to follow their consciences ought to be accorded to others, to follow theirs. This thought seems to underlie a remark by Frances Kissling of a group calling itself Catholics for a Free Choice: 'There is very little recognition that the conscience of the woman is as important, let alone more important, than the conscience of the provider.'[9] The organization seems particularly keen to stress the importance of conscience. 'Conscience' is the name they give to their newsletter.

This thought may seem persuasive if it is supposed that respect for the *providers'* conscience must indicate respect for their views or even for them. Were that so, Kissling would have a point. But the justification for 'respecting' the conscience of objectors which we have been exploring does not rest at all on the notion that objectors' views in general are worthy of respect. In the particular case, they may be worthy of very little, if any. And if we say that there is a sense in which any human being deserves respect, it is not under the aspect of the opinions they hold. Rather, what deserves respect is simply people's reluctance to do what they believe to be seriously wrong. This, we might say, is more a matter of showing respect for the moral law than of showing respect for any individual. Once that is understood, the parallel drawn by Kissling breaks down. Women seeking abortion do not as a rule believe that they are *obliged* to do so. Thus, if they are denied an abortion, they are not being compelled to act wrongly.

The Kissling line of thought turns on an ambiguity in the notion of 'following your conscience': between 'following' in the sense of obeying what it dictates – what you believe is obligatory – and 'following' in the sense of doing what your conscience permits – is comfortable with. There is, I have argued a world of difference between these cases.

The above claim that women do not as a rule believe that they are obliged to seek an abortion may be challenged. Admittedly, I have not produced evidence – and, of course, it may well be true that women seeking abortions quite usually *say* that they believe they 'must' do this. If so, that would hardly be surprising, and we need not suppose they are always insincere. All the same, there might understandably be an element of self-deception at work. Naomi Wolf reports the observation of an abortion clinic doctor writing in *The New York Times* that 'The only one reason I've ever heard for having an abortion is the desire to be a good mother'.[10] Wolf, not unreasonably, treats such professions with a certain reserve, and cites some other, not so lofty, reasons that women sometimes give.

But suppose that there are women who seek abortions who do honestly believe for one reason or another that they are obliged to do so. If they are denied the help they seek and cannot achieve an abortion without help, they are not being compelled to do wrong – that is, to act against their own consciences. No one, after all, is obliged to do the impossible. Imagine, by way of analogy, that a mother sincerely believes that it is her duty to see to it that her severely disabled child is humanely killed. Suppose the authorities get wind of this and take the child into care. She is not now able to do what she believes to be her duty. It is surely incorrect to describe what the authorities have done as compelling the mother to disobey her conscience.

Since talk of 'imposing values' is so very common in this connection, let us note that this hardly fits what conscientious objectors are doing. If Smith's shop is the only source of alcohol in my community and Smith becomes Muslim and refuses to stock alcohol any more, then I am out of luck. But Smith has not somehow hypnotically converted me to his opinion. My values have not been changed.

Misleading tolerance

There is, finally, a problem of what might be called misleading tolerance. It arises clearly in regard to those who object to abortion, but it might also arise, *mutatis mutandis*, about other matters – if, for example, your hospital were to offer female circumcision services.

Colleagues are expected to get along with one another, despite differences of opinion. And no doubt we are inclined to say, 'And long may this continue!' Tact is surely a virtue. However, tolerance may have a price. If you are conspicuously convivial with those who deliberately X, it might suggest that, whatever you *say*, you cannot really believe that X-ing is a great injustice.

Suppose your nurse colleague goes around saying that abortion is murder. Yet she seems perfectly happy to sit down in the hospital cafeteria day after day chatting affably with her colleagues who she knows routinely do abortions. Doesn't this suggest that she is insincere? She might indeed believe that abortion is 'a bad thing' – something 'that would not happen in an ideal world' – but surely she cannot really regard it as child killing.

Of course, this response rather assumes that we know how it would be appropriate to act if we believed that a practice, largely accepted in our community, was actually murderous. Maybe the matter is not so clear. If we lived in a society in which young men still fought duels, would it be inappropriate to sit down over a meal with someone whom you knew was prepared to kill in this way? Ought you to show more tolerance in such a case? After all, such a man would have grown up in a community in which readiness to engage in a duel would be considered honourable. In our own society, soldiers are trained to be prepared to launch nuclear weapons against civilian populations. If we sincerely thought such a policy to be murderous, as well we might, would we have to refuse to sit down at table or engage in social chat over a pint with such a soldier?

As I have already noted, if you think a practice is wrong for anyone to engage in, you must have *some* concern about others doing it. You are not, however, obliged to do everything possible to prevent others from engaging in the practice. This is very evident. That said, though, there is this other matter as to what your tolerance may lead people to suppose. People may interpret your tolerance as evidence that you do not really mean what you say. With regard to abortion, an inference of this kind has actually been drawn. There is a comfort doctrine that is put about regarding those who object to abortion, declaring it to be 'child killing'. It is suggested that these people cannot really mean what they say because they do not act as if they do – they are tolerant in a way which is inconsistent with the beliefs that they profess. There is this danger, then, that tolerance may mislead.

6

The Duties to Obtain Consent, Give Information and Respect Autonomy

The topic of consent is a big issue in texts on medical law as also in contemporary texts on health care ethics. Yet it does not so much as get a mention in the Hippocratic writings. Why the difference? Why, assuming that consent *is* as important a component of good practice as is nowadays supposed, was this not noticed before? Both the duty to obtain consent and the closely allied duty to inform are said to derive from the duty to respect patients' autonomy. According to the BMA's *Medical Ethics Today*, respect for patient autonomy has 'become a core principle of modern medicine'.[1] Jean McHale and Marie Fox observe that 'autonomy is regarded by many ethicists as the fundamental value in health care ethics'.[2] Ruth Faden and Tom Beauchamp say that 'Autonomy is almost certainly the most important value "discovered" in medical ethics in the last two decades'.[3] Now if the old ethic did indeed overlook this 'value', and if, in consequence, it failed to recognize the duties to obtain consent and to inform, if it even approved paternalist medical practices that would run counter to these duties, does this not show that the old ethic stands in need of a radical rethink?

In this chapter I will argue, though, that notwithstanding the lack of explicit notice accorded in times gone by to the duties to obtain consent and to inform, these duties are no new discoveries. As for the duty to respect patients' autonomy, it rather depends on how 'autonomy' is interpreted, whether modern talk about this marks a change of view. I will argue that in so far as there is this duty now, it is not new; rather, its recognition is implicit in what has always been considered good medical practice. And while nowadays there is less tolerance of medical paternalism, this does not reflect any fundamental change of view as to the duties of doctors and the rights of patients;

rather, it reflects how changed circumstances have altered what accords with these duties and rights.

Advances in modern medicine suffice to explain why the duties to obtain consent and to inform have become more onerous – hence, more in need of explicit debate, discussion and even regulation. Patients nowadays are literate. They generally want and need information about treatment options and attendant risks. And often there are treatment choices to be made among options whose medical benefits and harms do not by themselves determine which are better or worse for a particular patient. Further, doctors stand in need of information about their patients concerning their personal concerns and priorities before they are in a position to advise. The duty to inform becomes more challenging for doctors to fulfil, the more information they themselves have and the more options they are able to offer. And, since sharing information is likely to be time-consuming, their duty to inform has to be balanced against their other duties.

There are also problems that arise nowadays concerning the costs of medicines – whether, for example, patients are entitled to be told that there are better medicines available over the counter than those that are covered by the patient's insurance scheme or health service. For the present, though, I will ignore problems concerning the costs of health care – I take up this topic in chapters 8 and 9. For now, I want to investigate whether, in so far as obtaining consent, informing and respecting patients' autonomy really are duties, they have always been seen as such.

Obviously, the duty to obtain consent itself requires that patients be given *some* information. But just how much information and what sort of information there needs to be for consent really to be obtained is not so easy to establish. You do not consent to marry if you think that the ceremony you are taking part in is just a rehearsal. You may consent to undergo X, not knowing that X is also Y. In that case you may not have consented to undergo Y. Let us agree that in order really to be giving consent, you must be apprised of certain basic information at least. But does the duty to inform patients when seeking their consent to treatment require much more than that? Does it require full disclosure of risks and also of alternatives?

While we are inclined to think nowadays that, in the medical context, the duty to obtain consent and the duty to inform fully about risks and alternatives go hand in hand, we should not assume that they must always have done so. These duties are distinct, though it has to be admitted that there may be no neat, clear-cut division between what may be called the basic information that must be part and parcel of obtaining consent and the fuller information that has come to be expected from doctors. Thus, if in times gone by the duty to inform more fully about risks and alternatives was not acknowledged, we should not infer that the duty to obtain consent can't have been acknowledged either.

Since the ethical principles relating to consent have been enshrined in our common law tradition, it is instructive to take some note of how this tradition differentiates between the duty to obtain consent and the duty to inform.[4] The differences marked in the law are not mere historical happenstances. They reflect underlying differences of moral significance.

The duty to obtain consent in the common law tradition

Failure to obtain valid consent from adult patients of sound mind before any medical treatment or procedure that is invasive is carried out is both a crime (assault) and a tort (battery) of trespass to the person. The duty not to touch another person without consent is a general duty. It applies to doctors as it does to everyone else. Needless to say, there are, though, some defences for touching without prior consent, such as, for example, necessity in emergency situations, or where the person, if not touched, poses a danger to the lives or health of others.

How invasive must the touching be to count as a battery? Any intentional touchings of a person's body not consented to can count. They need not be hostile in intent.[5] (So a kiss or a hug, not consented to, could be actionable.) Exceptions are allowed for touchings that are inevitable and generally accepted in our daily excursions out and about (for example, when joining the crowd jostling to get on a train).[6] Recognition of this offence goes back a very long way. Danute Mendelson traces its origins to medieval times, when it provided a remedy to blood feuds that posed a threat to the King's peace.[7]

What conditions does the law require, then, for a patient's consent to be valid? The person who gives it must be competent to give consent, and the consent must be 'real'. The consent is not real if it is given under some form of duress, fraud or misrepresentation. Moreover, enough information must be conveyed to enable the one consenting to understand 'in broad terms' the nature of the treatment or procedure proposed. Understanding in broad terms requires that you are given some basic information, and with regard to medical treatment, this will include some information about significant risks as well as about the nature of the procedure (what it involves and what is its purpose).[8]

It stands to reason that doctors in times gone by were mindful of this legal framework and practised within it and, moreover, would have acted as if there were such a legal framework even if it did not in fact exist. The alternative hypothesis, that doctors once upon a time were wont to impose treatments forcibly on their patients (even on adults of sound mind) is incredible. Otherwise, as Jeremy Bentham, writing in 1802, observed, 'Distrust and terror would watch by the sick man's bed.'[9] That consent is not discussed in the Hippocratic writings proves nothing to the contrary. After all, the duty to obtain consent, as we have noted, relates to a general duty (not to commit assault). It is not, therefore, something special to medical law or ethics. There is, then, no particular reason why it should be included in the Hippocratic Oath, anymore than that this Oath should make mention of the general duty not to steal.

No doubt, though, doctors in earlier times would often, quite properly, assume consent. Actually, don't they still?[10] I go to my GP with earache. He hears my complaint. He asks which ear hurts, produces an auroscope, and asks me to tilt my head. He places one hand on my head, tilting it further, and with the other pokes the speculum of the auroscope in my good ear, then in the bad ear. He asks me if I am allergic to penicillin and then scribbles a prescription on his notepad and hands it to me to take to the pharmacist. Has he *asked* my permission to touch my head and poke the auroscope in my ear? No. But I allow him to do it. I do not resist or object. 'Qui tacet, consetire vedetur' (he who is silent is deemed to have consented). Has he explained the broad nature and purpose of his doing so? No. But it is obvious, or so he supposes – it would be another matter if I were a child or a confused adult: then careful explanation first might well be called for. Has he explained what he is prescribing? No. I presume it is an antibiotic and probably contains penicillin, since he asked if I was allergic. Doesn't my submission to the examination and accepting of the prescription amount to consent? If so, we should not take mere absence of explicit consent seeking in times gone by as proof that patients used to be treated without their consent.

The duty to inform in the common law tradition

The duty to inform patients does not arise just in the context of consent seeking. If you ask your doctors for general advice about your health, they may have to alert you to certain risks that you need to take precautions against. But here let us consider the duty to inform only as it arises in the context of their obtaining consent to treat. And let us distinguish the duty to impart basic information that is part and parcel of obtaining real consent from the duty to inform much more fully about risks and alternatives when seeking consent. We will hereafter refer to the latter duty as 'the duty to inform adequately'.

There are three particular differences in law between the duty to obtain consent and the duty to inform adequately that are instructive for us to take note of:

1 The duty to inform adequately (unlike the duty to obtain consent) is a special duty that applies only to those with a duty of care.
2 The duty to inform adequately (unlike the duty to obtain consent) is relatively new.
3 The duty to inform adequately (unlike the duty to obtain consent) does not have very clear-cut obedience rules. Thus, how much information is owed has to be weighed up in relation to the specific situation. Guidelines about how much information to give are bound to be somewhat vague.

I will comment on these features of the duty to inform adequately in turn.

The duty to inform adequately is a special duty

In law, failure to inform adequately falls under the head of negligence, not trespass.[11] Liability under the tort of negligence requires that there is a causal connection between the doctor's failure to inform adequately and some resultant harm to the patient (unlike liability for trespass, which does not require proof that a harm has resulted). Seeing that the duty to inform adequately arises from the duty of care, it binds only those who have this duty – unlike the general duty that everyone has to obtain consent to touch.

The doctor's duty to inform adequately is of relatively recent origin

Recognition in law of the doctor's duty to inform adequately dates in the USA from two landmark cases: *Salgo* v. *Leland Stanford Jr. University Board of Trustees* (1957)[12] and *Natanson* v. *Kline* (1960),[13] and in England from *Chatterton* v. *Gerson* (1981).[14] The development in law of this duty may be seen as part of a general trend towards providing more safeguards to people receiving services from professionals, non-medical as well as medical. If you seek financial advice, for example, your advisor will occasionally say such things as: 'I have to tell you that shares can go up as well as down', or 'I have to tell you that if you make this particular investment I will get a commission'. In *Rise and Fall of Freedom of Contract*, Atiyah chronicles a certain change. Old law: 'If you make a bad bargain, that is *your* affair, and the law only protects you against outright fraud or misrepresentation.' The new law is more solicitous of the foolish and ignorant. It is ironic that this social trend is portrayed in the medical ethics literature at least as evidence of our increasing respect for people's autonomy. Is it not, on the contrary, a trend towards more paternalism in the law, and hence evidence of our diminishing respect for people's autonomy? The statutory protections are deemed necessary to shield people who would otherwise contract imprudently – who cannot be presumed able to see to their own interests.

The doctor's duty to inform adequately does not have clear-cut obedience rules

It stands to reason that general duties to which serious sanctions in law are attached need to have clear-cut obedience rules, so that it is usually a straightforward matter to know if we are acting as the duty requires. Thus, in the case of obtaining consent, the permissible exceptions are normally obvious. What the duty to inform adequately requires of doctors is, by its nature, not so straightforward to specify. How much information is adequate will vary from case to case. The duty is only one aspect of the duty of care. Patients have other needs besides information, and these other needs may sometimes compete with and override the need for information. Hence, it is a duty which admits of many exceptions or qualifications.

The difficulty over specifying how much information is adequate and owed to patients is reflected in the ongoing debate over what standard the law should apply. Three standards have been mooted: a 'reasonable doctor' standard (what such a person would see fit to disclose), a 'reasonable patient' standard (what such a person would want to have disclosed), and a 'subjective' standard (what the actual subject, this particular patient, would want to have disclosed). In *Chatterton* v. *Gerson*, a reasonable doctor standard was applied – what in the UK has come to be known as the 'Bolam', after *Bolam* v. *Friern* (1957).[15] In 1972, three US cases ushered in a reasonable patient standard: *Canterbury* v. *Spence*,[16] *Cobbs* v. *Grant*[17] and *Wilkinson* v. *Vesey*.[18] Thus, in *Canterbury* it was said that doctors have a duty to disclose all material risks and went on to state that a risk is 'material' if the doctor knows (or should know) that a reasonable person in the patient's situation would want to know of it when determining whether or not to forgo the proposed therapy. In Canada, *Reibl* v. *Hughes* (1980) 114 DLR (3rd) 1 at 13 endorsed the reasonable patient standard. According to Beauchamp and Childress, writing in 2001, it has now gained acceptance in over half of the states in the USA.[19]

UK law may also be heading towards the reasonable patient standard. In *Pearce* v *United Bristol Healthcare NHS Trust* (1999)[20] the Court of Appeal judgement stated that it is normally the responsibility of the doctor to inform the patient of 'a significant risk which would affect the judgement of a reasonable patient'.[21] And the Bolam principle is anyway hardly likely to measure up to the rights implicit in the European Convention of Human Rights that was ratified in the Human Rights Act of 1998. In any case, even if 'informed consent' (the reasonable patient standard) fails to get a firm legal foothold in the UK, the medical profession, say J. K. Mason and R. A. McCall Smith, 'now accept it as a *fait accompli*'.[22] The General Medical Council's *Guidance on Consent: The Ethical Considerations* (1985) goes well beyond Bolam, emphasizing the need to provide patients with as much information as possible prior to their making decisions. It further states that doctors should enquire into their patients' individual needs and priorities when providing information.

Did doctors in times gone by overlook their duty to inform adequately?

Is it the duty to inform adequately that is missing from the old ethic? Has the idea that patients need to know all about risks and alternatives when they consent to treatment been something alien to the understanding of good medical practice until recent times? At least, there is no explicit mention of such a duty. Moreover, there are many sayings that caution against informing. The Hippocratic ethic enjoins: 'Conceal most things from the patient!' Thomas Percival's *Medical Ethics* (published in 1803) advises against dispiriting disclosures: 'For the physician should be the minister of hope and comfort to the sick; that, by such cordials to the drooping spirit, he may smooth the bed of death, revive expiring life, and counteract the depressing influence of those maladies which rob the philosopher of fortitude and the Christian of consolation.'[23] Much of this is repeated verbatim in the first American Medical Association Code (1847), though omitting the philosopher and the Christian. It is interesting, by the way, to note that Percival turns for guidance on the subject of truthfulness to a philosopher. The philosopher of the day was Francis Hutcheson. His advice? 'No man censures a physician for deceiving a patient too much dejected, by expressing good hopes for him, or by denying that he gives him a proper medicine which he is foolishly prejudiced against: the patient afterward will not reproach him for it.'[24] Consult philosophers of equally good standing nowadays, and they will with equal assurance repudiate Hutcheson's advice.

All these cautions against informing, however, far from showing that those who issued them did not acknowledge a duty to inform adequately, may rather have been put forward as exceptions to that very duty (the exceptions that prove the rule) – occasions for the exercise of what nowadays is recognized in US law (and tolerated in British law) as 'therapeutic privilege'. Mason and McCall Smith observe: 'even the most dedicated to patient autonomy will allow the doctor the "therapeutic privilege" to withhold information which would merely prove to distress or confuse the patient'.[25] For sure, doctors in earlier times may have been far readier to make exceptions, to withhold information, than would nowadays be considered reasonable. But this does not necessarily indicate any difference of opinion concerning what are the duties of doctors. Changed circumstances and new knowledge suffice to account for the present-day appreciation of the need for greater openness with patients. Though if your patients may be better off not knowing certain things about the relevant risks and alternatives, what is the use of your withholding the information when they will find it out for themselves anyway when they go 'on line'? In any case, even if your patients would be no better off knowing certain things, to avoid the risk of litigation, you had better not withhold information from them.

Consent, information and moral rights

It is often supposed that the duty to obtain consent and the duty to inform adequately, are both rooted in one and the same moral requirement on doctors: to respect their patients' autonomy (right of self-determination).[26] If this is so, we might note that the law does not (yet) firmly recognize this moral right. After all, if the duty to inform adequately derives from a patient's right of self-determination, shouldn't it be the patient's own wishes, not the wishes of the reasonable patient, let alone the reasonable doctor, that set the standard? A right to self-determination would be much enfeebled if it allowed patients only to make reasonable choices. Moreover, so long as the law ɔsumes the doctor's duty to inform adequately under the duty of ɹare, it does not support a patient's *right* of self-determination. If patients have a right (an entitlement) to know, then it is hardly relevant to ask, 'What do they need to know?'

But even if the law does not wholly support it, it may still be argued that patients do have this moral right. Is this, perhaps, what is new to medical ethics – the discovery of this right? In order to answer this question, we need to clarify what respect for autonomy might mean, and in what sense, if any, it might be owed to patients.

Autonomy

H. Tristram Engelhardt Jr. offers one insight into why present-day post-Christian Western societies may have only recently come to regard 'autonomy' as a human right – and, relatedly, why informed consent has come to acquire such prominence in contemporary accounts of medical ethics. The Enlightenment aspiration to replace Western Christian morality with a comprehensive secular morality, says Engelhardt, has failed. The failure is illustrated by the many irresolvable ongoing controversies and problems in medical ethics:

> The apparent triumph of secular bioethics is hollow. There are as many secular understandings as well as accounts of morality, justice and fairness as there are religions. There is no canonical sense or account of justice for the allocation of health care resources that is universally accepted or definitively justified. There is no settled general secular view of, or consensus regarding, the morality of abortion, health care allocations and euthanasia. There is deep disagreement about the propriety of many forms of third-party-assisted reproduction, indeed even of whether it is ever appropriate to provide medical treatment for individuals wishing to have sexual intercourse outside of the marriage of a man and a woman (e.g. to correct for impotence). More significantly there is no content-full, generally accepted understanding of the good life and of proper conduct. There is also no agreement about how one should proceed to remedy this difficulty and establish a canonical content-full ethics with its appropriate bioethics. Again, it is for this reason that bioethicists face a challenge in giving reliable advice. Depending on the ethics and the bioethics chosen as normative, dramatically different recommendations will be endorsed.[27]

In face of this difficulty, Engelhardt observes that 'secular bioethics turns to permission and procedural solutions such as free and informed consent'.[28] The default position where we cannot assume agreement in moral outlook is simply to seek agreement among those with whom we collaborate – for example, agreement between doctor and patient on a treatment proposal: 'If one acts with permission, one acts with the authority of those who collaborate.'[29] Thus, secular morality comes to have a 'libertarian cast' – 'the accent is unavoidably on free and informed consent' and 'we must be libertarians in our public lives, despite our private moral convictions'.[30]

Engelhardt's view points up a significant truth, but, as we remarked in the Introduction, makes over much of it. For sure, it stands to reason that differences between those whose outlook is wholly secular and those whose outlook is not are very likely to yield divergent views on what makes for living well and acting well. Some irresolvable disagreements on moral matters may well arise. That is the significant truth to which Engelhardt calls our attention. But do the differences run so wide and deep as to preclude our finding any rational common ground from which to tackle issues in bioethics? My project in this book challenges this comprehensive scepticism.

Engelhardt's explanation of the value we now attach to autonomy and consent implies that these have come to matter to us because we live in societies whose members have ceased to share a 'value perspective'. On moral matters, he claims, there is now 'foundational disagreement'. That being so, moral controversies are ultimately irresolvable through rational argument. Hence, 'gaining permission from persons is cardinal to secular bioethics because there is no other general source of secular moral authority'.[31] Even if Engelhardt hereby captures part of the explanation of why autonomy and consent are nowadays considered so central to ethics and bioethics, isn't there more to be said for our attaching value to these? Would a morally more homogeneous society – say, a traditional Christian society in the modern world – have no reason to make room for autonomy in its account of ethics and bioethics?

If respect for autonomy is a 'human' right, that implies that humans owe it to one another, whatever the nature of their society, be it 'fragmented' or not. But is there a human right to be 'autonomous'? What, anyway, are we to understand 'autonomy' to be? Are those who champion it as something worthy of respect and of cultivation all talking about the same thing? Gerald Dworkin suggests that they are not: 'About the only features held constant from one author to another are that autonomy is a feature of persons and that it is a desirable quality to have.'[32]

The term 'autonomy' derives from the Greek. Literally, it means 'self-rule', and it was applied by the Greeks to city-states that were politically independent. So, the modern sense of 'autonomy', applied to individual persons, relies on a metaphor. For our purposes, I think it suffices to distinguish three senses in which individuals can be 'autonomous'. In one sense, being autonomous is equivalent to being free – not, for example, constrained by others. In this sense I am not free to park my car in the street right outside my house if someone else is parked there already. My choice is restricted in this matter. Let us call this the *liberty* sense of autonomy. It is this sense of autonomy that corresponds to the right to privacy understood as a right to be let alone.

In another sense, being autonomous is equivalent to being in command of oneself. 'I am autonomous if I rule me and no one else rules I,' says Joel Feinberg.[33] Now what it might mean to say that 'I rule me' is not obvious. It might simply mean that I am not being constrained, e.g. by the actions of others (the liberty sense). Or, secondly, it might mean that I am in control of myself: able to make decisions as to what to believe or do and to act in line with them. Let us call this the *self-command* sense of autonomy. If I am flustered or in a temper, I may be substantially non-autonomous in this sense. Here my choice is restricted because of the state I am in. Maybe there is space to park right outside my house, but because I am in a temper, I cannot manage it.

Or thirdly, it might mean that I am self-reliant or independent in the sense that the decisions I make about what to believe or do are ones that I reach on my own, and not on the advice or direction of anyone else. Let us call this the *self-reliance* sense of autonomy. My choice may be interfered with in this way because my next door neighbours, seeing me trying to fit my car into the available space, hurry out to guide and direct me – maybe because they do not want their own cars bumped yet again. Many discussions of autonomy fail to distinguish among these three senses. However, in order to decide what importance to attach to a patient's autonomy, it matters which sense is in question.

John Benson, in 'Who is the autonomous man?', portrays autonomy as a moral virtue: a disposition that he says everyone needs in order to flourish. By 'autonomy' he means self-reliance – not self-reliance *per se*, but proper, 'right-minded' self-reliance. The virtue does not consist simply in being as self-reliant as possible in choosing what to believe and what to do, but in being self-reliant about the right things and in the right way – which involves judgement. It would be an insane ambition to strive to avoid as much as possible relying on others' advice and guidance over what to believe or what to do.

The extent to which we *can* work out 'all by ourselves' what to believe is obviously very limited; even more so, the extent to which it is at all sensible to try. Of necessity we rely on what we have been taught, or have picked up, in ways which we would find it difficult even to describe.

Thus, Benson maintains that those who have this virtue are neither over nor under reliant on the opinions of others. Those who are over reliant manifest deficiencies such as servility, submissiveness, credulity, gullibility. Those who are under reliant (too self-reliant) manifest 'excess' faults of arrogance or overconfidence. Benson says that this virtue is closely allied to courage. The under reliant show a kind of foolhardiness, and the over reliant show a kind of timidity. I suggest that this trait is even more closely related to practical wisdom (Aristotle's *phronēsis*). Indeed, isn't it actually an aspect of that very trait? Those who are practically wise will rely on others for advice and guidance just when that is the sensible thing to do. Autonomy in this sense, then, is no new discovery.

Medical paternalism: what is it? Is it always wrong?

We treat people paternalistically when we take steps to restrict their choices for their own good. Thus the motive behind paternalism is benign: to prevent people from making unwise choices that may harm them. So defined, it rules out the possibility of acting paternalistically towards oneself. But should it? Wasn't Odysseus being paternalistic towards himself when he got his crew to tie him to the mast while they sailed within earshot of the Sirens? Whether or not we choose to widen the definition of paternalism to include such an example, we should at least acknowledge that we can and sometimes should 'take our own selves in hand', so to speak. And if that is justifiable, maybe there are times when we can and should take others in hand too. But when?

Paternalist actions aim to prevent unwise *choice*. Thus, parents putting their infants in cots that have bars to prevent their falling out are acting protectively, but not with paternalism. Paternalism is exercised not towards infants but towards toddlers and older children – children able to make choices but liable, if left to themselves, to make bad choices. Parents who restrict what television programmes they allow their older children to watch, what books they allow them to read, what friends they allow them to associate with, may be acting paternalistically.

Paternalism may be manifested by omissions as well as by actions. Thus, for example, omitting to tell someone something because they are better off not knowing about it could be paternalist – but is not necessarily so. Suppose your teenage daughter faces an important exam on the morrow and you happen to notice that a film she would very much like to watch is on television late this very night. If you do not tell her, lest she insists on sitting up to watch it, that is a paternalistic decision. If you do not tell her merely to spare her disappointment, but knowing very well that she would be much too sensible to think of watching it, then that would not be a paternalistic decision, according to our definition: your intention is not to prevent her from making a bad choice – you know that *she* would not do that.

Similarly, if you withhold information from patients about to face operations concerning certain possible grim symptoms that very rarely result, you are not necessarily acting paternalistically. You are if you withhold the information for fear that the patients may change their minds and withdraw consent. But not if you know they would gamely face the operation but would meanwhile be made more miserable to no purpose. Admittedly, the supposition that you could 'know' this about your patients is not all that plausible.[34] Notice, at any rate, that your reason for withholding the information does not have to be *manipulative*. It need not be an attempt to interfere with or override the patients' freedom of choice. Of course, your lack of openness, even if not manipulative, may still be morally objectionable, for other reasons – as, for example, if you have actually promised to give your patients full information about all aspects of their operations and possible consequences.

It is often supposed that paternalistic interventions interfere with and disrespect a person's autonomy. Here it is important to consider what sense of autonomy is in question. Is respect owed to people's autonomous choices in all three senses we have distinguished? What if protecting patients' autonomy in one of the senses necessitates curtailing it in another of the senses?

Obviously, paternalistic interventions interfere with people's liberty (restricting their freedom of choice).[35] Often, too, they curtail a person's self-reliance. But does it interfere with their autonomy in the other sense: in respect of self-command? Why suppose that people whose freedom of choice is deliberately restricted must thereby be made less able to control their own actions? Was Bertrand Russell any less in command of himself while he was imprisoned, and writing *Principia Mathematica*, than he was when at liberty? When governments impose regulations that prevent us from choosing cheap but dangerous equipment or modes of travel, they interfere with our liberty and self-reliance, but do they undermine our self-control?

Given the importance to and for each of us of preserving our powers of rational agency, it is hard to see how the paternalistic motive – aiming at the individual's own *good* could justify infringing anyone's autonomy where this means interfering with their capacity for self-command, be they child or adult. In short, if we want to justify paternalism, what we need to defend is the restricting of other people's liberty and self-reliance.

John Stuart Mill, who famously opposes paternalism, makes some notable exceptions. One of these is to protect people from unintended self-harm. His example: intercepting a wayfarer about to step on to an unsafe bridge. The wayfarer exception suggests that restricting people's liberty when they will otherwise act against their *own* true preferences is justified. We assume that the wayfarer is not bent on suicide. For one reason or another, he does not appreciate the danger he faces.

Joel Feinberg distinguishes between soft and hard paternalism.[36] The former involves interventions which protect people from choices that are, in one way or another, substantially non-voluntary – not in accord with their *own* true wishes and aims. You bar the wayfarer from the unsafe bridge in the reasonable assumption that he does not want to fall into the river beneath. You stop your friends driving home when you realize, as they do not, that they have had too much to drink. You intervene to stop the post-operative, confused patient who wants to get into his car and drive home. You cajole and jolly the unwilling patient who needs to undergo painful exercises in rehabilitation, not (yet) letting on how bleak are the prospects for significant recovery of mobility. Arguably, soft paternalism is misleadingly described as a form of paternalism: the interventions stop people doing or bringing about things that they do not really mean to choose.[37]

Contrast interventions aimed at protecting people from unwise choices which really are their choices, which do indeed accord with their own values and aims – but which, even so, you consider to be perverse. Here you are imposing what you think their preferences should be – your idea of what is for their good. This is hard paternalism. Imposing a blood transfusion on the Jehovah's Witness patient might be a case in point.

Many commentators on medical paternalism approve the soft but not the hard variety. Clearly, it is easier to defend overriding a patient's current wishes when these seem in conflict with the patient's own settled preferences – where there is good reason to suspect that the patient's present 'choice', if you do not openly or covertly restrict it, would be substantially non-voluntary, as well as harmful. Yet, if one way in which a 'choice' can be substantially non-voluntary is where choosers are radically mistaken about their situation – for example, like the wayfarer, about the risks attending their choice – then even the hard paternalist interventions may typically be preventing people from doing what in a sense they do not really mean to choose. Jehovah's Witness patients would not persist in refusing transfusions if they discovered that they were quite mistaken in thinking that their doing so would incur God's wrath.

Does the idea that soft paternalism is defensible, but hard is not, rely on the shaky assumption that disagreements over matters of fact are decidable (so doctors may reasonably suppose they know better than their patients), whereas disagreements over matters of value are not (so doctors may not reasonably suppose they know better)? As Peter Geach has said, this assumption 'limps on both legs': factual questions are not always decidable, and there is no good reason to assume that moral questions are essentially undecidable.[38] Doesn't the distinction between hard and soft correspond to a distinction between differences of belief that can easily be resolved (like that between you and the wayfarer) and differences of belief that cannot be easily resolved (like that between you and the Jehovah's Witness)? In the case of hard paternalism, where you disagree about what is for the subject's good, the disagreement will quite likely itself turn on a difference of belief about matters of fact.

It is sometimes claimed that medical paternalism towards adult patients is insulting and demeaning because it treats them as if they were children. But paternalism towards adults is not necessarily insulting or demeaning. It is no insult in situations where their judgement is compromised through no fault of their own (if, for example, it is a result of the medication they are on). Sometimes contempt (low opinion) is deserved – contempt for a belief or an attitude. But contempt also implies a low opinion where better is to be expected. It shows no contempt for my dustbin that I deposit dust in it. But it does show contempt for a book (perhaps proper contempt) if I use it as a door-stop. If patients are characteristically depressed and resistant to post-operative treatments following traumatic surgery, having a low opinion of their attitudes does not signify any contempt for these patients – such attitudes are to be expected even of patients who happen also to be distinguished medical or nursing colleagues.

It is, however, somewhat simplistic to suppose that, provided doctors are acting in line with patients' own views of their best (health) interests, they cannot really be going against their true wishes. We do not, nor necessarily should we, always choose to put our personal welfare first. Acting against our own health interests is not necessarily irrational or in anyway reprehensible. Think of the heroic dedication of Lukwiya and of Urbani.[39] Often, though, when we act against our health interests in rejecting advice, we are acting irrationally and we know it – as when it is merely our own settled vices or whims that prompt our choices. Here the law, agreeing with Mill, upholds our liberty to choose imprudently, provided we are not thereby wronging others. Respecting this liberty clearly constrains what doctors and nurses can do for us in pursuit of their caring duties.

Medical paternalism is insulting, is a failure of respect, where doctors or nurses presume *unreasonably* that they know better. Given that patients' rational preferences do not always coincide with their best health interests, doctors and nurses are often not well placed to safely assume that they do know better. Freud refused palliative medication during his last illness, since it interfered with his capacity to work. That was surely a choice he was entitled to make, even if it was against his health interests. There should, then, be at least a strong presumption against hard paternalism in health care. Hard paternalism is in any case restricted by the duty that doctors are under to obtain consent. The patient who is legally competent (able to understand in broad terms what is proposed and to come to a decision) has the right to refuse treatment – in the words of Dame Butler Sloss (quoting an earlier ruling), 'A mentally competent patient has an absolute right to refuse consent to medical treatment, for any reason, rational or irrational, or no treatment at all, even where the decision may lead to his or her death.'[40]

Taking stock

The duty to obtain consent derives from a duty that we are all under, doctors included, to refrain from laying hands on other people without their consent. Since providing medical treatments often necessitates laying hands on patients, it is important to be clear about what constitutes valid consent. The law here gives straightforward and uncontroversial guidance. This duty is no new discovery, even if it scarcely gets a mention in histories of medicine. It is hardly credible that doctors have not always taken it seriously. True, it is not an item in the Hippocratic Oath. But what does that prove? According to a 1993 survey of Medical Schools in Canada and the United States regarding their use of the Hippocratic Oath, only 3 per cent prohibited sexual contact with patients.[41] Are we to suppose that the other 97 per cent condoned it? Surely not. Nor should we assume that the total absence of consent from Hippocratic writings demonstrates that doctors used not to understand the necessity of obtaining consent.

The duty to inform adequately, if seen simply as part of the professional duty of care, is nothing new. However, the duty is more complicated to specify than is the duty to obtain consent – particularly in regard to what standard of disclosure is adequate. Standards of good practice change, partly because knowledge increases. Consequently, the duty to inform adequately can be expected to become increasingly taxing. In times gone by, doctors would not have had so much information to share with patients – or so many tried and tested alternatives to canvas.

Nowadays, as we have noted, the duty to inform patients adequately may be said not just to derive from the duty of care. It may be said to derive also from patients' 'right' of autonomy. If so, which sense of autonomy is relevant and is compromised if information is withheld? By withholding information doctors would not be interfering with their patients' capacity for self-command, but they could be deliberately curtailing their self-reliance and their liberty.

Might this interference, though, be justified paternalism? Should patients always be helped and encouraged to be self-reliant, rather than simply allowing their doctors to decide for them? We have noted that self-reliance is a virtue only when it is combined with judgement – only when reliance on one's own judgement rather than that of others is reasonable. Thus, helping someone to be self-reliant is not always acting in their interests and is not always a sensible way of helping them to acquire the virtue of (proper) self-reliance. You do not help your young children to acquire this virtue by leaving them to work out for themselves how to handle fireworks safely.

Finally, we should recall that Mill's objection to paternalism concerns cases where letting people make unwise choices exposes them alone, not others, to harm. In clinical contexts it may be hard to find examples of unwise choices by patients that pose no risk of significant harm to anyone but themselves. Often the harm is *very* significant. We have all sorts of 'owings' to others which cannot be fulfilled if we allow ourselves to die or to be maimed. Beauchamp and Childress suggest that minor hard paternalistic actions are quite common in hospitals – and often justified.[42] They give as an example a 23-year-old patient who, after receiving his pre-operative medication, objects to the nurse putting up the side rails to his bed. He understands clearly the reason why the nurse wants to put up the rails, but he does not feel drowsy and has no intention of falling out of bed. But is the nurse, in over-riding his objection, merely acting paternalistically? Staying by the patient to see that no harm ensues in the busy ward will deprive other patients of attentions they urgently need. Leaving the patient exposes him to a risk. If he does fall, his operation may well have to be post-poned. That will be troublesome for others as well as for him.

7

'First, Do No Harm'

The teaching 'First, do no harm' has been solemnly repeated down the centuries, though its origin is obscure. Does it have a place in medical ethics?

Is this pledge (I will call it the *harm* pledge) supposed to be an undertaking to refrain from accidental harming or to refrain from non-accidental harming? Let us think first of accidental harming. A pledge to do no accidental harm would hardly be sensible. It is said that virtually every treatment carries risks. Suppose you interpret the pledge this way and accordingly spend all your time at the races. You might boast: 'Well at least I do no harm to my patients – I never go near them.' At this point someone might say that neglect, after all, counts as a harm.[1] What, then, can you do? Retire altogether from medical practice? You can't be harming patients if you don't have any.

A pledge has to relate to what you think is within your voluntary power. It is not within your power never to harm, even by accident. Harming through carelessness or incompetence is another matter. Resolving to avoid that does indeed make sense. Otherwise, we would not blame people for their careless or incompetent actions. Consider what is said to be the nearest phrase to 'first do no harm' that is to be found in the Hippocratic writings (in the *Epidemics*): 'to practice about diseases, two things: to help or not to harm'.[2] This seems to call attention to a humdrum necessity, a minimal thing – as if to say: 'The first thing, and it may seem platitudinous, is not rashly to harm your patients'. If we interpret 'first do no harm' along these lines – simply as a cautionary warning to doctors to know their limitations and to avoid rash proceedings, bearing in mind that the cure can easily be worse than the disease – it is a timely and important reminder. It could even be described as an axiom of medical ethics. Yet if it is so obvious (as axioms, after all, are supposed to be), does anyone need reminding of it? Well, perhaps it does deserve attending to; not because anyone doubts its importance, but because it is all too easy inadvertently or under pressure to act against it.

Compare now what is said about harm in the Hippocratic Oath. It contains a pledge to refrain from 'harm and injustice', and the immediately surrounding prose gives us some clue as to what is meant: 'I will apply dietetic measures for the benefit of the sick according to my ability and judgement; I will keep from harm and injustice. I will neither give a deadly drug to anybody who asks for it, nor will I make a suggestion to this effect. Similarly, I will not give to a woman an abortive remedy. In purity and holiness I will guard my life and my art.'[3]

This bit of the Oath seems to be making a different point about harm. It is not, as above, simply committing doctors to take due care and know their limitations. It is also committing them to refrain from using their skills for certain (harming or wronging) *purposes* – deadly purposes that seem hostile to healing aims. In other words, we are concerned here with non-accidental harm. More particularly, we are concerned with non-accidental harms that are deemed to be unjust (as non-accidental harms characteristically are – as, indeed, is reflected in the word 'injury', it being etymologically related to 'injustice'). Of course, it is possible to treat patients unjustly in other ways – for example, by robbing or raping. But these, so-to-speak, would not be *medical* injustices.

Let us understand the above bit of the Hippocratic Oath, then, to imply that doctors have a duty to refrain from recommending or administering treatments to their patients that they know or believe will do them harm. While the idea that doctors should not deliberately harm their patients may sound too obvious to need mention, we do well to meditate on it. Back in 1947, the Council of the British Medical Association issued a statement affirming its continuing commitment to the Hippocratic Oath: 'Although there have been many changes in Medicine, the spirit of the Hippocratic Oath cannot change and can be reaffirmed by the profession.' It immediately went on to observe that this Oath 'enjoins' 'the duty of curing, the greatest crime being cooperation in the destruction of life by murder, suicide and abortion'.[4]

More recent affirmations, however, make no mention of abortion, it being now accepted practice in most countries to provide it. As for physician-assisted suicide and euthanasia, these are not quite yet accepted practice except in a few places. But many people both inside and outside medicine are in favour of their becoming so, and modernized declarations if they do not yet explicitly embrace them no longer explicitly reject them either. According to a 1993 survey of Medical Schools in Canada and the USA, only 14 per cent included a repudiation of euthanasia in their Declarations, and only 8 per cent included a repudiation of abortion.[5] In the UK, the Royal College of Obstetricians and Gynaecologists these days describes induced abortion for unwanted pregnancy as 'a basic health care need'.[6]

Does this mean that the harm pledge is no longer thought appropriate? Not necessarily. It can perhaps be 'brought into line'. Those who approve of abortion may argue that it does not 'really' harm the developing individual whose life is cut short (maybe on the grounds that you cannot harm a creature merely by depriving it of a future). And those who approve of euthanasia are likely to argue that, far from harming, it is actually a form of helping. But let us leave these two contentious issues to one side for the present. Meanwhile, we might note in passing the remarkable sea change that has occurred since 1947 in what is regarded as compatible with the pledge to do no harm. It goes to show that so-called reaffirmations of Hippocratic values may mask deep differences of ethical outlook. It also goes to show that though the notion of harm is so familiar and not a bit technical, it is by no means easy to give a good account of what it means to harm someone. Harming makes us worse off; benefiting makes us better off. And we are interested here in what makes someone better or worse off overall. But noting this gets us not much further forward. To progress, maybe we shall have to revisit those fundamental questions with which we began our enquiries in chapter 1, asking, 'What constitutes doing well and faring well in life?'

For present purposes, though, let us narrow our focus to the notion of harm in the context of treatment decisions – that being what the passage in the Hippocratic Oath concerns. In the UK, the General Medical Council (GMC) issues a pocket-size card summarizing the 'duties of a doctor'. This is obviously handy information to have at your fingertips, especially if you are new to the job. While waiting for the next patient to enter, you can take a quick peek to check if your duties include protecting patients' confidences or being honest and trustworthy. The list of these duties begins with 'Make the care of your patient your first concern'. Presumably, this implies that the *other* duties which follow, like the duty to keep your skills up to date, are not meant to rival it. You are not supposed to hone your skills on your patients in ways that do manifest harm to them. Let us call this the *priority* view. We must now discuss it with some care.

There are two kinds of priority. We might call them *presumptive* (or rule of thumb) priority and *filter* priority. Presumptive priority can be illustrated in the following way. An avuncular professional is giving advice to a young tiro. 'There are these four principles for us to live by in our field. My advice to you is to take them in a certain order. Consider the issue of autonomy first: it tends to be forgotten. Make it your first concern. Of course, you may well recognize as your consultation progresses that you might have to abridge your patient's autonomy in the case in hand. Medical ethics is never simple . . .' Filter priority is quite different. It sets up a test. If the proposed treatment or practice fails the test, it is ruled out. If it passes the test, i.e. runs through the filter, it is time to take up other considerations. With this distinction in hand, which kind of priority should doctors give to 'do no harm'?

Does 'do no harm' have a merely presumptive priority or a filter priority?

Raanan Gillon, who has led the way in putting medical ethics on the map across the UK, can perhaps be regarded as a representative figure in the subject.[7] And he rather dismisses the teaching 'first do no harm'.[8] It is a phrase, he says, 'best consigned to the medical history books'.[9] It is 'too simple', 'too absolute', he maintains, to make out that this duty (or principle) has (what we are calling) filter priority. Rather, he argues, do no harm to your patient should be regarded as one very important, but *prima facie* duty, alongside others – alongside the duty to respect your patient's autonomy, for example.[10]

What Gillon says here is, up to a point, reasonable, at least if we interpret the do no harm pledge to have the broad implications he ascribes to it.[11] But by doing so, we may miss something of great importance. To see this, we need to peel away certain crass, or anyway, unsympathetic interpretations of the pledge, that may stand in the way of our inspecting its core. Thus, it would be crass to suppose that the pledge is meant to rule out doing some harm to a patient in order to prevent the patient from suffering a greater harm – for example, doing an amputation to prevent the spread of gangrene or cancer. To be sure, amputating a limb that has so deteriorated that it is no more use to the patient anyway is hardly a case of doing a harm to prevent greater harm. But some amputations will deprive a patient of something that is still of use: for example, the cautionary amputation of a healthy breast from a patient who is at high genetic risk of developing breast cancer. No one supposes in such cases that the patient's good is not the surgeon's first concern. The pledge rules out administering treatments that do *overall* harm – treatments that a patient would be foolish to choose to undergo.

We need also to understand 'first do no harm' to be referring specifically to doctoring of patients, to contexts where the patients are entitled to trust that the advice or treatment they are getting is from carers acting *in that role*. The pledge is not concerned with other ways in which doctors may do harm to their patients, sometimes justly and sometimes unjustly. 'First, do no harm' singles out the first duty of doctors *as* doctors *in relation to* the patients they are treating. Besides whatever duties doctors have in caring for their patients, they also have general duties. General duties apply to everyone, doctors included; like, as I said before, the duties not to rob or rape.

What then remains as the core of the pledge, once these misunderstandings are removed? It would appear to say that on no account may doctors (or nurses, or dentists, etc.) who stand in a fiduciary relationship with patients and are acting in that capacity, provide their patients with medical treatments which they know or believe are against their overall interests (which these patients would be foolish to choose). The 'on no account' indicates a filter priority. Is this still too simple, too absolute, a pledge for doctors to make? Gillon claims that duties of justice (arising from other people's rights) and duties of respect for patients' autonomy can both at times override the duty to do no harm to a patient. Even with our pared-down interpretation of the pledge, should we agree with Gillon that there will still be occasions on which one or other of these types of duty overrides the duty to do no harm?

Do requirements of justice owed to others ever oblige doctors to harm their patients?

There seem to be two possibilities here. First, occasions where doctors' citizenly duties might seem to override their duty to do no harm to their patients. Second, occasions where doctors deliberately withhold a beneficial treatment from a patient in order to provide scarce resources to others. From a utilitarian standpoint, no doubt, conserving resources for others would itself be a citizenly duty.

Citizenly duties

A GP who reports a patient who is ill-treating a child or who alerts the authorities upon incidentally discovering that a patient is planning to leave a bomb on an aeroplane, is acting just as a good citizen should. But he is not acting contrary to the harm pledge. The pledge, as we have construed it, concerns only treatment decisions that involve doing deliberate medical harm to patients in ways that are contrary to their overall interests – that they would be foolish to agree to submit to. Reporting patients may foreseeably be against their overall interests. But for all that, it does not involve doctors in deliberately subjecting them to a medical harm. The pledge is just about medical maltreatment. Imagine that you are an exceedingly able doctor – the best in the neighbourhood. Patient X is disagreeable and insulting. You tell him that you are removing him from your list. You are here acting against his overall interests. But this is not medical maltreatment. You are not breaching the harm pledge. It would be otherwise if you were vindictively to prescribe an inappropriate and toxic drug or to withhold an appropriate drug.

To be sure, patients who are reported may protest that their doctors have breached the duty of confidentiality – which duty is also enshrined in the Hippocratic Oath. But the complaint would be unreasonable. The duty of confidentiality, though obviously of great importance in medicine, is not plausibly to be thought of as having filter priority. Nor is filter priority suggested in the Hippocratic Oath when it says, rather: 'Whatsoever I see or hear in attending the sick, concerning people's lives, *which ought never to be published abroad*, I will keep silent' (my emphasis).

The same reason why it would be crass to suppose that doctors who report on patients who otherwise pose a serious risk to the lives or health of others are acting against the pledge explains why it would be crass to suppose that the pledge rules out doctors or nurses acting in self-defence or in defence of others (patients, colleagues) – maiming or even killing a patient who perhaps has run amok and is wielding an axe.

Consider, though, how in some countries doctors may be called upon to administer lethal injections by way of capital punishment[12] or to assist in carrying out sharia punishments – amputating the hand of a thief, for example, or branding a criminal. Doctors who engage in these activities are deploying their medical skills and judgement with the very reverse of healing aims, and obviously they know that they are inflicting harm on those who are subjected to such punishments. Now *if* these forms of punishment are unjust, then it is wrong, presumably, for anyone to assist in carrying them out. *A fortiori* it must be wrong for doctors to assist.[13] We might think it especially abhorrent for doctors to assist – just as, while it is wrong to ill-use any child, it is especially abhorrent if parents ill-use their own children.

Suppose, on the other hand, that some such punishments would not be unjust under certain conditions – let us not get enmeshed here in discussing what these might be. Then, where the relevant conditions applied, inflicting these punishments would be permissible under justice, and it would not be unjust for doctors to assist, assuming that they personally believed these forms of punishments to be morally defensible.[14] Indeed, they might feel under some obligation to offer to assist, in order to ensure that the punishments were carried out humanely. The guillotine, it is said, was invented by Dr Joseph Ignace Guillotin as a more humane and efficient way of executing the condemned.[15]

These doctors, it is true, would be using their medical skills in order to inflict harm. But would they be acting against the harm pledge? Not so. The pledge only concerns how they act *as* doctors *in relation to* their patients. Admittedly, there may be fringe cases where it is not clear whether or not the doctoring role is, or should be, in play. Suppose, for example, that by way of making the administering of the death penalty more humane, prisoners were allowed to have in attendance their own doctors. If doctors complied with such requests, would they be violating the pledge? Possibly not. In the circumstances it is not against their patients' interests that *they* administer the lethal treatment rather than passing on this task to someone else.

Is withholding a benefit from a patient to be counted as itself a form of harming?

Doctors working within a public health service are routinely obliged to trim the kinds of benefits they confer on this or that individual patient in fairness to the competing needs of other patients. Current guidelines suggest that NHS prescriptions of statins (drugs used to lower serum cholesterol levels) should be given only to those patients who have a risk of 30 per cent occurrence of heart disease in the next ten years. This is not because those with a lesser risk (say 20 per cent) would not benefit, but rather that the cost to the NHS would be prohibitive. [16] Here, then, is a case of withholding a preventative medical benefit from certain patients merely because of the resource implications. Does this illustrate how doctors deliberately (yet quite properly) do harm to some of their patients out of consideration for the competing needs of other patients?

It does not. The intention behind withholding medical benefit in the above kind of case is not in order to harm. Nor is someone harmed simply because they are benefited less than they could be. If I give a beggar £1 when I could easily have given him £2, I will not *ipso facto* be said to have harmed the beggar. If decisions to withhold help from a patient were deemed to be decisions to harm them, an overstretched nurse or doctor who could not be in two places at once would have to say, 'I often have to harm my patients'. Likewise, a nurse or doctor who chooses to work part-time, would be acting contrary to the pledge.

For sure, decisions *not* to help are *sometimes* rightly counted as a form of harming. There is such a thing as deliberate neglect – where it is part of your job to provide a particular service, but you choose not to provide it. But deliberately omitting to treat in the circumstances described above (having to eke out scarce resources) does not constitute deliberate neglect. The help which doctors owe their patients is to provide them with care of a good standard.[17] What constitutes a good standard partly depends on the resources available. Suppose you and I are on the waiting list for a kidney transplant and a kidney becomes available that is a good match for me but a still better match for you. If the transplant team decides to give it to you rather than to me, their choice leaves me worse off than I could have been, but that is not to say that they have done me a harm.

The importance of deciding which kind of priority to accord the harm pledge

Sympathetically interpreted, the harm pledge seems so far to stand up to challenges that might at first glance appear to tell against according it filter priority. It is easy enough, though, to find instances in times gone by when doctors of good repute have seen fit to treat the harm pledge as of merely presumptive priority: for example, putting the interests of medical science before the interests of their own patients. In 1796, Edward Jenner first tested his theory that cowpox would protect against smallpox on an 8-year-old boy, James Phipps. Luckily for young Phipps, the experiment was a success. In 1967, Henry Pappworth in the UK, and in 1970, Henry Beecher in the USA, documented many contemporary instances of medical research in which the interests of patients undergoing medical treatment were casually subordinated to the quest for knowledge. One such case was the notorious Tuskegee study, which lasted from 1932 to 1972. The subjects in this research, about 400 poor rural Alabamans, had syphilis and although a cure, penicillin, was discovered in the 1940s, it was withheld from those in the study so that the effects of the natural course of the disease could continue to be observed.

To illustrate the contrast between according the harm pledge mere presumptive priority and according it filter priority, it is instructive to compare the role of doctors to that of veterinary surgeons. In many ways their roles are parallel. The UK Royal College of Veterinary Surgeons even refers to animals under the surgeon's care as 'patients'. And, corresponding to the GMC's 'make the care of your patient your first concern', the first item of the RCVS Code of Practice is: 'treat all patients of whatever species, humanely, with respect, and with welfare as the primary consideration'. If doctors should pledge 'First, do no harm', why not vets too?

But how *can* vets take this pledge? At least, they can hardly accord it filter priority. Are they not routinely involved in doing harm to individual animals with a view to serving economic or other interests? For sure, in pursuance of these purposes, every effort is made to avoid causing animals 'unnecessary' pain. All the same, harm is deliberately done to individual animals. After the outbreak of BSE in Britain and its announced possible link with incidents in young people of Creuzfeld–Jacob disease, the meat market slumped. Many dairy farmers were driven to call out the local vet to kill off young healthy bull calves. From an economic standpoint these calves were simply an unwanted by-product. Consider too how culls are routinely carried out, sometimes to benefit the herd, sometimes to benefit animals of other species, but hardly with a view to benefiting the animals selected for culling. Take, for example, the recent cull of hedgehogs from several islands in the Hebrides. Hedgehogs had been introduced to the islands in the 1970s. Unchecked by any natural predators, they had proliferated. Because they ate birds' eggs, they became a threat to the survival of various native species of wading birds such as the Dunlin. The wading birds attract tourists to the island – an important source of income. If the veterinary code permits the (humane) killing of animals in pursuance of economic or other interests, that indicates that its requirement that an animal's welfare be 'the primary consideration' must be understood (at best) in what we have called the presumptive priority sense.

With medical practice, though, do we not expect doctors to make the interests of the individual patients they treat 'their first concern' in a stronger sense – in what we have called the filter priority sense? Isn't that anyway what we *should* expect? Isn't that why we regard the Tuskegee experiment as a scandalous episode in medical history; that the doctors conducting that study so readily subordinated the interests of their patients in the study to other interests?

In fending off 'justice' challenges to the filter priority view of the harm pledge, have we so hedged about our account of the pledge as to trivialize it – as if to say, 'Do no harm that you are not justified in doing'? Not a bit. If we take the harm pledge to be concerned with avoiding doing harm where this is a species of acting unjustly, there is still a substantial issue to debate: whether the harm or injustice at issue has presumptive or filter priority. Not everyone, after all, thinks that it is always wrong to do what is unjust. Rosalind Hursthouse, for example, maintains that 'circumstances may make it necessary to do what is, in itself, wrong'.[18] For those who take this view, the duty to do no harm, as we have interpreted it, will still be merely a presumptive duty, sometimes overridden by other duties. They will say: from time to time we have to do a lesser injustice to avert a greater injustice. Of course, those who think this may still deplore the Tuskegee study (especially on account of its being conducted on poor blacks) and agree that many experiments criticized by the two Henrys were indeed indefensible. But they will not take a principled stand against ever deliberately doing significant harm to a patient in order to advance science – harm that the patient would be foolish to agree to undergo.

Does respect for patients' autonomy ever allow (or oblige) doctors to do them harm?

Here we have to consider cases in which a patient (whom we will assume is adult and of sane mind) is set upon a choice which the doctor considers would be not merely sub-optimal but actually overall harmful – a choice that it is foolish for the patient to pursue. If doctors fail to dissuade their patients (or to be persuaded by them to revise their own opinions), are the patients entitled to have their wishes respected? That surely depends on whether 'respecting' their wishes only involves not imposing a treatment that the patients ill-advisedly refuse, or on whether it also involves acquiescing in providing treatments that the patients are ill-advisedly requesting. In the former cases, 'respecting' the patients' autonomy does not necessitate going against the harm pledge. The doctors do no harm. Rather, they fail to confer a benefit. Failing to benefit in such a case (in the face of a competent patient's refusal) is not harming.

So, to find examples where respect for patients' autonomy might override the harm pledge, we need to consider cases where 'acquiescing' means administering a treatment that the doctor knows or believes will do (overall) harm to the patient. This, the filter priority view does rule out. Can we find examples, then, that illustrate this possibility: treatment decisions which involve inflicting harm on patients but which, even so, seem justifiable since that is what *they* clearly want?

Apotemnophiles

The first possible example we will consider, although it is of a kind that few doctors will face, is interesting because it rather vividly illustrates how challenging some idiosyncratic patients' treatment choices may be to doctors who see themselves first and foremost as healers. It is easy to understand how it is for a patient's own good if a limb that is gangrenous is amputated. But suppose a patient wants to have a perfectly healthy limb amputated.

In 2000, a Scottish surgeon at the Royal Falkland Infirmary, Robert Smith, amputated a leg off each of two patients at their request. Their limbs were healthy, but they wanted rid of them. Smith said (in a BBC documentary) that why these 'apotemnophiles' (literally, those who love to have bits cut off themselves) feel this way is a mystery. But whatever the explanation, the feelings are persistent, acute, and (according to Smith) are unresponsive to psychotherapy. Apart from their bizarre obsession, these patients are said to seem perfectly sane. Their condition is all the same deemed to be an illness: bodily dysmorphic disorder. After the amputations were performed, both men said that they felt much happier as a result. Smith declared: 'It was the most satisfying operation I have ever performed.' A month later, he told a news conference: 'I have no doubt that what I was doing was the correct thing for those patients.' He was planning to do a third amputation, when the trust that ran his hospital stopped him.[19]

Is this an instance of a doctor flagrantly acting against the 'First, do no harm' injunction? Smith's action might be defended in either of two ways: (1) that he was not, in the circumstances, doing harm; (2) that he was doing harm, but justifiably. The filter priority view is not challenged by the first line of defence, but only by the second.

Consider, first, did Smith do these two men harm? On the face of it, he did. The limbs that were amputated were perfectly healthy – and there was no reason to expect that they might become a health threat (unlike the case of a woman who possesses one of the breast cancer genes and who wants her breasts removed now, even though there is no evidence yet of cancer in them). But Smith argued that he was *not* actually acting against the amputees' own interests. There was a psychological need that could not be alleviated any other way.

Comparison might be drawn with another surgical intervention: removing healthy parts of bodies to accommodate the wishes of transsexuals. Is objection to these proceedings no more than an unreasoned taboo in society against mutilations and maimings? Do they not have an overall healing aim? If so, there need be no breach of the harm pledge in these cases.[20]

Consider, next, the possibility that Smith was doing these two men harm, but justifiably. Ultimately, it may be argued, patients are entitled to choose the treatments *they* prefer. Doctors must make sure their patients understand so far as possible what the options are, and what the implications are, of choices they are minded to make. But provided the patients are competent (which might well be questioned, of course, in respect of apotemnophiles) and are freely choosing for themselves, and provided they are not by their choice interfering with other people's rights (we might assume that Smith's patients were paying the full cost of their treatment), then, on this view, doctors are not acting improperly in complying with their patients' considered wishes. Those who agree with this line of argument will repudiate the filter priority view. They hold that consent is not just necessary, it is sufficient. And doctors, like solicitors, can be expected to act on their clients' instructions, however ill-advised these are.

But should we expect doctors to acquiesce? If they do, they are aiding what they believe to be downright foolish choices (and most clearly so where the intervention requested is irreversible). Given that foolishness is a vice, it is bad to act foolishly, and bad therefore to aid and abet choices which we know or believe are foolish.

Elective sterilization

Perhaps a better example for our purposes is elective sterilization. Elective sterilization has been for some time the most common form of contraception worldwide. Clearly, it is generally regarded as justifiable (a good medical practice). Yet it involves doing biological harm – a mutilation. Moreover, unlike amputating a gangrenous limb, which is done with a healing aim, the aim behind elective sterilization is nothing to do with healing; it has only to do with the inconvenience of being fertile for those who want to have sex, but not children.

But does this form of mutilation inflict overall harm? It need not, and usually it does not. For sure, there is always the possibility that the patient will later come to regret the choice. Even so, the risk is often slight, and it may be more than offset by the likely benefits. Good sense, after all, does not dictate avoiding risks wherever possible. That is no recipe for living well. Here, then, is a case where a mutilation is inflicted only because the patient wants it. But assuming, as would normally be the case, that the patient's choice is not, all things considered, foolish, the doctor who acquiesces is not violating the harm pledge.

Suppose, though, the patient requesting a sterilization is a mere 20-year-old who is adamant that she has no wish ever to have children. A gynaecologist willing to comply forthwith surely is doing harm to the patient's own interests: the gynaecologist is depriving her of a capacity which she is foolish to dispense with at this stage of her life, whatever her present opinion. Gynaecologists who uphold the priority view will refuse such requests.

Elective maiming

Suppose someone has offered £200,000 for the little finger on a patient's left hand. The patient might be an ex-celebrity (Michael Jackson?) down on his luck. Would a surgeon willing to do the amputation be harming this patient in the sense under discussion? Suppose it was a toe, and the sum was £2 million? No reason in this case to suspect that the ex-celebrity seeking a surgeon's assistance is not in his right mind.

Here is a less fanciful example to illustrate how elective surgical maiming could be advantageous to a patient. Imagine a doctor receiving a request to be surgically maimed from a British youth about to be called up to serve his country back in 1916. The doctor would have had every reason to share the youth's dim view of his survival prospects. Better a lamed life than no life. Doctors who are willing to aid and abet in this way may be acting wrongly (unpatriotically, possibly unlawfully), but are they also violating the harm pledge? Philippa Foot mentions that 'humane doctors working in the hospitals (the "sick barracks") of Hitler's or Stalin's death-dealing labour camps were sometimes careful that their patients should not get back to work too fast'.[21] Obviously, these doctors were not being negligent. That is to say, they were not doing their patients a harm by giving less than a good standard of care. The doctors' 'neglect' was not against their patients' interests. The harm pledge only rules out treatments that the patient would be foolish to submit to.

Living organ donors

Where a physical harm done to a person is to be offset by a benefit to that same person, there is no (overall) harm to that person intended.

But how can this be said when the harm to one is to be offset not by benefits to that same individual but by benefits to someone else? Yet some practices that are accepted (considered good medical practice) seem to involve just this. Consider the practice of transplanting organs from living donors. The risks, harms and burdens that the donors take upon themselves are substantial, especially if what is being donated is, say, a segment of liver or even lung. Cutting out a living person's healthy organ would, in other circumstances, count as committing 'grievous bodily harm'. Undeniably, cutting out a healthy organ does the subject physical harm. But is it necessarily hostile to the overall interests of the donor to part with a healthy organ?

Suppose a mother wants to donate one of her own kidneys to her desperately ill child. Is such a choice necessarily foolish? So it might seem to a third party. However robust the mother's health is now, she forfeits an organ that she might well need in years to come. For all she knows, her own life may be cut short as a result of this decision. Simply thinking of her own *health* interests, the choice appears reckless. But good sense does not dictate that we always put our own health interests above all other interests. In view of the mother's overall interests and concerns, the trade-off she makes is, maybe, not unreasonable – if it stands a chance of saving the life of her child.[22]

Compare the recent case in Richmond, Virginia, of a 55-year-old woman who gave birth to triplets for her daughter who was medically unable to conceive.[23] The 55-year-old (interviewed on ABC's 'Good Morning America') said: 'Well, it was actually my idea with my husband. We had seen a movie many years ago that showed a similar predicament and when this opportunity presented itself, we knew we just had to do something to make a difference for Jason and Camille. And we think that this has.'

Consider the well-known Kentucky organ donor case of *Strunk* v. *Strunk* (1969). The critical issue for the court in this case, since the prospective donor was not himself competent to give consent, was whether, despite the harm that would be done to him, he still personally stood to benefit overall.[24] Tommy Strunk was a 28-year-old who was suffering from a fatal kidney disease. His family and various relatives were tested to see if they would be suitable donors, but the only person who proved compatible was Tommy's 27-year-old brother, Jerry. Jerry was a resident in an institute for the feeble-minded. He had an IQ of about 35, which was said to correspond approximately to the mental age of a 6-year-old. The boys' mother petitioned the county court for authority to proceed with the operation. The court gave permission. It was reported that Jerry was particularly attached to his brother, who regularly visited him. Tom was his only sibling, and the parents were already in their fifties.

Suppose that there was firm evidence[25] to support the claim about the close bond of affection between Jerry and Tom and good reason to suppose that if and only if Tom received Jerry's organ did Tom stand any chance of surviving. In such circumstances wouldn't it be reasonable to regard the procedure as in Jerry's interests as well as in Tom's?

There may be limits, though, to the risks that doctors should be willing to assist living donors in taking. Renada Daniel Patterson was born with only one kidney. It failed when she was 5, and she received a cadaveric kidney. Her body rejected it a year later. By the time she was 13, she was urgently in need of a new kidney. Her father, who had abandoned her before she was born and who was serving a seven-year prison sentence for burglary, offered to donate a kidney. He was 34. He turned out to be a good match. The transplant went ahead, and for a while Renada was in good health. But after several years the kidney began to fail, partly because Renada neglected to take the anti-rejection drugs. Renada's father, still in prison, offered to donate his one remaining kidney. Renada's surgeons sought the advice of their hospital ethics committee. It did not approve the transplant. Renada's mother protested that the decision should have been a private family matter, and that hospital officials had no right to interfere. Meanwhile, Renada's uncle, Randy Patterson, aged 42, offered to donate his kidney. He turned out to be a good match, and the transplant was successfully carried out.

In this case there was some doubt as to whether a second kidney from Renada's father would have transplanted successfully. But supposing it could have been, would it anyway have been unethical to proceed, however willing the father was? It was argued that the trade-off here was tantamount to saving one life at the cost of another. Is that a choice a donor is entitled to make? Was Renada's mother right to protest that the decision was a private family matter? Would it have been a form of altruistic suicide? If so, the surgeons would have been assisting a suicide. We are postponing discussion of that issue to later chapters.

Suppose, on the other hand, that though the risks for the father were huge, it was by no means certain that he would die as a direct result of donating his kidney. And suppose that the ethics committee had approved the donation. In that case, if the surgeons were, even so, unwilling to proceed, would they have had a duty at least to hand the case on to other surgeons who did not share their reluctance?[26] In some cases, handing on might seem appropriate. The reluctant surgeons might concede that esteemed colleagues elsewhere, maybe with more experience in renal transplantation, might come to a different judgement on the case. Handing on, then, would be entirely reasonable. Suppose, though, that the reluctant surgeons did not believe that any reputable surgeons would make a different judgement on the case. Then, handing on would be inappropriate – a mere charade. As I argued in chapter 5, if you think that providing a service requested by a patient is wrong not just for you to do, but wrong for anyone to do, you cannot think it is all right to 'pass the patient on' to those who think otherwise.

Respect for autonomy revisited

If doctors do not acquiesce in providing treatments that patients request on the grounds that the treatments would do them harm, are they interfering with the patients' autonomy? In chapter 6 we distinguished three kinds of autonomy: autonomy as self-command, autonomy as self-reliance and autonomy as liberty. Autonomy as self-command is not relevant here. Having our choices denied does not diminish our capacity for self-command.

Would doctors who refuse to comply with their competent patients' requests be disrespecting their autonomy as self-reliance? We noted, in chapter 6, how self-reliance or independence of character can be a virtue, provided, as John Benson argues, it is right-minded, well-judged. Otherwise, it is not owed respect. But in the kind of case we are considering here, where the doctors refuse because they think that what is requested is foolish, obviously the patient is not thought to be exercising well-judged self-reliance. Doctors can hardly be obliged to comply out of respect for the very kind of autonomy that is lacking.

Would doctors who refuse to comply with their competent patients' requests be interfering with their autonomy as liberty? It must be noticed here that the doctors who refuse would not be *invading* their patients' liberty, only *failing to assist* them in exercising it as they wished. We might here invoke the principle that the right to have our purposes furthered by others is not so extensive as is our right against their interference with our pursuit of our own purposes. Philippa Foot illustrates the principle with this example:

A sees B drinking some harmful stuff and judges that he, A, has no right to take it from him; nevertheless when the bottle starts to roll away out of B's reach he refuses to put out his hand to get it back for him. Surely he will be right to refuse, for while B may be able to get another bottle, possibly he will not. To take the bottle from him would be an impermissible paternalistic interference whereas it is a good thing to do to refuse to get it back.[27]

Analogously, while doctors have no right to impose treatments on competent patients – assuming that third parties are not being put at risk, they are within their rights refusing to assist patients in carrying out reckless projects. A doctor is not 'interfering' if he says to a student who wants a drug to keep him awake while he revises for exams, 'It could do you harm – so I wont prescribe it'.

Needless to say, doctors who refuse to comply with requests on the grounds that a patient's preference is foolish may well be mistaken in their judgement, sometimes culpably so. Since, as we have seen, judgements about what choices are sensible or silly often have to weigh up other interests besides health interests, medical expertise does not by itself equip doctors for discerning in every case what is or is not a sensible choice. On the filter priority view, doctors act badly if they comply with requests for treatments that they are convinced are foolish. It does not follow, however, that they must be acting well if they refuse to comply in such a case. Maybe they are mistaken in their judgement, and ought to know better. Recall the asymmetry between acting well and acting badly which we discussed in chapter 5: just because your act is good in some one way (for example, it may be well-intentioned), it does not follow that in doing it you are acting well.

Taking stock

Although, typically, good sense dictates that we protect our own health and bodily integrity, there are circumstances where it does not. Hence, the filter priority view does not rule out practices like elective sterilization and living organ donations. Though these do physical harm, they do not necessarily do harm relative to good sense. Engaging in these medical procedures becomes morally problematic where what is being done to a patient is, or appears to be, quite decidedly against the patient's own overall interests – as with Renada Patterson's father wanting to donate his second kidney.

I have defended the filter priority view of the harm pledge against some seeming counter-examples where either consideration of the rights of others or consideration of the (foolish) wishes of the patients themselves might seem to justify doing harm. None of the counter-examples we have discussed compels us to budge from the firm teaching: 'on no account may doctors (or nurses, dentists, etc.) who stand in a fiduciary relationship with patients and are acting in that capacity, provide them with treatments which they know or believe are against their overall interests'. We do still, however, have to address the issues of abortion, assisted suicide and euthanasia.

The defence we have mustered here for the harm pledge has all been directed against critics who complain that 'First, do no harm' exaggerates this duty's importance. They maintain that doctors are not always obliged to refrain from doing harm. Some critics might complain that the harm pledge as I have interpreted it is too modest. Shouldn't doctors aim higher than merely doing no harm?

Obviously, though, the strict requirement to do no harm does not by any means imply that doctors who observe this are doing all that is required of them. Nor should it be supposed that this requirement, though modest sounding, may not sometimes be very challenging to comply with. Consider, for example, how the pressures of defensive medicine may tempt doctors to acquiesce in requests from patients or their relatives despite their own convictions that what is sought is contrary to the patient's interests (relatives requesting cardiopulmonary resuscitation inappropriately, or inappropriate requests from patients for Caesarean section in childbirth).[28] Doctors here may very understandably be inclined to comply, not out of respect for autonomy but merely to avoid possible litigation.

8

Duties to Give, and Rights to Get, Health Care

In this and the next chapter I will explore some issues of justice in health care to do with duties to give, and rights to get, health care. First, I will consider justice in a non-comparative way: where what A owes B by way of service does not depend on what A does for C or D. Injustice, clearly, is not always dependent on comparison: a telephone company may be equally unjust to all its customers, overcharging every one. Many kinds of injustice are non-comparative in nature: the wrong of rape, torture, murder or theft is not that the victim has been singled out and treated differently from others in the same category: the thief who steals from my house cannot plead in mitigation that he has stolen from all the other houses on the block. Next, in chapter 9, I will consider justice in a comparative way – the idea that someone may be unjustly treated simply because someone else gets better treatment.

The primitive liberty of non-assistance

Let us begin with an important, though in a way trivial, point: that people are very often, even perhaps, characteristically, at liberty *not* to help others. Here we are interested in what may be called 'primitive liberty': the elementary liberty you have to do things which do not require justifying, as opposed to the liberty you may have to do what does need justifying and for which you have the appropriate justification. Suppose the job you have requires you to work on weekdays but not on Sundays. You are at liberty, then, to take a day off work during the week only if you have an appropriate excuse: for example, it is a public holiday or you are unwell; whereas, if you do not go to work on a Sunday, you are exercising a primitive liberty – no excuse is called for. Thus, to say that we have a primitive liberty not to offer help is to say that there is no duty of this kind – no presumption that help is owed just because we happen to be able to offer it. A notice is posted: 'caffeine drinkers, aged 18–45: volunteers wanted to help in a research project studying the effects of caffeine'. Suppose you fit the description, but do not volunteer. No excuse is called for here.

And this has nothing to do with the thought that you might have something 'morally more urgent' to do. It can be all right to go fishing, though you might instead be busying yourself with people in need of help. If someone asks, eyebrows raised, how this could possibly be so and calls for an explanation, we should answer that no explanation is to be sought, for what we have said is not in the least surprising, when things are thought out. It is just what we should expect. So, we would not need to make out, for example, that the world would be a better place for everyone if we 'allowed' people to go fishing in such circumstances. Any defence which might be necessary would be confined to removing obstacles there might be to thinking well in this matter. If someone were to object, for example, that morality is all about 'loving one's neighbour as oneself', we might reply (not necessarily accepting this view) that it is very often also all right *not* to do what helps *oneself* – to abstain from self-improvement and reach for the fishing tackle (and *not* because one needs a break). All this might upset the most elementary of utilitarian expectations, but perhaps it is high time they *were* upset.

To repeat: this point about the primitive liberty of non-assistance is not in the least surprising. It would be absurd to say that it results from an exercise of intuition, or that it relies on some particular tradition of thought. Nor does the mere assent to such a truism call for a partisan label: liberalism, laxism, libertarianism or whatever. If someone were to ask why this truism goes unnoticed, we might conjecture a partial explanation: we are apt to remember occasions in which we are called upon to help; we do not, by contrast, remember the times when we are *not* particularly called upon to do so – in fact, it would be comical even to attempt to list them. It might further be complained that what we have said is unattractive. But leaving aside the obvious point that the truth is often unattractive, we have nowhere said that our ordinary untheoretical opinions about the scope of our duty to assist are sound. It is quite compatible with what we have claimed that these opinions stand in need of correction – that they are too easy going and indulgent. This, though, would need to be argued separately.

In matters of justice, liberty is, as it were, the default condition. All-rightness, then, does not need to be accounted for. Needless to say, someone who refuses to help might be complained of on other grounds – for being stingy, unfriendly, etc. Recent writers on 'virtue ethics' often provide long lists of such characterizations. However, though it might be very annoying to me, it is clear that I am not being wronged if a builder declines to take on the job of repairing my garden wall, just because he happens to prefer to go fishing.

And isn't the same true in respect of those who have medical and nursing skills – that, *prior to any contractual commitments*, they are at liberty to choose if and when to offer their services? For example, no one is wronged if you, as a doctor, take on fewer patients in order to find time to go fishing, or if you only take on occasional cases that you happen to find interesting, as Sherlock Holmes must have chosen his cases.

Needless to say, the reality of working conditions for many doctors and nurses allows no such freedom: neither freedom over how many patients they treat nor freedom to pick and choose among those who come their way. In the UK almost all doctors work within contractual commitments. GPs in the UK are not allowed to close their lists to new patients even where they are already overstretched – as many are, in areas of doctor shortage. Nor is it easy for them to remove a patient – even if the patient, for example, has lodged an unfounded complaint against them. Consultants are expected to treat all those who are referred to them. They are not allowed to cherry-pick. Only if the treatment a patient needs is outside the consultant's or GP's skills do they have the freedom to decline to treat – or, if relations have broken down irretrievably (usually because the patient has acted violently against the doctors or their staff). But this lack of freedom all arises from their contractual commitments. Without these, would there be anything morally amiss in their cherry-picking like Sherlock Holmes?

Imagine that you are a forensic pathologist (in Ruritania?), newly qualified, but that your main ambition is to make a fortune writing detective stories. Meanwhile, you might want to keep your hand in as a pathologist, drawing on some of your experiences in that field for your writing. So you offer your services to a hospital on an occasional basis, as suits you. Where is the harm or the wrong in your doing that – assuming, at least, that you take care to maintain your skills and keep abreast of new knowledge?

In noticing the primitive all-rightness of casual helping, we need not make any presumptions in favour of free markets. It is important to recognize this. There is an ideology of praise for the free market. This may have its merits. But we do not need to consider them. After all, a retired nurse or doctor could be providing services out of mere kindness, where market considerations clearly do not apply. *Primitive all-rightness*, as I have said, signals something which does not need justifying. So it does not need justifying in particular by talking up the merits of the free market, such as they may be. Needless to say, there may still be good reasons for society to regulate in various ways what is primitively all right. Just as it is in the public interest that the sale of houses is regulated, so too, maybe, it is in the public interest that the medical helping of (say) retired doctors is also regulated – at least, where they are accepting a fee.[1]

Two caveats

There are two important caveats to make concerning the liberty of free-lance nurses and doctors to pick and choose when they give help. The first caveat applies to anyone working free-lance, whether or not they are responding to a health need. The second caveat applies particularly to nurses, doctors, dentists and the like.

The first caveat concerns the motive behind a refusal to help. As we have already noted, an act that is not bad in itself may be bad if done for a bad reason. If you are anti-Semitic and you withhold your (building or medical) service from me upon discovering that I am Jewish, you act badly. Notice, though, that the injustice of racist actions like this is not really to do with meting out *comparatively* worse treatment. Actions that are motivated by unreasonable hatred or contempt are bad whether or not those at the receiving end are being treated worse than others. In the above example, if you do not bestow your service on someone else instead of me, you have still acted badly.

The second caveat concerns those needing emergency help where, if you refuse to provide it, there is no one else available or willing to do so. How are we to understand here 'emergency help'? Not all emergencies are matters of life and death. The grinding pain of toothache is not life-threatening, but don't we reasonably expect a dentist to treat patients in such a predicament, as 'emergency' cases? And shouldn't emergencies also include patients who, if not treated, may suffer some permanent injury or damage to their health even if their lives would not be endangered? Let us bracket together all these predicaments as 'emergency' cases. Is there a general duty to rescue people from such predicaments, at least where the rescue is easy?

The common law tradition does not recognize a general duty to rescue – for good reason. It would be beset by two indeterminacies. First, who among those capable of acting on it would be held to account? Second, how much effort would they be required to make (for a duty to help has to depend upon the difficulty or cost of doing so)? Laws need to have fairly clear-cut obedience conditions (or criteria), so that those minded to obey the law know what they must and must not do, and so that those charged with enforcing the law know how to apply it. Do these reasons also tell against the idea that there is a general moral duty of easy rescue? Possibly, they do not. Moral duties that we do not attempt to enforce through the law need not have as well-defined obedience conditions. Still, if there is this moral duty, we need to find an explanation – *why* we owe one another easy rescue. Maybe, a community cannot hold together if its members are wont to stand aloof when faced with each other's need of easy rescue. Maybe at least this minimal degree of commitment to support one another is part of what enables people to live together in peace.

Do nurses and doctors, at any rate, have a duty to respond to medical emergency health needs when they know (or should know) that there is no one else available to do so – duties that continue to apply when they are on holiday or are recently retired?[2] It may be said that *being* a nurse or a doctor, taking on the role, involves not simply having skills that might be needed in certain kinds of emergencies but accepting some basic commitment to putting those skills at the service of others where the need is acute and meeting it is not difficult. We speak of nursing and doctoring as 'callings'. This notion of a calling involves a kind of commitment that is independent of contract and is somewhat open-ended. An old-fashioned butler might have this kind of commitment to the family he has served over the years. It would be more than a little odd, though, for computer-programmers or telephone engineers to think of their work as a calling, a vocation.

Does the second caveat apply only to emergency help? Suppose that you have invented a screening machine which detects incipient illnesses and provides a benefit to those affected.[3] Suppose that there is only the one machine, and you alone can work it. Now, though, you want to retire – to spend more time catching trout. But do you have a duty to stay at your post, manning the machine – at least until a replacement can be trained? You might protest: 'I have done some good to the community. It is mere cheek for it now to demand more.' On the other hand, you might declare: 'I simply cannot retire until a replacement is found.' That would, no doubt, be an admirable stance to adopt, but are we seriously to suppose this 'cannot' refers to a requirement of justice?

Compare again the builder who declines to build my garden wall. We do not suppose that he has a duty first to check whether there is someone else available to do the job for me. At this point, it may be said: but surely there is a *right* to health care. Health care is different in this respect from 'building care'. No one supposes that there is a right to have garden walls built.

Well, we have already allowed *some* rights to health care, because some would be included in the right to easy rescue. But the screening machine in the above example may not be needed to meet those rights. We need not suppose that the illnesses it screens for are serious – maybe, just a nuisance. Thus, the appeal to a right to health care is only relevant if it is an appeal to health care rights more generally (not just in response to easy-to-meet emergency needs).

The idea of a right to (non-emergency) health care

Rights, we are supposing, have to be rights *vis-à-vis* others who have corresponding duties. At least, rights that are not *vis-à-vis* anyone hardly seem worth discussing, let alone championing. Hence, if there are rights to health care, we need to consider on whom the corresponding duties to accommodate them are supposed to fall, and why. Duties of justice specify what we owe others by way of forbearance or help. It is quite usual to talk of rights in both cases: a right not to be mugged, a right to help from the police if we are mugged. A right to (get) health care would be a right to get help – what may be called a 'welfare right'. Is there any such right?

In asking this question, we are wanting to know whether there is, so to speak, a *general* right to health care. For, obviously, there can be a special right to health services, just as there can be to building services. If you have promised to build me a garden wall, then I have a right to this service. Or A may have a special right to a health service from B because B has negligently been responsible for A having the health need. Or A may have a special right to help from B because B is A's guardian, with duties of care, including attention to A's health needs. The interesting question is whether, special contexts apart, there is a right to health care. A needs it, B can supply it: can A call upon B to supply it? Declarations and Charters of Rights often include a human (i.e. general) right to health care, along with other welfare rights, without indicating who has a duty to jump to, should a demand for help be made. If this is left entirely indeterminate, we might doubt whether any intelligible claim has been made at all.

Notice that what makes the idea of a right to health care problematic is not simply that it is a welfare right, or simply that it is a general right. Rather, it is the combination of being a welfare right *and* being a general right that raises a problem. Clearly, the notion of welfare rights makes sense. As we have just remarked, A has a (welfare) right to B's assistance if B has promised to give it. Clearly, too, the notion of general rights makes sense. Your right not to be raped is a right *vis-à-vis* everyone: everyone has a duty to forbear from so acting. General duties to forbear do not give rise to the problem of indeterminacy, flagged above, that dogs the notion of a general duty to rescue. The same indeterminacy problem attends the closely allied notion of a duty to offer health care.[4]

Yet we should not simply despair of making sense of general welfare rights and duties. Nor, on the other hand, should we rest content with claims that we are under such duties that we cannot back up with any explanation. Consider, for example, the general right that people on trial have of access to legal counsel. That right relates to a public interest: that due process is observed in trials. Unless due process is observed and is seen to be so, people will cease to trust the law, will take the law into their own hands, and break the peace. Isn't preserving the peace the first duty of a state – its *raison d'etre*? Maintaining the peace and security are bound up with upholding due process. In other words, a story can be traced connecting the general right of access to legal counsel with a human necessity. We can see why in any society, it is vital to uphold this right and no less so than the negative rights against assault, etc. Can a similar story be traced to support the idea of a general right to non-emergency health care?

The story would need to explain why the state has a duty to provide for our health needs, in so far as it has the resources to do so – for who else is in a position to provide comprehensive health care? But *why* should the state assume responsibilities relating to its members' health needs? Some health needs would seem to fall within its ambit as part of maintaining peace and security. To this end the state has an interest in public health and hygiene, and in preventing epidemics of AIDS or SARS or the like. It is hard to see, though, how people's health needs more generally – the needs, for example, of people with Alzheimer's or heart disease or Parkinson's – impinge on the security concerns of a state.

Whether there is such a thing as a human right to (receive) health care tends to be something of a partisan issue between the champions of liberty, on the one hand, and the champions of equality, on the other hand. Briefly, champions of liberty fear that people will be forced to provide medical services, and champions of equality fear that only the rich, or those fortunate enough to have medical friends, will be able to obtain treatment. Side-stepping this debate, we might simply say that even if there is no such right, many people might still like there to be one, and a government could accordingly create such a right for its citizens without thereby seriously interfering with any supposed right to liberty. Admittedly, though, while the government could be especially mindful of the liberty of health care providers, it would not be able to avoid making some inroads on people's liberty: the minority opposed to the scheme who would still have to pay taxes to support it. Perhaps this is pretty much what happened in the UK when its National Health Service was introduced after World War II. Let us briefly review what happened.

The Beveridge Report (1942) envisaged a health service that would 'ensure for every citizen there is available whatever medical treatment he requires, in what ever form he requires it'. The occasion for setting up this particular comprehensive health service can be explained, I think, simply in relation to specific circumstances that held in Britain at the time. First, there was a recognition that sacrifices had been made by both civilians and the military forces, and there was a general feeling that some public acknowledgement was owed. Secondly, there was a desire to realize something good out of the war effort, beyond the restoration of peace. Thirdly, there was a realization that as a result of the measures taken to co-ordinate services during the war, it was now feasible to introduce a comprehensive health service. (There was at that time widespread faith in the efficiency of planned economies.) And doing so gave fitting expression to the palpable sense of solidarity and fellowship that then existed. The sense of solidarity and fellowship could have been given expression some other way. But establishing a comprehensive health service did seem an appropriate, and popular, way to make something good of the hard-won victory, to build on all the sacrifices that had been made, to bring about something permanently better – the New Jerusalem.[5]

Notice that this case for creating a NHS that I am suggesting is localized: it explains why the scope of the duty that was assumed extended only to members of the British community – not to people in need of health services throughout the world. This case makes no appeal to some supposed human right to health care. But it does explain why it was thought appropriate to create new rights as of 5 July 1948. We do not have to believe that prior to that NHS Bill the right already existed, unrecognized. We might still agree with David Owen (who was Minister of Health in the UK Labour government 1974–6) that it was then 'quite simply right' to create the NHS, given the opportunity and the shared need: quite simply 'fitting' – a reasonable state venture. [6] It was what virtually everyone wanted and voted for, and it was perceived as vastly preferable to the shambolic and humiliating health provisions for the poor and not so poor that had existed before World War II.

Those earlier provisions had been introduced with a view to improving national efficiency, military and industrial, and, once again, not in response to any notion of people's right to receive affordable health care. Lloyd George set up a National Insurance Scheme in 1911 (modelled on one established by Bismarck in 1883), to enable low-paid workers to have free medical care. (Employers, employees and the state paid into the scheme.) The underlying aim was to prevent the workers from falling into poverty through illness and becoming a burden on the state. [7]

Yet the idea behind the founding of the NHS, that no one any more should have 'money worries in times of illness' (White Paper 1944), may be said not to rely on mere historical happenstance, which might make it reasonable at a certain time and place to set up a public health service, but rather to acknowledge a duty any state that is sufficiently affluent owes its citizenry.

This thought that no one should have money worries in times of illness, and that states able to prevent this have a duty to do so, relies on some notion that it is unjust if *money* gives some advantages over others in regard to health needs. How is this supposed injustice to be explained? Essentially, I believe, it stems from the assumption that it is unfair to allow sheer luck to determine who gets better health care. By 'sheer luck', I mean what Ronald Dworkin calls 'brute luck', as opposed to 'option luck'. He draws the distinction thus: 'Option luck is a matter of how deliberate and calculated gambles turn out – whether someone gains or loses through accepting an isolated risk he or she should have anticipated and might have declined. Brute luck is a matter of how risks fall out that are not in any sense deliberate gambles.'[8] In the case of option luck, the victim bears some responsibility for the outcome. In the case of brute luck, the victim bears no responsibility at all. Suppose, for example, that A and B, who are both fair-skinned, are given the very same advice by their GP regarding the need to take extra precautions to avoid skin cancers. A takes careful heed of the advice and does not get skin cancer. B ignores the advice and gets skin cancer. B is unlucky, but at the same time partly responsible for the bad outcome. B had the option to take care and did not. The fact, however, that A and B are both fair-skinned and are therefore more vulnerable to skin cancers is a matter of brute luck. There is nothing that either could reasonably have done to avoid being fair-skinned.

It is particularly where ill luck is of the brute sort, where the victims could not in any way be said to deserve their fate, that some are wont to suppose that its occurrence amounts to an injustice, and that those in a position to rectify it have a duty to do so. Accordingly, they suppose that in so far as the state has a duty to protect its citizens from injustice, it has a duty to prevent sheer ill luck barring people from access to health care. Let us notice, however, that if undeserved advantage *per se* is unjust, it is unjust not only where the advantaged have better access to basic health care but also where they have better access to non-basic health care. In other words, the assumption implies a duty on the state to assure all of its citizens equal access to health care generally – in so far as it can muster the resources to do so.

Can we seriously suppose, though, that states have a duty to remove (all) money worries in times of illness?[9] If there is a right to affordable health care, is it not more plausible to take it to be a restricted right relating to basic health needs? Can't we expect the very well-off to foot the bill for their visits to luxury health farms? And can't we expect successful sportsmen to pay for the services of their specialist medical advisors? Even the wealthiest state cannot meet every health need of its citizens. Lord Beveridge, who pioneered the NHS, had the idea that once the system got established and the country became more affluent, the demand for health care would fall. It did not. Affluence simply brings in train different, not fewer, health problems – e.g. childhood obesity, more elderly people living on and succumbing to Alzheimer's disease.

Still, the claim that the state has a duty to remove all our money worries relating to health care may not be as extravagant in its implications as it sounds. It is not, if the duty is understood to be merely a *prima facie* duty, – one duty the state has to balance alongside its various other duties. So understood, the extent to which a state is obliged to iron out differences between the monied and the unmonied in matters of health might not in practice reach beyond provision of basic health care.

We have yet to explore, though, the underlying idea that it is unfair if the monied are allowed to get better health care. This leads us to issues of comparative justice – the subject of the next chapter.

9

Distributive Justice in Health Care

In this chapter I will consider (1) if and how issues of distributive justice arise in relation to people's health needs and (2) some implications both for front-line providers of health services and for those who decide policy over who gets what by way of health benefits in a community, hospital, clinic or practice.

The phrase 'unjust distribution of health care' is not at all clear. Compare the following scenarios:

Case 1: A is employed only to nurse B, but neglects B.
Case 2: A is employed by a hospital board to nurse B and C. A takes exceptional care of B, but in order to do so, neglects C.

In both of these cases A acts unjustly: patients are wronged.[1] But are both cases examples of *distributive* injustice? In Case 2, C is wronged because care is bestowed on B that is owed to C. In Case 1, B is wronged but not because care that is rightfully B's is bestowed on someone else. We may call both cases instances of distributive justice, inasmuch as both involve care not being distributed properly. Or we may call only Case 2 an instance of distributive injustice, inasmuch as there the injustice is, it seems, bound up with a comparison.

If we understand distributive injustice in the first sense, then any case where people are denied the health care they are owed (whatever the circumstances) will count as a case of distributive injustice. Thus, if A denies B the care that is owed to B, B is wronged however A treats others. (Of course, comparisons are often instructive, since they show up what is available that could be differently distributed). Nothing hangs on which way we use the phrase 'distributive justice' as long as we decide what we are including under it. Here, let us understand it in the narrower, comparison sense – where fair shares is at issue.

But when we home in on this narrower 'comparison' sense, it turns out to be surprisingly difficult to come up with an example. Let us revisit our Case 2. C is neglected because A spends too much time on B. The wrong C suffers is neglect. That is a wrong, whether the cause happens to be that A is lazy or that A is distracted by her enthusiasm for gardening or, as above, by her enthusiasm for treating another patient. In other words, the comparison is causally relevant to the injustice, but not of its essence. Fairness is not really the issue here. Hence, our Case 2 does not, after all, illustrate injustice in the narrower sense. The suspicion arises that maybe nothing does in a health care context. But let us proceed with an open mind and see if what are commonly treated as instances of comparative unfairness in health care confirm or correct this suspicion.

The Hippocratic Oath makes no mention of a duty to treat patients 'fairly' in relation to one another, though it does mention the duty to avoid what (would have been called) injustices. The examples that occur in the Oath, however, are not to do with issues of *distributive* injustice in the narrow sense but with injustices of other sorts (assault, invasions of privacy, breaches of confidentiality, abortion and administrating or supplying poisons). As was noted in the Introduction, injustice at least from Plato to J. S. Mill did encompass matters of this kind, and I remarked that in the medical ethics of our day this broader notion of injustice has damagingly been lost sight of.

Why is there no mention of distributive justice in the Hippocratic Oath? One reason might be that the duty to treat patients fairly in relation to one another was too obvious to need mention. Maybe, though, a more plausible (and interesting) explanation as to why distributive justice gets no mention is simply that issues of this kind would scarcely have arisen for doctors. I don't, of course, mean to insinuate that doctors used to be less perceptive about these issues. I mean, rather, that if we consider the *elementary* way in which someone provides a service, either *pro bono* or for money, comparative questions would seem out of place. This has nothing to do particularly with nursing or doctoring. If you choose to offer help to A, B and C, you cannot be faulted simply for helping one more than another, even assuming their needs are the same.

The primitive liberty of casual 'unequal' helping

In the previous chapter it was argued that, contracts and emergencies aside, doctors and nurses are entitled to pick and choose whom they take on as patients, just as self-employed builders and jobbing gardeners are entitled to pick and choose whom they work for. They have this same elementary freedom – primitive liberty.

We must now take this consideration further. Not only are self-employed builders and jobbing gardeners at liberty to pick and choose *whom* they serve, they are also at liberty to give *more* help to some of their customers than they give to others – though we may be inclined to insist that they owe a good or reasonable standard of service to each and every one of their customers. But a builder is not to be faulted simply for doing a better job for one customer than for another, which he might do without being aware of it, and therefore unintentionally. And even if the favoured customer is intentionally given extra service, where would be the wrong in that? It may be argued that doctors and nurses do *not* have this liberty: they should give the *same* good standard of service to every patient. Yet how would this argument go? Let us suppose that you conscientiously provide a good standard of service to all your patients. Would it make sense, as a reprimand, to be told: 'You have treated all your patients well, but one of them you treated especially well. What is your excuse?'

Dr Lydgate in George Eliot's *Middlemarch* paid extra visits to Fred Vincy when Fred was clearly on the mend, recovering from a serious illness. Lydgate had his eye on Vincy's pretty sister. His showing this partiality might have been imprudent. But assuming that he was not neglecting his other patients, the mere fact that he bestowed extra attention on Fred, for non-medical reasons, is not an instance of unfairness. And if, in being so attentive to Fred, Lydgate *was* neglecting other patients, the complaint should have been about the neglect *per se*, not about the unfairness of neglecting some of his patients when he was not neglecting others.

In other words, if Lydgate was competent by the standards of his day, and was providing a good standard of service to all his patients, who was wronged or harmed if he gave still better to some? Obviously, as we have already acknowledged, a lot of doctoring and nursing these days is conducted by individuals who are not working free-lance. They are working within hospitals, clinics, nursing homes or group practices, and they are bound to act as their contracts dictate. Even so, there may be ways of offering extra help to some without thereby deviating from their contractual obligations.

Suppose that you are a midwife and that your sister, pregnant for the first time, regularly rings you up for advice. Suppose you encourage her to do so, saying, 'Don't hesitate to ring me!' Are you remiss in making this offer to her, if you do not offer the same encouragement to all your clients? Suppose your usual practice is to give clients only the phone number of the agency you work for. They will be put through to you just when you are on call – otherwise they get put through to a colleague. To your sister, though (and maybe occasionally to some clients to whom you take a special liking), you give your mobile phone number so that she can always reach you. Are you being unjust or in any way unprofessional?

A nurse who happens to be a close friend of yours arranges to syringe your blocked ear on a Friday evening (after hours), so that you don't have to wait all weekend. Do I have a ground for complaint if I too ring up on the Friday asking to have my ear unblocked and am offered an appointment on the Monday morning?

The general point which these examples illustrate is that providing a service, basic or extra, be it free or for money, is (presumptively) a voluntary activity, and as such is something in a person's gift.[2] What I am saying here, I take to be a mere matter of ordinary good sense. It must be admitted, though, that many contemporary philosophers think it obvious that we owe 'equal consideration' to everyone.[3] They then have to finesse their view, with secondary principles and various qualifications, in an attempt to square it with good sense. They have to explain away the seeming innocence of arbitrary 'unequal' helping. Nosing along the road in heavy traffic, sometimes I wave in a car waiting to join the flow from a side road. Sometimes I do not. Do I need a justification for letting in this one and not that one? Is there even a presumption in such a matter that if I am a 'conscientious moral agent' I will strive to be even-handed? On the contrary, isn't it only in rather special contexts that even-handedness is morally required? To be sure, even-handedness, or at least the appearance of it, is often prudent, for which reason it might be wise policy for staff to be discouraged from openly lavishing extra care on favoured patients. But this is nothing to do with fairness.

What it *means* to say that everyone is owed 'equal consideration' is not obvious. One way of taking this phrase is as indicating simply that *everyone* is owed consideration. So understood, saying that everyone is owed *equal* consideration in respect of health needs is adding nothing to saying that *everyone* is owed consideration in respect of health needs. Be it so. The question then arises: how much consideration is owed everyone? Let us suppose that the answer is: the standard owed should be fixed to correspond with what it is reasonable to expect in the circumstances. Suppose a nurse more than meets that standard. No one can levy complaints of negligence against her. But suppose that she also does more for some patients of whom she is fond. Is this unjust?

Suppose that, owing to some breakdown in laundry services, there is a temporary shortage of blankets in a ward. Normally each patient on the ward is assigned three blankets. To be issued only one blanket would be sub-standard care. To be issued two would not be sub-standard, but patients are even more comfortable with three. Because of the laundry crisis, nurses are instructed to give each patient two blankets only. Plainly, for nurse A to give patient B three blankets, meaning that she has only one blanket left for patient C would be, not only contrary to orders, but unjust (*qua* negligent) to C. Here, it would not do by way of excuse for A to protest that B was her best friend.

But suppose that nurse A distributes the blankets as directed, and then finds that there is one blanket left over. She might then think, 'Great, I'll give it to my friend B,' or she might think, 'I must give all the patients an equal chance, so I'll draw lots,' or she might think, 'I must leave this blanket in the cupboard so as to avoid giving any one patient an unmerited advantage.' Is one of these responses to the situation the right answer – the only fair thing to do? Is the first of these responses, at any rate, unfair? Is equalizing the distribution of health benefits a duty of justice? We will revisit this nurse's dilemma shortly. Meanwhile, we need to reflect further on the notion of 'fair shares' in the context of health care.

Fair shares and access to health care

Many countries nowadays have introduced more or less universal health services, and other countries are urged to follow suit. The costs of these services are everywhere troublesome. Measures are therefore adopted to contain the costs – including what is commonly called 'rationing'. An editorial by Steven Schroeder in the *New England Journal of Medicine* in 1994 claims that (medical) 'rationing occurs in some form in every country, including the United States'.[4]

Often what is called 'rationing' in the health care context is simply any practice or policy, applied for selecting who gets access to what, that is adopted in the face of scarce resources. For example, the lifeboat rule, 'women and children first', would count as a form of rationing. Likewise, the practice in libraries of putting popular books on short loan only. Used in this loose way in the context of health care, there is no such thing as an individual citizen's ration as a certain delimited quantity. Ronald Dworkin says that rationing of health care in the USA at the present time is 'largely on the basis of money'.[5] Presumably, he means no more than that the monied get better treatment, not that there is a policy to this effect, still less a rationing policy. What, we might ask, would a rationing policy based on wealth look like? Maybe, it would involve issuing tokens for health care, portioning them out in some relation to wealth, and allowing access to health care only in exchange for these. No one has ever proposed such an odd scheme. Perhaps, Dworkin's thought is that what happens in the USA is *as if* such a scheme were in operation.

Where there are public health services, can those who feel let down by what they are offered complain that they are not getting their 'fair share'? Does it make sense to speak of 'fair shares' in this context? Compare the kind of context in which the notion of 'fair shares' seems unproblematic: a child's birthday party, where a cake is to be divided. In this case there is (1) a divisible entity to divide up – the cake; (2) a definite number of individuals entitled to a share – the constituency; and (3) a reason for doing the share-out, in that cakes on such occasions are regarded as, so to speak, 'joint gifts' to all invited – the cause.

None of these conditions seems easy to distinguish in trying to apply the notion of 'fair shares' to the distribution of a country's health resources. What aggregate is supposed to correspond to the cake? Presumably, a country's health resources. But what sort of aggregate do these constitute? The difficulty here is not simply that estimates of a country's health resources are likely to be rough, since the boundaries of what counts as a health resource are vague. The difficulty is deeper. What are we to *understand* as a country's health resources? Do they include all the health services that are available? What counts, then, as 'available'? The services of all trained nurses? Do we include trained nurses who, for whatever reason (they've gone fishing or are having babies), are not nursing? Do we include nurses who could be lured away from their own poorer countries to meet our needs? Do we include people who could be, but are not, trained to nurse or to contribute in other ways to providing health services? In estimating what resources are 'available', do we include resources currently spent on defence that could instead be spent on health services?

As for the constituency, those entitled to a share of the health resources, do we have even a rough idea of whom to include? Do we include future generations? Do we include people stricken by disaster in other countries who appeal for our help? We are dealing here with a number that is not even roughly determinable.

As for cause, what entitles us to regard the country's resources as the common property of its citizens? By what right does a country regard your skills and talents as a jointly owned asset? If you want to go abroad to nurse people stricken by some disaster, do you need your own country's permission, since you will be depriving it of 'available' resources (i.e. your skills)?

Now let us return to the 'dilemma' faced by the nurse with one blanket left over. What should she do? Should she give it to her friend? Draw lots? or put it back in the cupboard? What entitles us, though, to presume that there is an answer to this question: the right or fair solution? Maybe questions of fairness do not arise here. At least, the disanalogies we have just noted between making sense of fair shares of a birthday cake and making sense of fair shares of a country's health resources tell against the very idea that the nurse has a duty to distribute the last blanket according to the dictates of fairness.

Health care for free

A public service need not be free. People expect to have to put stamps on their letters at the public post office. It is sometimes said that a public service cannot be free. Don't we pay for it through taxation? But here the taxed do not actually pay for the services, if any, they receive, except in a manner of speaking. What they (are made to) pay for is the *existence* of the service. The same service, after all, is available to everyone in the relevant catchment area, irrespective of whether they pay a lot, a little, or nothing at all, in taxes.

Bernard Williams, in a well-known article, insists that money must not influence the way in which medical care is distributed. The proper criterion for medical care, he says, is medical need.[6] He declares that it is 'irrational' to distribute medical care except according to medical need. Of course, in the sense that medical care is for medical need, it is likewise the case that plumbing services are for plumbing needs. In neither case does it follow that those who provide these services are acting irrationally (or improperly) if they select which medical or plumbing needs they respond to according to some other criterion than degree of need – like, for example, how much money is on offer. If you choose to practise medicine, you are not rationally or morally obliged to distribute your services so as to meet the most acute medical needs in the community. You are being neither irrational nor unjust if you choose to specialize in addressing the career-specific health and fitness needs of ballet dancers or opera singers, just because you admire their artistry and want to be part of their world, or maybe because you see that in this specialty you can make a tidy fortune.[7]

Some say that 'respect for persons' is violated if money is allowed to give some an advantage over others when it comes to health care.

This is one of the reasons Amy Gutmann puts forward in support of her claim that it is unjust to provide a treatment to the monied in one's community if it is not made equally available to the unmonied. For practical reasons, she does not press for radical change to prevent this sort of injustice. All the same, it is in her view wrong that money should give some citizens an advantage over others in matters of health.[8] She contrasts the tolerability of our receiving inferior service on an aeroplane because we travel economy rather than business class with the intolerability of receiving an inferior service from the police or from nurses and doctors when we need their help. In the latter cases our having money should bear no part in how our needs are responded to. The former kind of discrimination is no threat to our self-esteem, says Gutmann, but the latter is.[9]

Inferior service, or access to a service, though, is not automatically an affront to self-esteem. Whether inferior service ruffles our self-esteem rather depends on why the service we get is inferior. If it takes an ambulance twice as long to answer my call as to answer yours, because I have chosen to live on an offshore island and you live on the mainland, my self-esteem should not be wounded. It is another matter if the ambulance takes twice as long answering my call if we are next door neighbours, both of us domiciled, say, in the town of Peterborough, Ontario, but you are a Peterborough man and I am not. (A 'Peterborough man' is one whose family has resided in Peterborough for at least two or three generations).[10] And don't many of us who are aware of our own health needs, and could afford to pay to have them attended to, choose to spend our time and money otherwise – sometimes, quite sensibly? If such private choices do not necessarily indicate self-contempt, why assume that a community's choice not to meet some health needs of their citizens indicates contempt for them?

Some say that people's rights to 'equal opportunities' are violated if money is allowed to give some an advantage over others in matters of health. Norman Daniels, for example, maintains that health care distribution is not just unless it arranges so far as possible to reduce barriers to equal opportunities in life that are caused by illness or injury.[11] Why so? He points out that illness and lack of access to basic health care put people at a considerable disadvantage in terms of equal opportunities. Such people lose out competitively, and often through no fault of their own. This is, of course, true. But what follows? How is the transition made from being unlucky to being wronged? Where does the duty come from to strive to equalize people's opportunities? The underlying assumption appears to be that a society has some duty to remedy (brute) bad luck.

As we noted in the last chapter, the duty to correct for brute bad luck, *if* it existed, would apply not just in respect of basic needs. We would continue to have this duty to strive to equalize opportunities even if we lived in a very affluent society in which the worst off were really pretty well off. This duty, then, is not to be confused with a duty to help the poor or with a duty of easy (emergency) rescue.

Michael Walzer (in *Spheres of Justice*) maintains that for people to be able to buy their way to better health care, or quicker access to it, is objectionable in the same way as it is objectionable if people are able to buy honours, prizes or degrees. But the cases are disanalogous in two significant respects. (1) Those who buy honours, prizes or degrees need to do so furtively, deceptively. The honours, etc. would be of no use to them if they did not pretend that they were earned. But medical treatment that is bought is no less useful to the recipient if the purchase is openly acknowledged. (2) If it is known that people can buy honours, etc., it undermines the value of those honours that people come by honestly through their own merits. But the known fact that some people can buy, say, hip replacement surgery in no way reduces the value of that surgery for those who get it free.

Walzer mentions another example of unseemly buying. In 1863, during the American Civil War, a Conscription Act was passed. Exemption was allowed for people willing to pay $300 (a large sum in those days).[12] Leaving aside any objection there may be to conscription *per se*, was it anyway unconscionable to allow the monied to buy their way out? If the monied are able to secure better or quicker health services than the unmonied, is this also unseemly, and for similar reasons? Are these both examples of unfair practices?

Yet again we must note that the mere fact that a practice happens to advantage some over others, even though the advantaged have not done anything to 'deserve' better, does not make the practice unjust. Thus, even if those who were able to buy their way out of conscription were putting others at a disadvantage, it does not follow that they were putting them at an *unfair* disadvantage. And indeed, they might not even be putting any others at a disadvantage. Suppose that every male in a certain age bracket is called up. But Jack buys himself out. Suppose that no other individual is now conscripted to take his place. All that happens, perhaps, is that the army has an extra $300 to buy better rifles: from a military standpoint, a reasonable exchange. All the same, the practice may indeed be indefensible – but for some other reason than that it is *distributively* unjust.

Similarly, the mere fact that some people – for example, the monied – are lucky in being able to get quicker or better health care than others, does not show that these others are being unfairly disadvantaged. Suppose that you persuade a retired nurse to come and look after you. I might wish that she would come to me instead, and maybe my nursing needs are more pressing than yours. Maybe, too, I have some reason to believe that had you not turned up, she would have agreed to look after me. She, however, is not *obliged* to tend either of us. And it so happens that she prefers to help you: it might be because you can offer her more money, or it might be that you are luckier than I in some other way – maybe she happens to dote on your spaniel. Is this unfair? Am I wronged? I am unlucky, and perhaps I have done nothing to 'deserve' my predicament, not being able to match your offer and not having a winsome spaniel to rival yours. But, once again, sheer bad luck is unfortunate – not in itself unjust.

The like-cases principle

It is said that fairness requires that 'like cases are treated alike'. The conventional, but in truth distracting, response to make to this pronouncement, is to say that it settles nothing: everything hinges on what should be counted as a 'like case'. Two babies need a heart transplant, and one becomes available that is an equally good match for either baby. One baby has Down's syndrome, the other does not. Are they like cases? Two couples seek fertility treatment. One couple already has a child, the other does not. Are they like cases? A heart and lung become available for transplant and are an equally good match for two patients, one of whom has been a heavy smoker, the other of whom has cystic fibrosis. Are they like cases? Two patients need a hip replacement, only one of whom is able to pay (go private). Are they like cases?

There is something more interesting to notice about this like-cases principle. It sounds innocuous – if somewhat unhelpful, for the reason suggested. But appeals to it are liable to smuggle in the assumption that an issue of comparative justice arises. That, however, is just what needs to be established. We need to ask in the particular context (here, access to health care), if the context is one in which the principle applies.

There are distinct ways, perhaps, in which the principle might properly be invoked: (1) in contexts where it is remiss to allow even *accidental* differences to occur in how benefits or burdens are distributed among 'like cases'; (2) in contexts where it is remiss to allow *personal preferences* to influence how benefits or burdens are distributed. If you are a trustee charged with the duty to share out an inheritance equally among the beneficiaries, you are obliged to apply the principle both ways. If you are a magistrate passing sentence, the principle obviously applies in the second way. But does it in the first?

Suppose that you and I are magistrates and we are passing sentence on like cases; but you pass a sentence of two months, and I pass a sentence of three (assume that both sentences fall within the range of reasonable sentences for the type of offence in question). If we cannot find any relevant difference between our two cases, must we conclude that at least one of us has got things wrong? Must we think that there is a 'right sentence to pass'? Is the accidental difference an instance of distributive injustice?

These points about the 'like cases' phrase in the context of sentencing have an important bearing on controversies over policy decisions in health care. Suppose that two neighbouring towns have a windfall, and both decide to put the money towards local citizens' health needs. Suppose that in one town they decide to put the money into improving hospice facilities, whereas in the other they put it into improving programmes for drug rehabilitation. Let us suppose further that the populaces in both towns are as similar as can be in relevant respects – the same needs for hospice improvements and the same too for drug rehabilitation. Must we then say that at least one of these allocations is wrong (since like cases must be treated alike)? Provided that in both cases the decision has been reached impartially and thoughtfully, why should the difference be a ground for complaint or embarrassment?

In the UK, the complaint is often made that people do not have the same access to health benefits throughout the country. For example, the ease with which they can get access to fertility treatment varies from one region to another. This inequality of provision is commonly referred to as the 'post code lottery'. The present government is pledged to rid the country of this 'inequity'. Yet, the mere fact that different regions, to whom portions of a national budget have been distributed to be allocated within their respective areas, do not adopt the same distributive policies, does not by itself indicate that there is any injustice afoot.

It would be another matter, though, if the government responsible for allocating health resources from a central budget was not itself 'even-handed' in its allocations to the various regions. Isn't the government *vis-à-vis* its citizenry analogous to a trustee *vis-à-vis* beneficiaries with equal entitlements?

Medical triage

The term 'triage' (from the French for 'sorting' or 'choosing') was first applied in the medical context of sorting soldiers wounded in battle, according to their needs and prospects. Nowadays the term is applied in other medical contexts where sorting and prioritizing of patients is necessary – as when, for whatever reason, there is a shortage of intensive care unit beds. The individual who mans the reception desk of the Accident and Emergency Ward these days is often called the triage nurse. Obviously, sorting and prioritizing of patients also takes place away from life-and-death situations – as in our example of the parcelling out of blankets during a laundry crisis. In such situations choices have to be made between patients, to bestow medical benefits on some rather than (or, in some cases, sooner than) on others.

Now if someone asks, 'What does fairness permit or require in these triage situations?', we should pause to consider whether these situations give rise to an issue of fairness. You (being a doctor) turn up at the scene of an accident and think that you are unlikely to be able to help A, who is too badly injured, hardly need to help B, and pick on the middlingly injured C to help. Why would 'fairness' so much as cross your mind? You want to do some good – that is all. If you help C, you are unlikely to tell yourself that fairness permits you to do so. Indeed, the very idea of fairness 'permitting' is unnatural. What is not unjust is just. But should we say that what is not unfair is permitted by fairness? It is more natural to think of 'just' as a residual category, like 'legal', than to think of 'fairness' as a residual category. If 'just' is a residual category, then everything we do is just if it is not unjust. I am suggesting, that we should *not* similarly suppose that 'fair' is a residual category, and that everything we do is fair if it is not unfair. Rather, we should understand that questions of fairness and unfairness arise only in certain sorts of contexts – contexts, as with our birthday cake example, in which there is a divisible entity for distribution, a constituency of those entitled to a share of it, and a cause or reason for doing a share-out.

Consider the following scenario: two patients, A and B, are candidates for a kidney transplant. A kidney becomes available which is an equally good match for both. A is 75 years old, and B is 57. In the absence of further information, how should a doctor choose?

Needless to say, in reality it is unlikely that there will not be further information about A and B which the doctor might find relevant. Adding years to a patient's life is just one of a range of benefits that doctors reasonably have in view. Other benefits in the range will include making patients more comfortable, less anxious, more mobile or otherwise more able. Then, too, there are considerations beyond the medical benefits that a doctor can bestow directly on a patient that, rightly or wrongly, might enter into the choice: like what this patient is likely to do with mobility or sight restored (rob a bank? complete the writing of a novel?), or whether by treating this patient first, you can bestow more health benefits generally (inoculating doctors and nurses first in face of an epidemic, so that they will be available to help deal with it).

But let us return to the simple scenario. Even here we can expect there to be different views over how to proceed. One doctor might give the kidney to B, hoping to bestow more years of life. Another doctor might draw lots, thinking this is 'only fair'. Which of these responses, if either, is the right response? *Is* there a right response?

Suppose that when the kidney becomes available, there is only the one patient A to hand and the doctor has begun preparing A to receive it when along comes patient B. Would it be unfair for the doctor to stop the preparations on A and transfer the kidney to B instead? Might it be unfair *not* to do so? Or might either choice be defensible, and neither the required (only fair) way of proceeding?

The doctor might be working in a hospital which has certain efficiency targets. In that case, the doctor may be contractually obliged to choose B over A. Would such a policy itself be unfair? Or would a hospital be at fault and, act unfairly if it refused, or even omitted, to adopt a policy that would use resources more efficiently?

Assume that the hospital is government-funded. If governments have a duty to be 'even-handed' in how they treat their citizens, would they be wrong to impose efficiency on triage choices in their hospitals? Wouldn't these in effect make certain categories of citizens second class; like older patients and patients with chronic diseases (e.g. arthritis, asthma)? A government could still encourage efficiency in treatment of individual patients – encouraging the use of generic drugs, for example.

If, on the other hand, the hospital is privately funded, has it any duty to be 'even-handed' in triage choices? Is it unfair if it adopts and announces a policy of prioritizing war veterans? Suppose that Polish émigrés set up a hospital for descendants of Polish émigrés: is it unfair in triage choices if they give preference to patients in that category? Saving the leg of a Pole before the life of a non-Pole appears to be unjust in view of the duty on doctors of easy rescue. But if the triage choice is between patients with equally acute needs – say, for renal dialysis – is it unjust (because unfair) for this hospital to say, 'Poles first!'?

Taking stock

At the outset of this chapter the suspicion was raised that, while it is easy to find examples of patients being denied the care they are owed, it is not so easy to find examples of patients being treated unfairly where the injustice depends on comparison with others who are better served. That suspicion seems to have been confirmed. For sure, there are many situations in which patients are unlucky compared to others in regard to the health care to which they have access. But once we cast off the very common, but irrational, assumption that those who suffer brute bad luck are necessarily victims of injustice, it becomes difficult to find *any* examples of distributive injustice (unfairness) in health care contexts.

Scarce health resources confront providers with hard choices. Hospices, for example, may agonize over whether to stick with a policy of caring for every patient till death or to switch to a policy of transferring out (back home or to a nursing home) patients whose symptoms have been brought under control but who are not dying very quickly, in order to make room for others with urgent need of hospice care. We should not assume here that there must be 'the right choice' – the better, fairer policy.

In the course of the discussion in this chapter, I have flagged a number of questions where it may be supposed that there should be a right answer if only we had a better understanding of justice, especially distributive justice (fairness). But with some of these questions the right answer may be: 'There is no right answer – no one alternative which fairness dictates.' And this *not* because the alternatives are equally fair, but because fair shares is not an issue in this context.

Let us now rejoin the question I raised in chapter 8 as to whether people have a right (against the state) to have their health care needs provided for, whether or not they can pay. We have explored one way of defending this right: making out that it is *unfair* if, through ill luck, those who cannot pay do not get their (non-emergency) health care needs attended to. This popular route of support for a state's duty to provide turns out to be no good – at least, if it relies, as we have supposed, on the mistaken assumption that victims of brute bad luck are victims of injustice. Perhaps there are other ways of accounting for the right to non-emergency health care. At any rate, it is not simply to be assumed that there is this right. Explanation is called for.

10

Abortion

That the Hippocratic Oath repudiates abortion is something of an embarrassment nowadays, and modern, updated versions of the Oath soften or expunge this item. The Canadian Medical Association boasts that its current Code of Ethics has as one of its sources the Hippocratic Oath. But, unlike that Oath, it side-steps issues to do with medical killing, such as abortion and euthanasia, which it relegates to separate policy statements. The 1994 Declaration of Geneva reads: 'I will maintain the utmost respect for human life from its beginnings even under threat', which wordage leaves it conveniently vague when human life is to be deemed to have begun. This is hardly surprising, given that in many countries abortion has been decriminalized and is available virtually on request, in the first trimester of pregnancy at least.

The prevailing view of professional bodies is that abortion, where not illegal, is, in the words of the World Medical Association, simply 'a matter of individual conviction and conscience' – and, accordingly, the medical (and nursing) profession itself need not (and should not) take sides on the issue. This policy *sounds* even-handed (and is agreeable in that it allows people to avoid uncomfortable discussions), but it is, for all that, actually taking sides on the issue. Anyone who says that abortion is merely 'a matter of individual conviction and conscience' does not view the possibility that abortion involves child killing, or something akin to it, as an open question. If it does or may involve precisely that, it needs more by way of justification than simply that providers of this service are acting in accordance with their own convictions and consciences.[1]

The thought that abortion might involve child killing is something that many will naturally want to play down. Rosalind Hursthouse, in a much admired and anthologized article, maintains that 'virtue theory' 'quite transforms the discussion of abortion. It does so, by dismissing the two familiar dominant considerations as, in a way, fundamentally irrelevant.'[2] The two dominant considerations she has in mind are: (1) what a human foetus *is*, and whether this sort of thing can justifiably be killed, and 2) the scope of a woman's rights over her body, and whether these rights include a right to have an abortion. Both considerations, of course, relate to the virtue of justice (as I have characterized it in chapter 2). Hursthouse wants to bring into the discussion of the morality of abortion a range of other considerations. Even if women are acting within their rights in requesting an abortion, they may still, we are told, be acting very badly. They may still, for example, be doing something 'cruel, or callous, or selfish, light-minded, self-righteous, stupid, inconsiderate, disloyal, dishonest . . .'. Anyone is bound to agree with that. But can virtue theory also brush aside the other consideration as to whether the killing involved in abortion is a wrongful killing in the way killing so often is? How can that be 'fundamentally irrelevant'? Hursthouse herself remarks that the cutting off of a new human life is 'in some sense' always a serious matter.[3] That being so, how can it not feature prominently in any enquiry into the morality of abortion? At any rate, our discussion here will be what Hursthouse calls 'killing-centred'.

First, a brief note about terminology. There is a tendency to adopt euphemisms wherever doctors are involved in killing. Tom Beauchamp and James Childress, for example, say that they do not like to talk about 'killing' in regard to physician-assisted suicide or euthanasia. They delicately prefer to ask when, if ever, doctors should be involved with 'intentionally arranged deaths'.[4] And although induced abortions are commonplace in many countries, the doctors and nurses who perform them do not describe what they do as killing. They prefer to talk of 'terminations'. Needless to say, *every* pregnancy ends in a termination of the pregnancy. And sometimes this termination is quite uncontroversially 'induced'.

How to explain what makes killing wrong

Bioethicists commonly adopt the following perfectly natural strategy for resolving disagreements over controversial types of killing, such as (elective) abortion. First, they say, select some examples of killings that are uncontroversially indefensible (the easy cases). Secondly, single out the feature(s) shared by these examples that make these killings wrong.

Thirdly, inspect the hard cases where the wrongfulness of killing is in dispute, to see if the same features are present there too.

Yet, though nothing, in a way, is more obviously and indisputably wrong than a plain murder, it does not follow that the *explanation* of this wrongness is easy and uncontentious. Far from it. The usual accounts of what makes killing wrong when it is wrong that go the rounds among bioethicists seem (to me, and I hope, presently, to you) inadequate. The quest is for an understanding of how murder is wrong *non-incidentally*. Thus, we know in advance that we cannot explain how murder is wrong by pointing out that it causes distress, since this will sometimes not be the case. This is not to say that the distress commonly caused might not feature in an account of the wrongness of killing in an indirect way, as part of a complex story. The usual accounts of what make certain killings wrongful locate this essentially in the harm or injury done to the one who is killed: that a valuable life is ended. Accounts differ over what makes human lives especially valuable: is it that people have distinctive rational capacities? Is it that they (most of them) want very much to go on living? Is it that they (most of them) stand to miss out on good things if their lives are cut short?

Whatever further explanation is offered as to why human lives are so valuable, each explanation rests on the same assumption that the wrong-making feature of homicide is that it involves cutting short a valuable life. That assumption, though, appears to imply that the duty not (deliberately) to kill and the duty to rescue are morally on the same footing. If it is wrong to decide to kill a patient just because by so doing you cut short a valuable life, for the very same reason it must be wrong to decide not to rescue a patient where rescue is possible. The two duties should be similarly binding if they share the very same grounding. But are they? Do the considerations that justify doctors deciding on occasion not to attempt to rescue a patient equally justify their deciding to kill the patient? If we say 'No' to both these questions, we must seek elsewhere an explanation of the duty not to kill.

The assumption that the wrong-making feature of homicide is that it involves cutting short a valuable life and the questionable implications of this assumption may both be illustrated from Don Marquis's analysis of the morality of abortion. In another much anthologized article,[5] Marquis commends the strategy described above (first explain what makes killing wrong in the easy case, and then use this insight to shed light on the harder cases) and applies it to the issue of abortion. The essential wrongness of killing (when it is wrong), Marquis argues, is that the one killed is deprived of a future of value. Marquis says that it is this feature of wrongful killing: that it inflicts on the one killed the misfortune of premature death, which explains why we regard killing as 'one of the worst of crimes. My being killed deprives me of more than does my being robbed or beaten or harmed in some other way because my being killed deprives me of all the value of my future, not merely part of it.'[6] On this account of the essential wrongness of killing, it is unimportant how many of what contemporary ethicists like to call 'features of personhood', if any, a developing foetus or new-born baby already has. It is its future prospects that we need to focus on – what sort of life it would miss out on if killed prematurely. Marquis believes that on this account abortion involves a serious wrong except in 'rare instances'. But he notes that premature death is not always a misfortune – it is only a misfortune for those who are deprived of a life worth living. (Marquis supposes that any such life must be a conscious life which contains some of the goods of human life).

Consider, now, two implications of this account. First, it puts the duty not to kill on the same footing as the duty to rescue. Both the decision to kill patients and the decision not to rescue have the same consequence: that the patients miss out on the rest of their lives – the life they would have had but for the decision. If this consequence of killing is what makes killing wrongful, and if not rescuing has the very same consequence, both duties should be equally binding. Let us dwell for a moment on what this means.

The duty to rescue is obviously a qualified duty. No one supposes that doctors and nurses are obliged to do everything in their power to prevent or delay a patient's dying. And one of the relevant considerations in deciding whether or not to rescue is indeed the kind of life that the patient would miss out on if not rescued. If the quality is bleak, and the intervention needed is burdensome to the patient or is expensive, it may be reasonable not to attempt it. Another way in which the duty to rescue a patient is qualified is by the pressing needs of other patients. If two patients suffer cardiac arrest at the same time, and the medical staff have to choose which patient to attempt to resuscitate, they must let one of the two die. What they *must* do, they *may* do. Here too it seems entirely reasonable, though not obligatory, to rescue the one whose future life prospects are better. At least, it would not be wrong to be moved by such a consideration.

Now is the duty not to (deliberately) kill patients qualified by the same sorts of considerations as is the duty to rescue? If the Marquis account of the wrongness of killing is correct, it seems so. Thus, the duty that doctors and nurses have not deliberately to kill their patients,

like the duty they have not deliberately to let them die, would turn out
to be merely presumptive. Just as they sometimes need to decide which
patient to rescue, so too they would sometimes need to decide which
patient to kill. Suppose that a hospital declines to attempt to rescue a
particular patient because it is estimated that the treatment needed
would cost a million pounds. That, surely, could be a reasonable decision – and the hospital would not even be *obliged* to spend the money
saved on saving other lives. Compare now a hospital agreeing to accept
the offer of a million pounds to kill one of its patients. Could that be a
reasonable offer to accept?

Secondly, on the Marquis account, what fundamental objection
can there be to killing one patient, thereby depriving the patient of a
valuable future life, if that is the only way doctors have of preventing
the premature deaths of several other patients who will, if let die, be
likewise deprived of valuable futures? So long as the wrongness of
killing derives from the value of the lives that are ended, there is no
way of resisting the claim that it is not only permissible, but obligatory, to kill one (say, in order to harvest transplantable vital organs)
to save several, if there is no other way of saving the several. However
special the value of the one life, is not each of the several lives special
in just the same way? 'Always remember you're unique! Just like
everyone else.'

Anyone who supposes that the duty not to kill is on a *different*
footing from the duty to rescue, or who supposes that it is *never* a justification for killing one patient that it is your only way of saving
several others, must find accounts of the wrongness of killing that
dwell on the *value* of the lives that are taken unpersuasive.

Admittedly, not everyone will find these implications disturbing: not,
for example, Peter Singer who defends driving over one trapped person
should that happen to be necessary in order to save five other lives.[7]

An alternative, 'securitarian' account of what makes killing wrong

According to John Stuart Mill, the duties of justice have a singular
importance, in that 'it is their observance which alone preserves peace
among human beings'.[8] He picks out as the 'most marked cases of
injustice' wrongful aggression and the wrongful exercise of power over
someone. He dwells on the 'extraordinarily important and impressive
kind of utility' that duties of justice have: 'The interest involved is
that of security, to everyone's feelings the most vital of all interests.'[9]

In chapter 2 I labelled this type of account 'securitarian'. From it we might extrapolate what we might call a 'securitarian' explanation of the essential (non-incidental) wrongness of homicide.

Now this explanation has some merits. The securitarian account avoids the two disturbing implications of the accounts so far discussed that focus on the value of the particular life being taken. This is because the focus of the securitarian account is not on the value of the life taken, but on the social need for some kind of strict teaching against people killing people. The emphasis is on the general *duty* not to kill, rather on people's (derivative) *right* not to be killed.

Moreover, the securitarian account of the wrongness of killing perhaps allows us to offer a unified explanation of the exceptions that have most generally been thought justifiable killings. If ever exception is to be allowed, is it not most plausibly where the killing is done in defence of one's own or another's life? Going to war obviously commits us to killing people. But we may defend our doing so if that really is necessary (and effective) for preserving our collective security. Allowing the police the authority to kill in some situations rests with the same security need. Similarly, those who defend capital punishment believe that it is a necessary measure for collective security – a measure that may indeed have been necessary in societies which could not afford to provide life imprisonment as an alternative. Of course, my remarks here are sketchy, but still, I hope, plausible.

All these conventional exceptions to the duty not to kill (and we are not going to examine them further here) might be bracketed under the notion of the duty not to intentionally kill 'innocent' humans, provided we interpret 'innocent' correctly. We would have to understand 'innocent' here *not* to refer to absence of moral responsibility or blameworthiness, but to absence of the immediate threat of harm. 'Innocent' in this sense means simply 'not engaged in harming' (from the Latin *nocens*). It is only an immediate threat of harm that allows us the securitarian excuse that killing certain individuals is our only way of defending one another.

The securitarian account of the wrongness of killing makes it easy – all too easy, it may be thought – to add abortion to our list of justifiable killings – and infanticide too, since, as Jeremy Bentham famously put it, this practice is 'of a nature not to give the slightest inquietude to the most timid imagination'.[10] As we have already remarked (in chapter 2, pp. 23–5), if the duties of justice are grounded only in our need for peace and order, then their scope is limited to those with whom we need to live in peace. And this explanation does not square with the common presumption that the general duty not to kill human beings

applies equally to those who live far away and those who live close by –
and equally to those who do not have powerful friends and allies to rally
to their defence as to those who do.[11] From a securitarian standpoint,
it would seem that distance could be morally relevant: if those killed are
remote, we may have nothing to fear from them or their kith and kin.
But nobody seriously maintains that it is morally defensible to poison
people provided they are far off. Thus, the securitarian account seems
inadequate to explain the essential wrongness of those killings we consider to be wrong.

The strategy of explaining the wrongness of killing by first selecting
examples of uncontroversially wrongful killings, then singling out
from these the wrong-making feature or features and applying that
insight to the more controversial types of killing, turns out to be of
little use, since the second step eludes us.

There are, however, other ways of addressing the abortion issue that
do not not rely on our having this insight. Thus, the general duty not
to kill may be interpreted in such a way that abortions (some anyway)
do not fall under the prohibition – do not have to involve *intentional*
killing. Or it may be conceded that abortion does involve intentional
killing, but argued that what is killed is merely a human being and
not what the author proposes to call a 'person' – not a human being
who 'counts', who has rights or, anyway, the right not to be killed. Or
it may be argued that abortions (some anyway) do not kill human
beings, but merely precursors of human beings. We will consider these
arguments in turn.

Judith Jarvis Thomson on self-defence and on the duty to rescue

Thomson does not herself believe that if an abortion is carried out
very early in pregnancy, what is aborted is already a human being or
person (she does not distinguish). But, she says, let's suppose, for the
sake of argument, that what is being killed when an abortion is performed is always a person. Suppose too that everyone has a 'right to
life', and that this right is more serious than a woman's right to choose
what happens in and to her body. Even so, she argues, it by no means
simply follows from these two assumptions that no abortions can be
justified. She develops two independent lines of argument which
could be used to justify some abortions: one line appeals to a person's
right of self-defence; the other relies on the idea that the 'right to life'
does not automatically impose on individuals who are (uniquely) able

to rescue a life the obligation to do so – at least, in cases where the rescue would be significantly onerous. [12]

The first line of argument would apply in cases where continuing the pregnancy threatens the mother's survival. It is not so clear if it would also apply if the pregnancy would do some lesser damage to the mother's health. Thomson supposes that at least where the mother's own survival is threatened, she is justified in defending herself against the threat posed by her unborn child. Thomson further argues that third parties need not be neutral in such a predicament over whose life to defend, since it is the mother who *owns* the body that can support only one life or the other. Whether it makes sense to think of our bodies in this way as items of property is questionable. Arguably, they are significantly *like* items of property. Be that as it may, we should not, anyway, assume that we can always do as we like with our own property. But let us leave this aside. It is at any rate not wrong (unjust) to help these women to have abortions, given that the earlier supposition is sound, that people have a right to defend their very lives and may need help from others to do so.

This argument, Thomson maintains, shows that sometimes it is defensible to kill rather than let die: here, that it is defensible for a third party to set about killing the foetal person rather than let the mother die. Let us notice, however, that if an abortion is justified in this way, the death of the foetus would have to be seen as a regrettable and inevitable consequence of the procedure, and not something independently aimed at by the mother or her rescuers. There would be an obligation on them to save the foetal life if that were possible without thereby endangering the mother's life. Hence, this right of self-defence justifies only a small proportion of induced abortions.

Thomson's other line of argument draws our attention to the notion of a 'right to life'. What exactly are we to suppose that it is a right to? Is it a right to have our basic survival needs provided for, no matter how onerous providing them happens to be? Away from debates about abortion, Thomson doubts if anyone believes in such a right (to another's help). If a stranger happens to need your help to survive, and only you can supply it, are you morally obliged to rescue the stranger, however disruptive of your own plans and projects that might be? Arguably, as Thomson acknowledges, a foetus is not quite like a total stranger happening to need your help. Often, the mother is at least partly responsible for the predicament of the foetus lodged inside her body. Still, Thomson maintains, the mere fact that only she can sustain the foetus's life does not oblige her to do just that. If she chose not to rescue, she would be within her rights. Her refusal to rescue would not be a wrongful (unjust) act, though it might be unfriendly. This seems reasonable enough. It is not obvious that the woman has a duty to rescue, especially if doing so would be onerous.

But how plausible is it to portray the woman and those who provide assistance as simply involved in detaching the reluctant host mother from the baby – as if killing it were incidental to what they are all about? At any rate, this line of defence, at best, only excuses pregnant women from a duty to sustain the lives of their foetuses. It does not extend to excusing their aiming to kill their foetuses. Nor, either, does it justify abortionists in having that aim. Yet, just because late abortions do sometimes result in live births, abortion techniques have been altered to avoid this untoward result. Greg Pence, commenting on late abortions, mentions that in the USA 'the use of prostaglandins to induce abortions is now avoided, since prostaglandins, although safer than suction or surgical techniques, resulted in 30 times more live births'.[13] And in the UK, obstetric departments doing terminations at a stage of gestation where there is a risk of the baby being born alive, use an intercardiac injection of potassium chloride before administering prostaglandins to avoid that awkward result. Such practices would not square with Thomson's defence of abortion. Of course, most late abortions these days are likely to be of foetuses found, through prenatal screening, to have genetic abnormalities, where it is decided that the babies should not survive. Thomson's article pre-dates this development.[14]

Moreover, while, as Thomson quite properly reminds us, a right not to be killed does not imply a right to be rescued, isn't her portrayal of abortion as a mere ceasing to rescue, rather than as an assault on someone else's life, altogether misleading? The picture implicit in her portrayal of pregnancy is of a woman who is performing a rescue throughout its duration: providing the developing foetus round the clock with food and shelter. But the mother is continually 'providing' only in the sense that she could be said to be continually 'pumping' – that is to say, pumping blood around her own body. And if it is correct to portray the mother as rescuing the foetus in so far as she 'provides' for it, it is equally correct to portray the mother as rescuing herself in so far as she 'pumps' blood around her own body.

A situation might arise, however, where a pregnant woman really would be faced with a decision as to whether or not to attempt to rescue her foetus. For example, her foetus might be discovered to need emergency surgery while still in the womb. There is nothing specious in describing the choice this woman would face as a choice over whether or not to rescue. And in such a case, we might well agree with

Thomson that the mother would not be morally obliged to consent to the surgery. At any rate, if she refused, she would not have killed the foetus. But in the normal course of pregnancy the issue of whether or not to rescue does not arise, and a decision to abort can hardly be represented as merely a refusal to rescue.

Michael Tooley on persons and human beings

As we have noted, Judith Jarvis Thomson does not herself think that the foetus or embryo is a human being from the moment of conception, though she believes it most certainly is a human being 'well before birth'. She remarks, in passing, that 'the prospects for "drawing a line" in the development of the foetus look dim'.[15] Her own argument bypasses this problem.

Michael Tooley also bypasses this problem.[16] Instead of engaging in debate over when the conceptus is properly described as a human being, he asks, rather, when it acquires a right not to be killed. To qualify for this right, says Tooley, one must be the sort of thing that is capable of certain mental experiences: specifically, one must be capable of wanting one's own life to continue. Why does Tooley treat the capacity to desire to go on living as key to the right not to be killed? He observes that to say 'A has a right to X' is to say, 'if A desires X, then others are not to deprive A of X'. Thus, it seems that being able to desire X is part and parcel of having a right to X.

Tooley proceeds to qualify this requirement to allow for certain situations where people might retain the right not to be killed although they temporarily lack the capacity to want to go on living. He envisages three kinds of situations: where they are in a disturbed state of mind; where they are temporarily unconscious; or where they have been conditioned or hypnotized out of a desire to go on living. These kinds of situations we might bracket off as aberrant conditions in someone who may still retain or recover the requisite capacity.

Now it seems pretty obvious that not even the new-born baby, let alone the foetus, has yet got the relevant concepts and desires. It does not think of itself as being the subject of a life which it wants to continue. Thus, Tooley supposes that the new-born baby does not yet have a right not to be killed. The notion of a 'capacity', however, may not be so straightforward to apply to foetuses and babies as Tooley seems to suppose. It is a modal notion, and modal notions are tricky. Is baking a cheese soufflé within your capacity? Maybe, it depends: are we asking about your capacity at this very moment, or less specifically, about your capacity generally when opportunity presents? Perhaps you would be able to bake a soufflé now but for the fact that you have just downed two whiskies and are feeling pleasantly befuddled. Perhaps you could if you were provided with a recipe book. Perhaps you could only if also provided with a microwave oven to bake it in – or the money to buy the ingredients. If we are allowed to ascribe capacities to you even when you are asleep or drunk, or not yet instructed or equipped, on the grounds that when awake, sober, instructed and equipped you could do these things, maybe we can also ascribe to babies the capacity to want to go on living on the grounds that, if we do not interfere, they will come to be able to want this. After all, Tooley himself acknowledges that your inability to exercise a capacity does not of itself suffice to prove you lack it.

Notice that Tooley's argument treats the 'right to life' (the right to keep one's life and not be deprived of it) as a kind of property right. But maybe, as I have already surmised, property rights are a misleading model. Do you own your life in the same sense as you own your books or your clothes? Notice too that this argument assumes that justice (not wronging) is *only* a matter of respecting rights. Hence, only individuals who have rights can be treated unjustly.

Yet, while it is true that since rights are rights *vis-à-vis* others, they imply duties (either to help or not to hinder), it does not follow that all our duties derive from others' rights. The general duty not to kill human beings may be a case in point. If it merely derived from others' rights, they could waive it and permit us to kill them. The law, however, treats consensual killing – duelling, for example – as a crime. It does not rest the duty not to kill on a waivable right. Compare the duty you have to provide for your children's education. You have a duty to provide for this even if they blithely permit you to neglect it. The duty is not subject to their consent – it does not *derive*, therefore, from their right.

When does the human conceptus change from a something to a someone?

At what stage in gestation is it correct to describe the human conceptus (the products of conception) as a human being? This question is one for biology to answer – in the very same way as it is for biology to determine how far on in gestation a foal exists in the womb of its mare.

Anti-abortion propaganda sometimes proclaims: 'Every abortion stops a beating heart!' That is not strictly true (if it means an already beating heart). The heart begins to beat only in the fourth week after fertilization occurs.[17] Admittedly, most induced abortions occur later than this. But let us here consider the very early abortion that occurs within the first four weeks. This may not stop a human heart, but does it all the same stop a human life? Does the life of each human being begin when fertilization is completed? The single-cell human zygote is undeniably live and human. But then so too is the human ovum – and for that matter, a human sperm or blood corpuscle. Yet fertilization results in a *new* substance – a new organism. As Elizabeth Anscombe observes, it is not like two lumps of clay becoming one, where there would be no substantial change, 'only the deletion of boundaries'.[18]

Granted that there is a new human organism, it does not follow that the zygote is already a human being. What goes into the oven when you bake a cake is not yet a cake, even if you have not left out any of the vital ingredients. A cake has a different structure from cake batter. Admittedly, a cake is the normal expected outcome, barring some disruption or interference – for which reason the cook might well say, 'The cake is in the oven'. Strictly speaking, though, it is not, when it has only just gone into the oven, already a cake. An unmade bed is a bed, but an unmade cake is not a cake.

A three-day-old mouse embryo is not a tiny mouse if it does not yet have the organs or parts of a mouse. An acorn may be rightly described as 'oak'. That is its nature, its kind. All the same, it is not a tiny oak-tree. It is not a tree at all, even if, under propitious circumstances, that is what it will develop into. Trees have a certain structure (anatomy). They have roots, trunks, branches. A tree might still be a tree with its branches removed. But if roots and trunk are also removed, it is no longer a tree. The mere fact that the DNA blueprint out of which a human being (or possibly two, if identical twinning occurs) exists by the time of fertilization does not suffice to show that a human *being* already exists. The plan for a building is not itself a building.

But if not from fertilization on, at what point in the course of human gestation does a new human being begin to exist? Close attention to the biological facts will not yield a definitive answer. The development being gradual, there is no such point to be found – any more than there is a point in time when day becomes night. Nevertheless, close attention to the biological facts may still enable us to determine a point *before* which it is certainly not an actual human being and possibly also a point *after* which it most certainly is.[19]

Embryologists customarily distinguish three stages: the first two weeks (from fertilization), as the period of gastrulation, by the end of which implantation is completed; the third to eighth week, as the period of embryonic development, by the end of which the main organ systems have been established; and the ninth week to birth, as the period of foetal development during which the body grows and the organ systems mature. Can we use this terminology to fix when killing a human conceptus is killing a human being? I suggest that it affords us a clear answer to the question before which a human being definitely does not yet exist: viz. not before gastrulation is complete; and a clear answer to the question after when a human being definitely does exist: viz. by the foetal period (after eight weeks).

How do we know that the human conceptus is definitely not a human being within the gastrulation period? For one thing, as Norman Ford observes, humans are multicellular individuals. But by the time the conceptus reaches the uterine cavity on the third or fourth day after fertilization, it is not yet a multicellular individual. To be sure, someone might say that human beings become multicellular *after* their zygote stage. However, by the morula stage (when there is a cluster of sixteen cells), what exists seems rather more like a colony of individuals than some one individual. The individual cells of morula and blastocyst have too much independence to constitute an individual human being.[20] The cells are not yet differentiated. Furthermore, when the blastocyst is formed from the morula, the embryo proper is still not distinguished from what will become the placenta and extra embryonic membranes.[21] At this stage, it is not as if these parts already exist but are still joined together. Rather, these parts are not yet formed. Hence, it is implausible to regard either morula or blastocyst as a human being. It is the material out of which a human (or two) might develop – though it is also possible that what develops from this very same material is merely a hydatidiform mole. Nobody would consider *that* to be a human being.

It is only when the blastocyst is implanted that the human body begins to form. Arguably, from then on what is developing is an actual human being. But surely not *before* then. In other words, we can at least establish that prior to the completion of implantation a human being has not yet begun to exist. What has come into existence with the formation of a zygote may develop *into* a human being, but it is not, prior to the completion of implantation, the developing *of* a human being.[22]

How do we know that after the first eight weeks there is a human being? Quite simply, by that stage all the main organ systems are in place, although they still need to grow and mature. Once foetal development has passed the point when all the essential organs are discernible, the foetus looks like a baby inside and out – because it *is* a baby.

Needless to say even if we are right to claim that there is a human being after eight weeks, this of itself does not show that abortion beyond that time is indefensible. Nor, indeed, does the claim that there is not a human being before three weeks of itself show that abortion then is defensible.

How can people so readily come to terms with abortion if it really does involve killing human beings?

Induced abortion is 'one of the most commonly performed gynaecological procedures in Great Britain. Around 180,000 terminations are performed annually in England and Wales. At least one-third of British women will have had an abortion by the time they reach the age of 45 years.'[23] The fact is that in many countries nowadays abortion is basically available on request at least in the first twelve weeks or so – and abortion later on in pregnancy is offered on the back of prenatal screening if that is what the parents want. There is, besides, a convenient loophole to facilitate late abortions: to protect the mother's health. Nowadays, advances in medicine have made medically induced abortions safer for women than child birth. Furthermore, 'health' is interpreted generously to cover all aspects of the woman's 'well-being'.[24]

Thus, if the argument presented in this chapter is sound, very many women are choosing to have their own unborn babies killed with the willing assistance of their doctors. Is that an unthinkable thought? Evidently, it is not.

However, as we have noted, many who defend abortion rights do not dispute that what is killed, at least in the third trimester of pregnancy, is a baby. They argue that a baby, though a someone, is not a someone who counts – who has rights that might override the mother's rights. Or they argue that the baby does have some rights – it would be wrong to get rid of it for light-minded reasons – but not if it is done regretfully and after much thought. Here we come up against the difficulty of explaining what makes killing humans wrong when it is wrong. Jeff McMahan observes: 'No one to my knowledge has ever offered an account of why killing is wrong that even begins to do justice to the full range of commonsense beliefs about the morality of killing.'[25] He should know, as one who has studied the philosophical literature on this subject in some depth. That said, the only cure for confused thinking is further thinking.

The idea that abortion is a matter of 'personal morality'

As I noted at the beginning of this chapter, the prevailing view in many countries in which abortion has been decriminalized is that the morality of abortion is now a private matter – of 'individual conviction'. Compare, for example, the stance adopted by the British Medical Association towards abortion with its recent stance towards euthanasia. 'The Association itself makes no policy statement about the morality of abortion. Nevertheless, this implies that there are circumstances in which the BMA considers that abortion is acceptable, unlike euthanasia, which the BMA unreservedly rejects.'[26] The former issue is deemed to be one on which the Association need not have a view: it is an issue, so to speak, of 'personal morality'. The latter issue has been deemed to be very much one on which the Association has seen fit to have a view and air it. But both issues have to do with doctors killing human beings.

How, though, can duties of justice, to which surely the duty not to kill belongs, be seen as merely personal issues? Duties of justice have to do with what we owe *others*. That hardly sounds merely personal. The BMA feigns to be neutral, in regard to the abortion issue. But to be neutral, it would have to profess itself undecided as to whether abortion involves intentionally killing babies, or as to whether doing so is morally defensible. If it really is undecided, can it consistently uphold a woman's moral right to abortion, committing the profession to ensuring that women who want abortions get ready access?

The very notion of 'personal morality' (or private morality) is itself of some interest. What might it mean to say of some moral view that it is merely 'personal'? It might mean that it is a belief held by some persons, and not by others: a matter on which there is no consensus. Obviously, any morally controversial issue is 'personal' in this sense. This cannot be the sense in which the BMA views abortion as merely personal, since it considered that doctors should strive towards a thought-out consensus on the controversial issue of euthanasia.

It may be said that reproductive choice is personal in the sense that it concerns a realm of life each of us is at liberty to arrange without interference. Some reproductive choices (for example, maybe, using contraceptives) do indeed qualify as personal in this sense: where the choice does not impose on others. Abortion, however, does (except if it is very early) impose on an other – the individual who is killed.

It may be supposed that abortion is personal because disagreements on this issue hinge on religious differences, and people must let each other alone to live by the lights of their religious convictions.

This too ignores the possibility that abortion involves killing other human beings – hardly a matter of merely religious concern.

Perhaps it is thought that morality is personal in the sense that each of us should act in accordance with the dictates of our *own* conscience. This, as I remarked in chapter 5, is in one sense true; in another, false. In the true sense, we each of us act badly if we act *against* the dictates of our own conscience (doing what we personally believe is wrong). Then, we act badly even if it so happens that what we believe is wrong is not. On the other hand, suppose our conscience is easy. We do not think that what we are doing is wrong. By no means are we entitled to assume here that then we cannot *be* wrong and, possibly, at fault for being so. Talk about morality being 'personal' invites us to overlook this possibility.

What the law regarding abortion should be

Even if many abortions are unjust, it does not follow that they should be made illegal. John Stuart Mill (in chapter 5 of *Utilitarianism*) maintains that our notion of unjust deeds essentially concerns what we deserve punishment for doing – what we ought in some way to be compelled to do. However, he does not think that the law should always be the means of compulsion. When it is sensible to use the law to prevent people forcibly from acting unjustly is a pragmatic question. Sometimes it is better to rely on the influence of public opinion or personal conscience. Criminalizing abortion is unlikely to stop women with unwanted pregnancies from getting abortions. In developing countries, where abortion is illegal or highly restricted, mortality rates from abortion are much higher than elsewhere.[27] Even if the law could be effective as an enforcer, recourse to it might be inhumane. Given these realities, it may be a good thing if, around the world, the trend is to decriminalize abortion. It by no means follows, though, that the issue is correctly portrayed as a mere matter of personal morality.

Taking stock

I have argued that abortions conducted during the foetal period do involve the killing of a baby, whereas abortions conducted during the gastrulation period (as, for example, with the so-called morning-after pill) do not. As for the period between, these, the embryonic period, the biological facts may not be compelling one way or the other. But in order to judge the morality of abortion, we need to do more than establish if what is being killed is a human being; we need further to explain when killing people (human beings) is unjust. Those who defend euthanasia, after all, maintain that while this obviously involves killing people, it is not an unjust kind of killing. If they are right about this, then some abortions on the heel of prenatal screening might be justified along these lines – though not, surely, abortion of babies found to have Down's syndrome.

But finding a satisfactory answer to this question as to what makes killing people wrong, when it is wrong, has proved much more troublesome than might have been expected. The usual explanations on offer seem not to be adequate. This difficulty, which we have been unable to resolve, has a bearing not just on abortion, but also on the other life-and-death issues such as suicide, assisted suicide and euthanasia, to which we now turn.

11

Suicide, Assisted Suicide
and Euthanasia

In this chapter we will consider what stance doctors and nurses should adopt regarding suicide, assisted suicide and euthanasia. Whereas the medical and nursing professions in many countries have come round to seeing abortion as a service to which women are entitled to as a matter of right, these professions have been much more reluctant to abandon traditional teachings against assisted suicide and euthanasia. Yet, on the face of it, killings of the latter sort would seem the easier to justify. At least, it seems so if we approach the issues from the standpoint of the one killed. In the case of assisted suicide and voluntary euthanasia, the one killed is consenting. Not so in the case of abortion. In the case of assisted suicide and voluntary euthanasia, it is plausible to suppose that the motive of doctor or nurse is compassionate towards the one killed. That is not so likely in the case of abortion. In the case of assisted suicide and voluntary euthanasia, those who do the killing may be presumed to think that the life they are cutting short is no longer worth living. Again, that is often not the case with abortions.

Curiously, though, the health professions on both sides of the Atlantic have largely kept up their opposition to euthanasia while accommodating demands for abortion. In the United States, shortly after *Roe* v. *Wade*[1] offered constitutional protection to abortion, the American Medical Association could say: 'The intentional termination of the life of one human being by another – mercy killing – is contrary to that for which the medical profession stands and is contrary to the policy of the American Medical Association.'[2] And as we have just noted (p. 130), the British Medical Association contrasts its attitude to abortion and euthanasia: 'The Association makes no policy statement about the morality of abortion. Nevertheless this implies that there are circumstances in which the BMA considers that abortion is acceptable, unlike euthanasia, which the BMA unreservedly rejects.'[3]

The concept of euthanasia

'Euthanasia' (literally, 'good death') has come to mean the intentional ending of someone's life to relieve their suffering – that is to say, mercy killing. Before we can sensibly discuss what stand to take regarding euthanasia, we need to clarify more precisely just what kind of practices we are referring to under this heading. Philippa Foot, in her essay on euthanasia, says: 'The first thing to notice is that it is wrong to ask whether we should introduce the practice of euthanasia as if it were not something we already had. In fact we do have it.'[4] She proceeds to describe some of the 'common practices' she has in mind. One of these is: 'If someone very old and soon to die[5] is attacked by a disease that makes his life wretched, doctors do not always come in with life-prolonging drugs. Perhaps poor patients are more fortunate in this respect than rich patients, being more often left to die in peace; but it is in any case a well recognized piece of medical practice, and a form of euthanasia.'[6] This suggestion that poor patients are more likely than rich ones to be left to die in peace does not hold true in countries where most acute, critical care is provided by a public health service (as in the UK). But in any case, is what Foot describes here as common practice rightly described as 'euthanasia'? It is not, if the reason that 'doctors do not always come in with life-prolonging drugs' is just that patients refuse them. In that case, doctors are not withholding the drugs *in order to* kill.

If, however, some doctors do withhold life-prolonging drugs just in order to put an end to a patient's suffering, that is indeed a form of euthanasia. It is what is called 'passive euthanasia'. Interestingly, the 1994 *Report of the Select Committee on Medical Ethics*, which advised firmly against legalizing euthanasia, declined to discuss 'passive euthanasia', saying that the term is misleading.[7] But passive euthanasia seems to be at least part of what Foot has in mind when she says that euthanasia is recognized medical practice. A doctor, commenting on the trial in 1991 of Dr Nigel Cox, who administered a lethal dose of potassium chloride to a patient who was terminally ill and in great pain, declares: 'Euthanasia is practiced in hospital every day, in silence and in secret' (Dr Luisa Diller, *Guardian*, 10 Sept. 1996). Just what sort of practices does this doctor have in mind? Presumably, she is not claiming that doctors are every day secretly administering lethal injections of potassium chloride. Obviously, whether her claim is true depends on what practices she is referring to, and whether these are properly described as forms of euthanasia.

What, then, would it be best for us to take euthanasia to be? There is a range of practices that might fall within the scope of this concept, and various puzzles arise, especially as we move away from clear-cut typical cases. But the basic idea seems to be that someone is deliberately killed for what appears to be their own good. I say 'appears to', however someone might argue that a killing does not count as euthanasia unless it actually *does* benefit the one killed. This requirement is built in to Jeff McMahan's account of euthanasia. He says: 'Even if an act that brings about a person's death is intended thereby to benefit the person, it does not count as euthanasia if it is not in fact good for that person. If it would have been better for the person to continue to live, the act may be an instance of intended euthanasia or attempted euthanasia, but it is not actually euthanasia.'[8] Isn't it, though, peculiar to speak of such a case as 'intended euthanasia'? Isn't all euthanasia intended? And isn't it misleading to speak of such a case as 'attempted euthanasia'. Won't this be taken to mean that the killing was botched – that the person did not die, just as an attempted suicide is understood to be a botched suicide?

There are a number of points worth noting about the basic idea of euthanasia, before we move on to discuss the morality of it. First, let us note that instances of killing people for their own good need not occur just in medical contexts. The moral issues surrounding euthanasia require that we seek an understanding of the morality of killing not just in the context of health care, but more generally.

Secondly, if our basic idea is correct, what is essential for an act to count as euthanasia is *why* a death is brought about, not *how*. Thus, gentleness in the manner of killing is neither sufficient nor even necessary for an act of euthanasia. It is not sufficient: a humane person wanting free of a marriage might find a gentle way to do down her spouse. It is not necessary: perhaps the only available way of preventing someone dying in a worse way is itself messy and painful. Nor need the aim be to bestow on someone a better death than they would otherwise incur. Someone might be 'euthanased' to spare them suffering before their actual dying, though it might be predictable that after the horrible suffering they would eventually lapse into a coma and die serenely.

Thirdly, the basic idea stipulates only that the killer intends to benefit the one killed. This leaves open the possibility of the killer having other intentions besides – such as to benefit the relatives (who might include the killer, of course) or to free up a hospital bed for another patient. The presence of other intentions behind euthanasing someone does not rule out the presence of the essential intention. But it does make it more difficult to establish if the essential intention is really present. Notice too that benefits can be big or little. Maybe the killer believes that the patient being killed is thereby benefited though only in a small way (the patient is likely to die very soon in any case), but someone else will benefit in a big way – another patient waiting for that bed. Is this still to be counted as a case of euthanasia?

Fourthly, the basic idea covers straightforwardly clear-cut cases of euthanasia. But when we look to more marginal cases, the basic idea does not show us so clearly what is to count as euthanasia. Implicit in the basic idea is the presumption that death can be a benefit in some situations. In what sort of circumstances might death be a benefit to someone? We need not suppose that this could be so only if the person's *present* circumstances are intolerable and not otherwise remediable. Someone not presently suffering might want to be 'euthanased' to avoid future impending suffering – to die, for example, before they encounter breathing difficulties. Or someone might want to be euthanased for reasons unrelated to the avoidance of their own suffering. At least, this seems to be so if we recognize that we can be benefited if causes or projects that we particularly care about are furthered. Thus, someone might view his own death as a benefit, even though he still finds life worth living: suppose, for example, that he does not want to see most of his hard-earned savings which he means to leave to his children swallowed up in the ongoing costs of his care in a nursing home. (This predicament is a very real possibility in England at the present time.)

Arguably, death can be a benefit for someone who is incapable of suffering – such as someone who is permanently comatose – hence, past all experience. It may still be the case that this individual is killed for his own sake. It may be thought, for example, that it is what *he* would have wanted. Benefits do not need to be experienced to be for a person's good. Isn't it possible to benefit even the dead? Can we not do things for their sake: tending their graves, caring for their children, supporting the causes that were dear to them?[9]

It is not important for us to attempt to resolve whether the less clear-cut cases should be described as cases of 'euthanasia'. Our concern is rather with the morality of killing in this or that circumstance. Thus, for example, we do not need to settle whether or not killing someone who is permanently comatose should be called an act of euthanasia. What we want to enquire into, rather, is whether killing someone like that could be morally defensible. Before we pursue this enquiry, some common distinctions need to be noted.

It has become customary to distinguish voluntary euthanasia from both non-voluntary and involuntary euthanasia. Euthanasia is said to be voluntary if those killed themselves (freely) request this service. Euthanasia is said to be non-voluntary if those killed are unable to request or to decline this service (as with animals, babies and individuals who are severely cognitively impaired, or who for other reasons are apparently unable to communicate – as in some cases of Locked-In syndrome). Euthanasia is said to be involuntary if it is performed on persons who are able to request it but do not do so (either they decline it or they are not asked). Campaigners for euthanasia to be legalized typically repudiate involuntary euthanasia (as a matter of either tactics or conviction).

John Harris maintains that society already permits and practices non-voluntary and involuntary euthanasia: 'By far the most massive administration of non-voluntary and involuntary euthanasia is the result of government policy or action.'[10] Harris proceeds to illustrate this startling observation with several instances of the UK 'government's euthanasia programme' – viz. instances of government cutbacks and economies on health care spending which foreseeably result in people dying; people whose lives could be saved, if only more resources were made available. Clearly, what Harris here describes as instances of euthanasia are not so according to our definition. On our definition, a death has to be intended, not merely foreseen, to count as euthanasia, and furthermore, it has to be intended as a means to benefit the individuals who are being killed. Neither condition is met by the example of government cut-backs. No one can suppose that governments do this *in order to* kill off the patients who are denied access to the health care they need or that it is thought to be a benefit to these patients to be denied this.

Needless to say, John Harris is not operating on the basis of the definition I have proposed. Here is his definition: 'Euthanasia is simply the implementation of a decision that the life of a particular individual will come to an end before it need do so – a decision that a life will end when it could continue.'[11] On this definition, euthanasia occurs whether or not the killing is benignly motivated, and whether or not the death is intended or merely foreseen. He gives as one example of euthanasia the policy advocated by John Lorber, back in the mid-1970s, for the management of severe cases of spina bifida babies.[12] Lorber put the case for selective non-treatment of these babies. He argued that nothing should be done to prolong their lives – that they should be fed only on demand, given no tube feeding, no antibiotics for infection, no oxygen. In this way he aimed to minimize the suffering of these patients. Was the policy advocated by Lorber a policy of euthanasia?

It plainly is according to Harris's definition. On our definition, the answer is not so obvious. While the intention behind the policy is benign, not to prolong the suffering of the babies, it is not immediately clear whether the non-treatment is *aimed* at speeding up dying or whether more active treatments are being rejected as not in the circumstances of net benefit. Harris observes that Lorber's policy is 'calculated to bring about the speedy deaths of the patients', and his quotations from Lorber rather support that interpretation. If the policy was indeed aimed at briskly killing off these babies, then we should concur with Harris in counting the policy as an instance of euthanasia.

Compare, though, the policy of a government which cuts back on the health care resources it makes available. According to Harris's definition of euthanasia, this policy involves it. But according to our definition, as we have just noted, it does not. Whereas the Lorber policy may well have involved decisions to let babies die which were *also* decisions to omit in order to kill, government cut-backs involve decisions to let die which are plainly *not* also decisions to omit *in order* to kill. We will take up the question of when decisions to let patients die are defensible and when they are not in the next chapter.

The relatedness of euthanasia and suicide as moral issues

In exploring the morality of euthanasia, we are naturally led to reflect on the subject of suicide. *If* suicide is permissible, it is hard to object to assisted suicide. After all, if you are justified in doing X, you are, generally speaking, justified too in getting help in doing X – though, not of, course, if it so happens that you are obliged to do X on your own, as if, say, you are sitting an exam. And if assisted suicide is permissible, it is hard to object to voluntary euthanasia. Would it not be arbitrary to teach that people can be helped to kill themselves only if they are able to play some active part, however small, in the killing? Dr Jack Kervorkian, the doctor who achieved notoriety in the USA for openly assisting clients to kill themselves, designed a device to which his clients could be hooked up. It contained a lethal chemical, and the client could activate the device simply by pressing a button. Then Kervorkian got a client by the name of Youk, who suffered from amyotrophic lateral scelerosis. Youk was too disabled to manage the button. He asked Kervorkian to press it for him. It is hard to see the difference between doing it oneself and having it done at one's request as of moral significance.

But, then, if voluntary euthanasia is permissible, killing a person who requests this for his own good, why not non-voluntary euthanasia, which is also killing a person for his own good – a person who is unable to make the request? Those who argue that euthanasia should be restricted to the voluntary obviously intend in this way to safeguard against abuse. Arguably, though, this safeguard is not very reliable – it could even be counter-productive. People are notoriously vulnerable to despair in the face of serious illness or impairment. They may be mistaken in their estimation of the worthwhileness of their own lives continuing. But where voluntary euthanasia is in question, those who provide it may be inclined to assume that the requester's estimation is reliable. In the case of non-voluntary euthanasia, the providers are forced to think out for themselves if death would be a benefit in each case that comes up.

In a way, I suggest, suicide may be morally the more fundamental issue to explore. At least, if it turns out that a moral teaching *against* suicide is something we need to uphold, then the moral case for assisted suicide, and for euthanasia, cannot get off the ground. If, on the other hand, it turns out that suicide is not a bad type of action, and a moral teaching against suicide *per se* is unwarranted, then further discussion can get off the ground regarding assisted suicide and euthanasia. My hunch is that suicide is the more fundamental issue – and that we do need to hang on to (or recover) a moral teaching against suicide itself. It is this hunch which I now want to explore.

The concept of suicide

The notion of suicide gives rise to complexities similar to those we have discussed in relation to euthanasia. Here too there is a range of cases. Accordingly, there are problems over what to count as suicide as we move away from the clear cases. The basic idea, though, I take it, is that of intentional self-killing.

It may be argued that this is too bare an account – that we should add in the idea that you only commit suicide if you kill yourself from a certain motive – out of a desire no longer to live an unhappy or painful life, or in order to avoid future misery. This fits the most common kinds of case – the kinds that are counted by mortality statisticians. If we build this feature into our account of suicide, it will allow us to exempt from 'suicide' some of the altruistic self-sacrificing acts which might otherwise have to be included. A mother who in a famine starves herself to death, passing on all the food she gets to her children, does not do this because she thinks she'd be better off dead. But in this case, it may be said, she does not refuse food in order to kill herself – her death is foreseen, not aimed at. In short, even on our bare account, we do not have to say that this woman committed suicide.

Consider the case of Maximilian Kolbe. He was a Polish priest imprisoned in Auschwitz, for having harboured Polish refugees, including Jews, in his friary. In Auschwitz, if a prisoner escaped, the Nazi officers would randomly select ten prisoners to be starved to death by way of reprisal. On 14 August, 1941, a prisoner went missing, and ten prisoners were duly selected for 'punishment'. One of these was a Pole, Franciszek Gajowniczek. He wept: 'My poor wife! My poor children! What will they do?' Kolbe then stepped forward and said to the commandant: 'I am a Catholic priest. Let me take his place. I am old. He has a wife and children.' The request was granted, and Kolbe and the others were led away to die. (It later turned out that the missing prisoner had drowned in the camp latrine. Kolbe was canonized in 1981, and Franciszek lived on to the age of 95, never forgetting his indebtedness.) Should we say, then, that Kolbe committed suicide?

Presumably, he would not have been canonized had the Pope thought so. As with the former case of the mother starving herself, here too we need not suppose that Kolbe acted with the intention of killing himself, or even of getting himself killed. His own *death* was not an essential means to preventing the killing of Gajowniczek. As it happened, Kolbe outlasted the others who were selected to die, and as he was still alive nine days later and the guards wanted his cell for other purposes, someone was summoned from the camp hospital to give him a lethal injection. It is conceivable that, instead, a sympathetic guard might have spirited him away and saved his life. Had that happened, there is no reason to suppose that Kolbe would have objected. This is not to say, however, that someone who deliberately gets himself killed by someone else might not, even so, be a case of suicide. Imagine, for example, a prisoner in a concentration camp who confides to a friend that he wants to kill himself, that he finds his circumstances intolerable. The friend advises him to run towards the prison perimeter fence. If he does this in broad daylight, he will be shot. He follows the advice, shouting out to make sure that he is noticed by the guards, and they shoot him. In this case, as in Kolbe's, the prisoner gets himself killed by someone else. But in this case, unlike Kolbe's, that is precisely what he intends. Thus, again, we do not need to embellish our basic idea of what suicide is so as to make out that Kolbe was not a suicide.

Compare the case of Henning von Tresckow. He took part in the July 1944 plot to assassinate Hitler. When he learned that the plot had failed, he took his own life (blowing himself up with a hand-grenade). Before he went off to do this, he explained what he intended to do, saying that he did not trust his capacity to withhold names of accomplices under torture. Did Tresckow commit suicide? His case firmly fits our basic idea. Clearly, he aimed to kill himself – though not, presumably, because he was tired of life and felt that life was no longer worth living.

As with euthanasia, so with suicide, once we move away from clear-cut cases to consider cases at the end of a spectrum of possible cases, it becomes difficult to adjudicate in a non-arbitrary way what to count in or out. But, more important for our purposes than trying to settle how to describe various problematic cases, is sorting out, if we can, the morality of suicide.

Suicide as a right

The very word suggests that this is a bad type of action – an offence against the moral law, or an offence against the law of the land, itself reflecting a moral teaching. Thus we talk of '*committing* suicide'. That signals how suicide has been viewed historically. Yet, in recent years, many countries have decriminalized suicide while retaining *assisted* suicide as a criminal offence. This might seem an anomalous, half-hearted kind of reform. If the move to decriminalize suicide was justified, wasn't it arbitrary and indefensible to preserve the law against assisted suicide? We might go further. Doesn't the law already recognize, if in a confused and back-handed sort of way, a right to kill oneself? If so, surely this right should be extended to patients who cannot exercise it without assistance? And should it not also be available to those who are unable to perform any part in the killing beyond requesting it?

These complaints about the law are fuelled by two distinct elements: (1) the seeming anomaly of decriminalizing suicide, but not assisted suicide; (2) the seeming anomaly of certain court rulings which appear to support assisted suicides in some cases, where assistance can take the form of withholding or withdrawing life-saving treatment, but refuse to support assisted suicides in other cases, where assistance has to take the form of active intervention, like the administering of a lethal injection. I will comment on the first of these elements now, and on the second in the next chapter.

The seeming anomaly of decriminalizing suicide but not assisted suicide

Has the law in those countries that have decriminalized suicide but not assisted suicide failed to keep pace with changes of outlook on the morality of suicide? Suicide used to be considered an evil act – 'self-murder'. Antony Flew makes fun of this characterization, drawing a comparison with the notion of 'own-wife adultery'.[13] Richard Hare treats Kant's portrayal of suicide as self-murder (*selbst mord*) as some aberration, which Hare puts down to Kant's curious, rigorous, religious upbringing[14] (although we might well wonder whether any such special explanation is needed, given that this characterization has been standard through much of our history[15]).

At any rate, isn't the prevailing view about the morality of suicide quite different nowadays? It is, after all, in essence something you do to yourself – which sounds like a personal matter, a final 'life-style' choice, to be put alongside the arrangements, possibly somewhat eccentric, you make for your funeral. Admittedly, suicide is a singularly momentous life-style choice, more like deciding to marry someone than like choosing a new hat or even arranging your own funeral. Even so, if the choice to kill yourself is, sometimes, just a personal matter, why in such cases is it not equally a personal matter if you want to end your own life and if, needing assistance to do so, you seek help from those willing to provide it? Maybe, then, the move to decriminalize suicide itself reflects only a partial, incomplete accommodation of the law to the new way of thinking about the morality of suicide. Has the law failed to square with the implications of the new way? Has it failed to appreciate that there is no good reason to persist in denying a right to assisted suicide, once the law has recognized a right to suicide?

This line of thought assumes that the law decriminalized suicide to keep up with the new thinking among reputable, representative citizens about the morality of suicide – the thinking that suicide is essentially a private matter, and not something for the law to concern itself with. There is, though, an alternative explanation of why it was decided to decriminalize suicide, which, according to John Keown, was also the actual explanation in respect of the English 1961 Suicide Act. Keown quotes the government minister who steered the Act through the House of Commons:

> Because we have taken the view, as Parliament and the Government have taken, that the treatment of people who attempt to commit suicide should no longer be through the criminal courts, it in no way lessens, nor should it lessen, the respect for the sanctity of human life which we all share. It must not be thought that because we are changing the method of treatment for those unfortunate people, we seek to depreciate the gravity of the action of anyone who tries to commit suicide.[16]

What, then, was the motive for decriminalizing suicide if the reformers had *not* changed their view as to its morality? Keown suggests that it had come to be seen that the criminalizing of suicide was not much of a deterrent and, besides, that it imposed unduly harsh consequences on the offenders' families.[17] This explanation shows that there need be no inconsistency in supporting the decriminalization of suicide but not of assisted suicide. Those who would assist suicides *can* be effectively deterred by the threat of prosecution. And *their* families need not be already having to cope with a sudden and shocking bereavement. All the same, and even supposing that Keown is correct about the actual thinking behind the 1961 Suicide Act – that it did *not* reflect a change of view as to the morality of suicide and was *not* intended to underwrite some supposed moral right, say of self-determination – the question remains: is the historical view of the morality of suicide mistaken? Should it be jettisoned?

Towards understanding the way in which suicide is bad

Some types of acts are in themselves essentially unjust – for example, stealing, cheating and raping. Since we have characterized 'justice' as a virtue concerned with what we owe others (by way of help or forbearance), and since we have characterized 'suicide' as intentional self-killing – something, that is, that we do to ourselves – suicide is not in itself unjust. But, of course, an act of any type can wrong others incidentally. Even the innocent-sounding choice to go for a walk can be incidentally unjust – as, for example, if it so happens that you are supposed to be at your post in the ward or the office. Not only can acts of suicide be incidentally unjust, and seriously so, they typically *are* unjust in this way. Consider, for example, how many suicides are committed by people whose parents are still alive and upon whom the suicide of their offspring inflicts a grievous and lasting injury. In some cases, maybe, the parents deserve no better. But in many cases they do.

All this may be true, but the possibility remains that some suicides are not unjust in any way. If suicides are not necessarily unjust, should we reject the historical teaching that suicide is a bad type of action?

Injustice is only one of the vices. If suicide is a bad type of action, maybe we should look elsewhere, at other vices, to explain this. Let us recall the distinction we drew (p. 26) between social and personal virtues. We noted that these categories overlap. There is moreover considerable intertwining of the personal and the social among, and even within, the virtues and vices. Think, for example, of intemperance (bad judgement or lack of discipline with regard to bodily indulgences): with regard to eating, the vice seems primarily personal; with regard to drinking or sex, maybe not. We followed Aristotle in identifying human virtues as traits that it is advantageous to acquire – advantageous, that is, to those who have them. They naturally included such traits as courage, wisdom and temperance. On this understanding of virtues, the social virtues, as we saw, seem more problematic than the personal, it being less obvious how the possessors of these are advantaged.

From this Aristotelian standpoint it is readily intelligible that a trait that is of its nature *self*-harming will be a vice – if, at least, it is a trait that people can voluntarily arm themselves against. One trait that fits this description that is often impugned in suicides is lack of courage, or of hope, which itself might be seen as an aspect of courage.[18] Besides fear or despair, any of the following – anger, grief, hatred, self-pity and shame – can put someone in a suicidal frame of mind. The temptation to suicide is something that is liable to come upon people especially when their normal defences are down, when good sense is hardest to hold on to. Given the many adversities of life, and given that most suicides are irrational acts, the result of yielding to an impulse that ruins the prospects of faring well in life, the historical teaching that suicide is a bad type of action, because it is characteristically irrational, and that it is a *very* bad type of action, because its bad consequences are irreparable, seems to be a sound teaching.

Champions of a right to commit suicide often use analogies which down-play the enormity of the mistake that a suicide can be. Seneca, for example, famously says: 'Just as I shall select my ship when I am about to go on a voyage, or my house when I propose to take a residence, so I shall choose death when I am about to depart from life.'[19]

This sounds well; but no one supposes that mistakes in choosing a ship in which to sail or a house to inhabit are necessarily irreparable. The choice of suicide is.

Nothing said so far, though, indicates that *every* act of suicide is bad. Stealing is a bad type of act, essentially unjust. Likewise, lying. It does not follow, though of course it might be true, that every act of theft or every lie is morally indefensible. Maybe the suicide of Tresckow was wholly honourable. Assume that he had no way of avoiding capture and torture. In that case his act was not irrational. Nor was it unjust, cowardly or inhumane. In short, no vice was indicated. Even Kant, intensely hostile to suicide as he was, invites us to consider the following case of suicide as possibly justified: 'A man who had been bitten by a mad dog already felt hydrophobia [rabies], and he explains in a letter he left, that since, so far as he knew, the disease was incurable, he killed himself lest he harm others as well in his madness, the onset of which he already felt.'[20]

Let us characterize as 'hard cases' suicides that appear neither irrational, nor unjust, nor cowardly, nor even unkind to others. These are hard cases to square with a teaching that says that every suicide is a bad act. In fact, we may say that these cases are not just hard, but impossible, to square with such a teaching. If an act is morally bad, *some* vice must be involved. But what we are calling 'hard cases' are cases where we find no vice is involved. Maybe, then, we should stop talking of 'committing' suicide – this language may beguile us into an unreasonable prejudice against suicide. Would it not be better to approach the topic of suicide in a more open-minded way, bearing in mind that there are cases and cases?

The trouble with such a stance is that it neglects the particular danger that the temptation to suicide typically poses: that it hits people when they are unlikely to be able to judge well their own situation and prospects. That is why there is sense in adopting a protective teaching against suicide – a teaching that this kind of act is *not to be thought of*. There is sense in adopting this protective teaching, even though we acknowledge that there are some hard cases. The point of a teaching against a practice does not necessarily come out by close examination of this or that particular case. The protective teaching against suicide is what is needed to save many of us from irretrievable imprudence.[21] This need is overlooked by David Hume, who declares, incredibly, 'I believe that no man ever threw away his life, while it was worth keeping.'[22]

Some types of acts are properly regarded as only bad presumptively. And with these we expect people to use their discretion. Take, for example, promise keeping. No one can sensibly advocate a teaching that promises must *always* be kept. Other types of acts are always bad – rape and perjury, for example. Such acts are, by their nature, indefensible. That is why a non-discretionary teaching repudiating them as unthinkable is in order. The reason for adopting a non-discretionary teaching against suicide is different. Arguably, at any rate, not every act of suicide is by its nature indefensible. But even if it is true that some particular suicides and assisted suicides, the hard cases, are not in themselves bad acts – that is to say, they do not indicate any vice at all – we need a protective teaching against suicide that denies us discretion. This, I suggest, is the only safe teaching about suicide and assisted suicide for humanity, doctors and carers included. Adopting this teaching does not, it must be emphasized, commit us to a particularly punitive approach to those who in great distress are tempted to kill themselves. As we have seen, there are good reasons for approving the decriminalization of suicide even if we stand by the protective teaching.

What kind of teaching is needed against suicide and euthanasia?

But is the teaching that repudiates suicide and euthanasia overly protective? Does it exaggerate the risks of those many suicides which are bad in the various ways that have been suggested and underrate the hardship that a total ban on suicide and euthanasia imposes on some persons and on their carers? It might be easier to accept the teaching if hard cases were very exceptional. But, are they? Maybe some doctors and nurses routinely encounter hard cases. If so, perhaps a more balanced, nuanced teaching on suicide and euthanasia is needed: one which acknowledges the seriousness of suicide and euthanasia and the importance of rallying the spirits of people for whom this would be a bad choice, but which at the same time makes provision for identifying and helping the hard cases, by legalizing physician-assisted suicide and voluntary euthanasia.

The usual objection to adopting a more 'balanced teaching' is that legalizing physician-assisted suicide and voluntary euthanasia is too risky. Obviously, what are called 'safeguards' would surround any legalisation. But these, it is said, are very likely to be flouted – as some say already happens in the Netherlands, where euthanasia is now legal and has been so in effect for some years.[23] This, however, does not settle the matter. Supporters of a 'balanced teaching' may argue that the risks are a price worth paying. After all, regulations are never wholly effective. Regulations to prevent road accidents are flouted by some road-users. But nobody says that we had better close down the roads.

The case, then, for adopting the protective teaching is thus far hardly demonstrated. Critics may ask: where's the evidence that we need it? Perhaps, its supporters will be somewhat impatient with the demand for 'evidence'? Is evidence really needed here? Are there not certain familiar facts of life that make it obvious that we need a protective teaching? Is it not a fact of life that people are susceptible to moods of despair and self-loathing that are liable to tempt them to suicide? And don't we know that people in the grip of these moods are not well able to think clearly and reliably about their own situation and prospects? That is why, as we have argued, they need to arm themselves against even entertaining the idea of suicide or euthanasia as a solution to their problems.

Let us now add a further fact of life that supports the case for repudiating assisted suicide and euthanasia. People are wont to undervalue the lives of those who are seriously disabled, terminally ill, or frail and elderly. This undervaluing reflects a widespread prejudice – and one that is shared by many who themselves fall within one or another of these categories. Since patients who seek assisted suicide or euthanasia are particularly likely to be in these categories, the chances are that those from whom they seek help will mistakenly concur in supposing that they would be better off dead. The case for a discretionary stance on assisted suicide and euthanasia rests on the assumption that various safeguards can be put in place to prevent mistakes being made. But since there is this prejudice, that assumption is unsafe.

Yet these facts of life that are appealed to, though relevant, hardly suffice to demonstrate to a sceptic that humanity needs the protective teaching. Someone might well say that those who appeal to the risks of adopting a more relaxed teaching do so *because* they think that no one should set about killing a patient. This would be a significant observation, worth taking seriously. It is partly true and partly not true. It is partly not true, in so far as there really are risks to worry about, as we have just observed. But it is partly true, in so far as supporters of the protective teaching do not *derive* their belief about the need for this *from* the observed risks. Rather, they are already convinced that there is this need, and in casting around for an explanation of this need, they hit on risks. Risks offer some explanation, but they do not by any means do the whole job.

There is a point of interest to note here. The elementary badness of certain kinds of acts – of rape, of lying, of the killings we call murder – is something we seem to understand in a way prior to enquiry, and not as a result of evidence-based research. That is not to say that we can adequately explain their badness. We have seen (in the previous chapter) that the usual accounts of what makes it wrong to kill people, when we all agree that it is wrong, turn out in this way or that to be inadequate. In these matters the convictions come first, and the conjectures in support of them come later. That ordering is not peculiar to ethical convictions; nor is it irrational. On the contrary, it would be impossible to jettison all our convictions, Descartes-style, and refuse to believe anything that was not 'evidence-based'. So-called evidence-based beliefs can only rest on beliefs many of which are not themselves evidence-based.[24]

The previous section of our discussion was headed, 'towards understanding . . . ' to signal that our treatment of the subject is incomplete. This cannot be helped so long as we remain unable to explain well the badness of killing people even in cases where we are all agreed that killing would be bad. All the same, we need to decide on a teaching to live by meanwhile: either one that allows euthanasia or one that does not.

In the next chapter we will explore some of the implications of the quite unsurprising teaching that decisions to kill patients are never justified.

12

Killing and Letting Die

In this chapter I will consider some implications of the teaching discussed in the last chapter: the hardly novel teaching that doctors should not kill their patients. Suppose, as occasionally happens, maybe because of a local shortage of appropriate drugs or nursing skills, a patient is suffering horribly, and no effective palliative relief is available. Does the teaching leave doctors powerless to help such a patient? In certain cases, it may. This does not, of itself, undermine what I have said. *Whatever* our understanding of morality, or justice, we are going to believe that it forbids the adoption of certain means to secure benefits for those in our charge. Pretty well anyone's teaching will sometimes be a *hard* teaching.

A much more damaging criticism may be made of the teaching. If we say that doctors must never kill their patients, are we saying that they must never let them die, where that is preventable, either? If that is our teaching, it sounds not just hard, but incredible. No one seriously supposes that doctors must never let patients die where life saving or prolonging would be possible. If, however, we are saying that doctors must never decide to kill, but may sometimes decide to let die, we are assuming that deciding to let die is not itself necessarily deciding to kill. It may be suspected, though, that the difference between doctors' decisions to 'let die' and their decisions to 'kill' is merely cosmetic.

'Letting die' as a defence, and its abuse

Obviously, doctors sometimes let their patients die accidentally, and this may be excusable or inexcusable. I am not concerned with that here. I want to take up cases where doctors *decide* to let their patients die. In particular, I have in mind cases where doctors defend what they have done, saying, 'We did not kill the patient, we only let the patient die'. Let us first ask: could this be true? Are some decisions to let die not decisions to kill? The answer to these questions must surely be yes.

It will be yes where a life-saving drug or procedure is withheld for any of a range of reasons, including the following: (1) because the patient needing saving refuses the treatment; (2) because a hospital cannot afford to bestow as much treatment as would be needed to save the patient's life; (3) because it is decided to treat another patient, who also requires immediate rescue, instead, there being not enough resources on hand to treat all. Where any of these reasons explains why a doctor has let a patient die, no one would say that the doctor had killed the patient.[1] Needless, to say, a doctor's decision to let a patient die for any of the these reasons may still be open to criticism. Maybe the doctor should have taken more trouble to persuade the patient to accept treatment. Maybe the doctor was mistaken in thinking that the treatment this patient needed was unaffordable or in thinking that another patient should be rescued instead of this one. But that is another topic. Here I am simply concerned to establish that where any of these reasons explain a doctor's decision to withhold a life-saving treatment, it is simply not true to say that the decision is a decision to kill.

There are other cases, however, where doctors might be tempted to say that they did not kill, but only let die, where this defence would be a cheat. It could be a cheat in either or both of the following ways: (1) if the doctors were withholding a vital treatment *in order to* bring about death – that is to say, in order to kill; (2) if the patient was not dying in the first place *before* the decision was made to withhold a needed treatment.

Consider a cheat of the first sort. A patient is dying, but this could quite easily be prevented. Nevertheless, doctors in charge of his case decide to let the patient die. Why? Because in the circumstances, and for one reason or another, they want the patient to die. Perhaps, the patient is a seriously disabled baby who needs surgery. The parents might refuse the surgery because they would rather that the baby died.

Duodenal atresia is a complication that sometimes afflicts Down's syndrome babies, who are born with an internal blockage that prevents them from digesting food. They need surgery to clear it, and that surgery is pretty straightforward and usually successful. Sometimes, however, parents refuse to consent to the surgery just because they do not want the child to live. One such case which went to court and engendered heated public debate in the United States concerned a baby born in Indiana in 1982. To preserve anonymity, the baby was described in the court records and press coverage as 'Baby Doe'.[2] The obstetrician, supported by some other obstetricians, advised against the necessary surgery, whereas a paediatrician called in to advise, recommended the surgery, as did some of his colleagues. The parents accepted the obstetricians' advice, apparently in the belief that Down's syndrome children have a poor quality of life. Now in such a case are we to say that the decision not to operate is merely a decision to let the baby die, or are we to say that it is a decision to kill – by omission? If we are to say the latter, we must be able to attribute the baby's death to the decision not to operate on it, and we must further suppose that the decision was taken in order to cause the baby to die. Both suppositions, I will argue, seem correct in this case.

Consider, first, whether that decision can be said to have caused the baby to die. Killing is a causal notion: A kills B if and only if A causes B's death. But the question of when we are to say that one thing causes another is not a straightforward matter. Perhaps we need to distinguish kinds of cause. It is evident that much work needs to be done on such questions by philosophers. Of specific importance to us here is the question of whether *absences* can be causes, and something fairly elementary can be said. If one has the primitive thought that every cause must involve something like a push, then there clearly cannot be causes of the absence kind. But this is perhaps a bad thought. We are quite happy with attributing a disaster to a drought. Overwatering might make a plant droop, but so might underwatering. Leaving out the baking powder spoils the cake. Absence, they say, makes the heart grow fonder. In view of such examples, wouldn't it be rash to insist that one could not literally kill a baby by arranging for it to be on short rations or by withholding a life-preserving drug or procedure that is routine? A court would not dismiss a murder charge on the ground that a nothing cannot produce a something. And this is quite striking when one reflects that in the common law tradition there is no duty to rescue.

One way in which we might be tempted to assert that an absence cannot really be a cause would go like this. 'It was not the doctor's inattention which caused the patient's death, it was the physiological action of the wrong dose that he gave!' The answer here is to give up thinking that in a causal happening there is just one thing, describable as *the* cause, at issue. Of course, we can give true causal accounts in different ways. For example, we can say that the driver's inattention caused the accident, *and* say that the driver's speed caused the accident, *and* say that the wet leaves on the road caused the accident. This can be important in medical ethics. (Careless doctor: 'I am *not* responsible.

It was the *disease* which caused the patient's death.') If you throw some-body off a high building, blame gravity. Nature 'takes its course'.

We cannot, then, rule out the possibility that A might properly be said to cause B's death by an omission. However, since killing is a vague concept, it will not always be clear at the margin when it is correct to say that A causes B's death – i.e. A kills B. Compare these two cases: (1) a doctor faced with two patients needing emergency care leaves one patient to die and goes to the other; (2) a doctor faced with a patient needing emergency care, whom he recognizes to be his worst enemy, says to the patient, 'At last I can get even with you!' and walks away from the patient, and goes for a smoke on the balcony. Now the first case is, I take it, very clearly *not* a case of (intentional) killing. The doctor leaves the one patient foreseeing, but not aiming at, that patient's death. What about the second case? Here the doctor, if asked, 'Why are you not treating this patient?', might well answer (confiden-tially), '*so that* this dreadful man will die – and soon!' Now, as we have just established that not-doings can be causes, we should not dismiss the claim that this doctor has killed merely because he did not *do* any-thing to the patient. All the same, someone might argue that, however culpable the doctor's conduct, he has not 'literally speaking' killed, but only let die. Let it be so. This only shows what the speaker is going to *take* as killing. If this is not killing, it is anyway tantamount to killing. And that is enough for our purposes. So let us, hereafter, treat as killing, cases where doctors or nurses refrain from providing some needed treatment *so that* the patient will die.

Let us now return to the decision not to arrange the surgery that Baby Doe needed. In the circumstances of the case, it appears that the decision not to operate explains why the baby died. Plainly, if this was killing – and we have just agreed to say that this sort of decision is a decision to kill – it is intentional killing. *Why* was the decision made against surgery? Honest answer: *so that* the baby would die. Hence, it is a cheat to say in such a case that the doctors only let the baby die.

Consider now a cheat of the second sort. Here the cheat is in doctors making out that they are taking a decision which is correctly described as a decision to let the patient die. For it to be true that you let X happen, it must be the case that X was going to happen, would happen, unless you intervened. Thus, it is a cheat to make out that you are only letting die if the patient is dying for no other reason than because of what you have been up to – in that you have been withholding essen-tial attention calculated to bring it about that the patient is dying. Only of some babies can we truthfully say, 'This is a dying baby'. It is not true of *all* babies merely on account of the fact that any baby will soon

be dying if it is not fed. Not feeding hitherto healthy children you have
in your care might be a deliberate policy aimed at ending their lives.
Michael Burleigh in *Death and Deliverance: 'Euthanasia' in Germany
1900–1945*, quotes from the following account of a visit to an asylum:

> After we had visited a number of other wards, the asylum director, who
> was called Pfannmuller, led us into the children's ward. The ward made a
> clean and cared-for impression. In about fifteen beds there were as many
> children, all aged between one and five years old. In this ward,
> Pfannmuller explained his intentions at some length. I remember the fol-
> lowing as a condensed account of the sense of what Pfannmuller had to
> say: 'As a National Socialist, these creatures (he meant the aforemen-
> tioned children) naturally represent to me a burden upon the healthy body
> of our nation. We don't kill [he may have used a more circumlocutory
> expression instead of the word 'kill'] with poison, injections etc., since that
> would only give the foreign press and certain gentlemen in Switzerland
> new hate-propaganda material. No: you see our method is much simpler
> and more natural.' With these words, and assisted by a nurse who worked
> in this ward, he pulled one of the children out of bed. As he displayed the
> child around, like a dead hare, he pointed out, with a knowing look and a
> cynical grin, 'This one will last another two or three days.' The image of
> this fat, grinning man, with the whimpering skeleton in his fleshy hand,
> surrounded by other starving children, is still clear before my eyes.
> Furthermore, the murderer declared that they were not suddenly with-
> drawing the food, but gradually reducing the rations. A lady who also took
> part in the tour asked, with an outrage she had difficulty suppressing,
> whether a quick death aided by injections would not be more merciful.
> Pfannmuller sang the praises of his methods once more, as being more
> practical in terms of the foreign press.[3]

No one, not even, I suspect, Dr Pfanmuller (with his talk of 'methods'),
would think that these patients were *only* being let die.

The question of whether a doctor had meant to kill was one of
the key issues in the celebrated English case of *R* v. *Arthur* (*The Times*,
6 November, 1981). In 1980, in Derby, a baby, John Pearson, was
born with Down's syndrome. The baby appeared to be otherwise
healthy – no suggestion of an intestinal blockage requiring surgery, for
example. Dr Leonard Arthur examined the baby in the presence of its
parents and then put in the records: 'Parents do not wish the baby to
survive. Nursing care only.' He prescribed a strong pain-killing drug,
dihydrocodeine, a drug not normally given to infants. Thereafter, the
baby was kept comfortable, but, it seems, was given water, not food.
By the evening of the first day he was already weakening, and over the
next two days his condition deteriorated. On the fourth day, he died.

Dr Arthur was prosecuted. Initially, the charge was murder, but that was changed to attempted murder, because of uncertainties as to the actual cause of the baby's death. The prosecution's case was that Dr Arthur had attempted murder, since both the administration of the drug and the instruction of 'Nursing care only' indicated an intent to kill – in the latter case, an intent to kill by omission, where he had a duty of care.

The prosecution's case rested on two charges: one involving a commission and the other involving an omission. It is the second that interests us here. Was it not by itself decisive evidence in support of the prosecution's case? In the trial, eminent medical colleagues testified in support of Dr Arthur's action. Judge Farquharson, in his summing up, put it to the jury that the jurors should 'think long and hard before deciding that doctors of the eminence that we have heard . . . had evolved standards which amount to committing a crime'. Dr Arthur was acquitted.

Suppose, however, that it had actually been established that the baby died of starvation – as a direct result of the instruction 'Nursing care only'. Clearly, this phrase must be taken in a somewhat technical sense, seeing that a healthy baby needs only normal care to survive, and in a hospital this would naturally be supplied by nurses. If the instruction in this case meant that certain life-preserving procedures were to be omitted, that calls for explanation. And what other explanation could there be for deciding to omit the normal feeding of a baby in an ordinary hospital context but the determination to kill it? ('Ordinary context': we do not suppose that the process of feeding is enormously burdensome for the child. Nor do we imagine the food to be in such short supply that some babies are going to starve anyway.)

Notice that in this case there was no reason to suppose that the baby was dying prior to the decision to give it 'nursing care only'. Once the baby was put on 'nursing care only', he caught pneumonia. Thereafter, the baby was presumably dying, and then it could be said correctly that the decision not to offer an antibiotic was a decision to let the baby die (though still not *only* to let die). Thus, to say that Dr Arthur only meant to let die and did not mean to kill seems a double cheat.

Some recent court rulings concerning killing and letting die

The distinction between what is killing and what is only letting die can be crucial in court rulings, as in two recent cases which we can usefully compare. In the first case, *B* v. *An NHS Hospital Trust* [2002] All ER 449, the patient was not dying so long as she continued on a life-support machine, but she wanted to have it turned off. In the second case, *R. (on the application of Pretty)* v. *DPP* [2002] 1 All ER 1 the patient was dying anyway, but she wanted to have someone kill her at a time of her choosing.

Ms B, a 43-year-old woman paralysed from the neck down who had been kept alive for more than a year on a ventilator, asserted her right to have it switched off so that she could die. The only issue that needed resolving for her legal right to be granted concerned her mental competence. Once a psychiatrist had pronounced that she was competent, the judge ruled that Ms B was fully entitled to refuse treatment.

Mrs Pretty, a 43-year-old, suffered from motor neurone disease. When the disease had progressed to the point where she was almost totally paralysed, having to be fed through a tube and scarcely able to speak, she sought an undertaking from the Director of Public Prosecutions that if her husband helped her to commit suicide, he would not be prosecuted. The DPP refused to give this undertaking, and Mrs Pretty sought judicial review of that decision. Mrs Pretty claimed that she had a right to her husband's assistance under the European Convention on Human Rights. The Law Lords unanimously dismissed her appeal, whereupon she took her case to the European Court at Strasbourg, where again it was dismissed.[4]

As the law in England presently stands, it is hardly surprising that Mrs Pretty's case failed. But is there something disturbingly arbitrary about this result when we compare these two cases? The mere happenstance that Ms B was ventilator-dependent and Mrs Pretty was not determined which woman got her way. Did the law in the case of Ms B rely on a cheating pretence that the doctors would 'only be letting die'?

While it may seem that in a sense both women were wanting the same thing: let us say, to die soon, what they were asking the doctors to do was importantly different in two ways.

1 Ms B, by withholding or withdrawing consent, was merely asserting her right against trespass; Mrs Pretty could not make use of this right to achieve her goal.
2 Granting Mrs Pretty's request seemed tantamount to authorizing assisted suicide; complying with Ms B's request arguably did not have this implication.

Consider the first point. As we noted in chapter 6, the duty on doctors not to treat without consent has its roots in everyday notions of battery, in the law of tort, and Dame Butler Sloss, the President of the High Court in the case of Ms B, plainly had this in mind when she made the declaration (previously quoted p. 71): 'A mentally competent patient has an absolute right to refuse consent to medical treatment for any reason, rational or irrational or no reason at all, even where the decision may lead to his or her death.' Thus, the reason why Ms B's choice was respected need not be presumed to rely on some supposed right (say, of self-determination or privacy) to be helped to end her life at a time of her choosing. It could rely simply on a right to refuse unwanted medical treatment (a right against trespass or battery).

Consider the second point. In the case of Mrs Pretty, accommodating her choice would have meant formally undertaking to turn a blind eye to the committing of a criminal offence. Yet, it may be asked, wasn't the ruling in favour of Ms B actually *directing* doctors to commit this offence – to assist a suicide? It might seem easy enough to rebut this suggestion. We have only to recall that where a life-saving treatment is withheld because the patient refuses it, the doctors concerned are merely letting die, not killing. In Ms B's case, the doctors would obviously foresee her death. But even assuming that death was *her* aim, it need not have been an aim that they shared. Aims sufficient to explain their action, we might say, could have been simply to avoid forcing treatment on her and to obey a court ruling – a ruling which should *not* be construed as permission to assist suicide.[5]

Without, however, gainsaying the general point that withholding life-saving treatment at the patient's request is not *ipso facto* killing, we may still hesitate to brush off the suspicion that doctors were actually killing in the case of Ms B. There is no doubt that she did refuse the treatment. The problem in her case is that there is so little distance between her death and what the doctors had to *do* to comply with her request. Let us grant that the doctors would not be acting in order to cause her death. But was the very action they performed in the circumstances (switching off a ventilator knowing she was dependent on it) an act of killing?

The difficulty in answering this question is not that we need more information about what the doctors who complied with the court order actually did. It is, rather, a difficulty about the concept of intention: what is to be counted as 'intentional killing'. Explaining this concept is by no means a simple matter. Elizabeth Anscombe's classic pioneering study may help to give us some bearings.[6] We will begin our enquiry by examining the distinction between consequences of what we decide to do or omit that are intended and those that are merely foreseen.

Consequences intended and consequences merely foreseen

We understand well enough the difference between the consequences of what we voluntarily do or omit that are intended and those that are merely foreseen – between outcomes we aim at and outcomes we realize we are bringing about, but which are no part of our aim. We pay our taxes, and in consequence have less money to spend. But we do not pay our taxes in order to have less money to spend. We foresee, but do not intend, when we enter our phone number in a telephone directory, to receive some unwelcome calls. A doctor foresees, but does not intend, the death of a patient when he decides, in accordance with the patient's direction, to omit some life-saving procedure which he would normally provide. These are clear cases. But not every case will be so clear. Suppose, for example, that you are attacked by someone when you are both standing on the edge of a cliff: if you push your assailant over the edge, do you intend, or merely foresee, his death?[7]

Sometimes what is merely foreseen is accidental, and sometimes it is not. Suppose you undergo cosmetic surgery, though you are warned that there is some risk of it causing a disfiguring scar. The risk materializes. It was not meant to happen, but the possibility was foreseen. In this case it seems right to say that it was an accident. But it is no accident, chance or mishap that a patient given chemotherapy suffers hair loss (assuming, at least, that this always, or nearly always, happens). That is just what the oncologist and the patient expect. Still, the oncologist does not subject the patient to chemotherapy *in order to* cause hair loss. This is simply a foreseen, regrettable, but accepted, effect of the drug that the patient needs. Where foreseen consequences are concerned, there is a spectrum of the likelihood of their materializing: at one end are consequences foreseen as remote possibilities; at the other end are consequences foreseen as inevitable, or highly probable. The nearer to the latter end of the spectrum a particular consequence is, the more difficult it may be to determine if it is merely foreseen, and not also intended.

Anscombe, in the course of her discussion of intention, introduces an example, well known to philosophers, of a man pumping poisoned water into a house. Suppose the man knows that the water is being poisoned by others who want to kill the occupants of the house, but disowns any intention on his part to kill them; he says that he is indifferent about their fate – is simply doing his normal job, earning his living. What the man says here *could* be true (that the poisoning is not intentional on *his* part), though whether it is so in a particular case can be hard to ascertain.[8] Contrast the case where the man is *hired* 'to pump poisoned water into the house'. Here he cannot disown the intention to poison the inhabitants on the grounds that he is *only* concerned to earn his living, since then the means he takes to earn his living is *by* doing the poisoning. The means we choose to bring about our purposes are always intended. We do them 'in order to . . .'.

Someone might question whether the distinction between consequences intended and consequences foreseen is of any interest in ethics. Consider Anscombe's example of the man pumping water who says that he was only doing his usual job. Anscombe observes, 'if what he said was true, *that* will not absolve him from guilt of murder'.[9] Though in this case the distinction may not be of ethical interest, elsewhere it can be.[10] Anthony Kenny offers a nice low-key example to show how the distinction can have significance. Compare fixing a meeting for a time that you know will sadly make it impossible for Professor X to attend, and fixing a meeting for that time just *in order that* Professor X cannot attend.[11] Maybe, we, as onlookers, are not able to tell which you are doing. Yet, doing the one is perhaps doing something significantly different from doing the other, for it may be your duty as convenor not to exclude people in this way.

The distinction is of particular interest to doctors, nurses and patients who are concerned to avoid intentional killing. That means, obviously, that they reject decisions to treat or not treat that are *aimed* at causing patients' deaths for whatever reason. But just what *that* rules out is not always clear, given that it can be indeterminate at the margin what counts as intentional. Whether a patient's death has been brought about intentionally is sometimes clear enough – as in the case of King George V. Lord Dawson, who attended at the King's deathbed in 1936, later disclosed that he had administered morphine *so as to* ensure that the king died in time for this to be announced in the morning papers.[12]

But consider a case where doctors administer a drug knowing that this will relieve the patient's pain *and* that the drug may well precipitate the patient's death. The doctors may claim that they are aiming only to relieve pain and not at all to speed up the dying. Could this be true? Could this make the difference between permissible and impermissible killing?

Doctors who defend their actions in this way are appealing, at least implicitly, to what are known as 'double effect' considerations. Voluntary actions, as we have said, can produce two kinds of effect: effects that are aimed at and effects that are merely foreseen. Teachings drawing on so-called double effect considerations seek to clarify certain convictions concerning what it is permissible to decide to do or not do. Specifically, they seek to cast light on how it may be permissible to bring about something as a side-effect of your action which it would not be permissible for you to bring about intentionally. Bringing about a patient's death intentionally, according to these teachings, is never permissible, whereas bringing about a patient's death where this is foreseen as a possibility is *sometimes* permissible. Thus, for example, it can be permissible for doctors to administer a pain-relieving drug that may very well kill – provided that there is no other way of relieving the pain, that the doctors are not for one reason or another (high-minded or low) trying to kill the patient, and that in the circumstances the benefit (pain relief) outweighs the risk of harm (causing death) – as when the patient is dying anyway.

Suppose, though, that a patient needs and is given pain relief in steadily increasing doses, and it is evident to you, the doctor, that at some point the dose will kill the patient, though you do not know just when that will be. Here the patient's death is foreseen as a certainty or near certainty. Can you still say that, even so, it is not intended? The man hired 'to pump poisoned water' might prefer not to be doing that, but the money is good and he accepts the terms. In this case, don't we have to say that he intends to poison, that is just what he is doing, even though he does not share the plotters' further aims. So, likewise, do you have to accept that you intend the patient's death if you know that the drugs you are administering are going to bring it about, but choose to administer them in spite of that? To answer this question, we need to enquire further into the notion of intentional doings.

Intentional doings

So far we have focused only on the intentions with which we act – the aims or purposes of our actions. Now we need to take note of what we do *on* purpose as against what we do *with* or *for* a purpose. We may do something on purpose (intentionally), whether or not we have any further end in view. People are wont to say, 'It is the intention that counts'. Here again, we should recall an asymmetry between acting well and acting badly (which was touched on in chapter 5, p. 46). If your intention is bad, then you are acting badly, whatever else is true about what you are doing. However, if your intention is good, it by no means follows that you are acting well, whatever else is true about what you are doing. So being well-intentioned is *not* all that counts.

One and the same action can be truly described in various ways. Under some of these descriptions, what is done is intentional. Under others, it is not. For our purposes we need to consider the following two kinds of case. The first kind is comparatively straightforward to handle. Where you do something, not *knowing* that a particular description is true, you are not doing that intentionally. You may know that you are filling a syringe, but not know that the fluid you are filling it with is contaminated. *Qua* filling a syringe, your action is intentional. *Qua* filling a syringe with contaminated fluid, it is not. Under the latter description what you do is accidental – hence, unintentional.

Consider next the more troublesome kind of case, where you do know that a description of your action is true, but regard this as something *incidental*, and not part of your plan – not part of what you are trying to achieve. Walking to work wears away the soles of your shoes, as you know. But this is incidental to your purpose. It is not part of your reason for choosing to walk, rather than drive. Anscombe, describing the man pumping water, mentions various true descriptions of what he is doing – some intentional, some not. Suppose the movement of his arm is casting a certain shadow on the rockery. He might notice this. But if asked, '*Why* are you doing this?', he might say, 'Not for any reason (purpose) – it is incidental to what I am about'. If you knowingly are doing something that is incidental to your purposes, is it right to say that you are not doing it intentionally?

Let us return to the case where a patient needs and is given pain relief in steadily increasing doses, and it is evident to you, the doctor, that at some point the dose will kill the patient, though you do not know just when that will be. Can you truthfully maintain that though you foresee the death as an inevitable side-effect of the drug as you are prescribing it, you do not intend this result? In a way, that seems correct, assuming that you do not administer the drug *in order to* achieve that result. But in another way, it seems incorrect. For how can you say you do not *mean* this to happen, are not doing it on purpose, if you know that what you are doing is bound to bring about this result?

Intentionally doing X, as distinct from doing X unintentionally, where it is a mere side-effect of what you are doing on purpose, implies that you know you are doing X, that your doing X is voluntary and that you are doing X for a reason. But now suppose that in doing X you know that you are bringing about Y, and that this side-effect is both immediate and certain. Can you still say that since Y is no part of your plan, you do not intend to bring about Y? Is Y merely incidental? Anscombe argues that it is 'at best a dubious business' to say that you don't intend a result of what you are engaged in doing if you know that the result will occur immediately and certainly. In such a case, you can hardly say that you are merely 'taking a risk' that this result will happen.[13]

It would seem, then, that we need to work with a slightly broader account of intention. Maybe we can dismiss as not intended and as merely incidental some noticed side-effects of what we do – side-effects which seem of no account or interest (like casting a shadow on the rockery), but if the noticed side-effect of what we are doing is inevitably and more or less immediately causing a patient's death, it seems very *artificial* to say that the death is not intended.

In the next chapter I will explore further some of the implications of our account of intentional killing for doctors' decisions that result in patients' deaths.

Patients' Deaths and Doctors' Decisions

In what circumstances is it true to say that a doctor's decision which results in a patient's death is a decision to kill the patient? Here it is helpful to set up several different cases to use as points of reference. Various cases that arise will differ in this way and that. We should not expect to reach clear verdicts in every case. There are bound to be borderlines.

Relevance of aims underlying the decisions that result in deaths

Case 1   Surgeons take vital organs from patient A, expecting A to die in consequence. They do this in order to save the life of patient B.

Suppose that the surgeons can truthfully say that A's death is immaterial to their aims and that, if by some miracle A survives, they will be delighted. Would this show that the killing of A is not, after all, intended? In the light of our broadened account of intention, it seems that it would not show this. While their overall intention is to save B's life, isn't the means they choose itself an act of intentional killing? They can hardly disown this result of what they do as an unintended side-effect of their action since they know well that removing vital organs from A in the circumstances will result more or less immediately and inevitably in A's death. The result is so immediate and certain that they could hardly be said to be 'taking a risk that that would happen'. The surgeons might truthfully say that they do not *particularly* intend A's death. The fact that we have this usage is significant. They can hardly say, though, that they did not mean this to happen: 'Things were not supposed to turn out like this!' In one way, this death was no part of their plan, inasmuch as if A had survived, their plan would not have been frustrated. In another way, A's death *was* part of their plan, since they accepted that their chosen route to save B would pretty well automatically result in A's death.

Case 2   Patient A is on a life support machine. Patient B, newly arrived, needs to be put straightaway on such a machine. There are no spare machines. It is decided to cease treating A, whose long-term prospects are bleak, and to treat B instead. A dies, as expected, in consequence of being taken off the machine. Is it right to say that the doctor who makes this decision is choosing to kill A?

This is a triage-type situation. The doctor, faced with a necessity of either letting A die or B die, chooses to rescue B rather than A. The letting die is clearly intentional. But is this a cheating use of 'letting die'? Is this a decision to kill by omission, by ceasing to treat?

In Case 1 we have said that since the surgeons know that what they are doing will result immediately and certainly in a patient's death, they intend this death. Applying that reasoning to Case 2, must we say that the doctor here intends to bring about the death of A? If so, the view that doctors ought never to choose to kill patients stands discredited: in triage situations they would not be able to do otherwise.

There is, though, a significant difference between Case 1 and Case 2. In Case 2, A's death results from a decision to cease to rescue A. That duty is a duty which is subject to certain qualifications. It may, for example, be overridden by other duties – as here, by the duty to rescue B. In this case the doctors change their mind about rescuing A and decide instead to rescue B. A's death is foreseen, not aimed at. In Case 1, A's death cannot be portrayed as a ceasing to rescue. (We need not suppose that before surgery is embarked on, A's life is at risk – A may be on the surgeons' list merely for a nose job.) Thus, it makes sense to say in Case 2 that A was let die, not killed, by the doctor, whereas it would be plainly a cheat to say this about A in Case 1.

Case 3   Surgeons operate on patient A, who is critically ill or injured, trying to save A's life. The aim is to save A's life. The surgeons know, however, that A is extremely likely to die under the knife. The operation proceeds, and A dies as a result. Is this a case of intentional killing?

Here, though the surgeons expect A to die on the operating table, that is no part of their plan. The surgeons are trying to save A's life. You cannot be intentionally killing someone whose life you are trying to save. This is a case of unintentional (accidental) killing. Needless to say, the surgeons may be open to criticism on other scores. The proceeding may be rashly undertaken, or rashly undertaken by *them*. Be that as it may, they are not intentionally killing A.

Futility

Case 4   Patient A is a premature baby in an intensive care unit. A's long-term prospects are diminishing as more evidence of brain damage and organ failure emerges. A also appears to be suffering. Doctors reviewing the case decide to 'let A die'. Hitherto, when A has stopped breathing, A has been given ventilation. It is decided not to do so the next time the need arises, but to let 'nature take its course'. Let us suppose that the reason given for this decision is that further treatment would be futile.[1]

The notion of 'futility' needs careful handling. Judgements of futility are sometimes clear-cut, uncontroversial and dependent solely on clinical matters – like, for example, the judgement that antibiotics are futile as a cure for colds. We should notice, though, that a treatment which is futile in respect of one objective may not be so in respect of another. A GP might persist in prescribing antibiotics for patients with colds, fearing that otherwise the patients would switch to other more biddable colleagues. Similarly, a treatment that is not futile for treating a particular condition of a patient may still be deemed futile to give to that patient in view of other aspects of the situation. Thus, it might be deemed futile to give a very elderly and frail patient an antibiotic for his pneumonia if he is refusing to eat, drink or be tube-fed. Here it may be said that the ultimate objective in providing a rescue treatment is to benefit the patient. But prolonging the life of those who are suffering may not be doing them a benefit – may be futile in relation to that objective.

Consider what Lord Goff said concerning the decision to cease to feed a patient who was permanently comatose.[2] He summed up his view of the case, saying, 'in the end, in a case such as the present it is the futility of the treatment which justifies its termination'. Now if the objective of feeding this patient was to keep him alive (as is the case with feeding rather generally), the treatment in question was clearly effective. Thus it was in relation to a different objective that Lord Goff made his judgement. In effect, he was saying that it is useless for someone who will never recover consciousness to continue living. This judgement, which appears to imply that being alive is not by itself a reasonable objective, that it is desirable only in relation to other objectives debarred to the permanently comatose, does not turn simply on clinical matters.

Let us return to Case 4. Here doctors might explain their decision by saying, 'Hitherto, we put A on the ventilator to stabilize the breathing so that we could treat A's other life-threatening problems. A has now deteriorated to a point where it is clear that even if the breathing is stabilized, it will not be possible to correct the other life-threatening problems.' In other words, stabilizing the breathing is not useful if A's other life-threatening problems are insurmountable – and imminent. In these circumstances putting A on a ventilator is indeed futile and the decision to let die is not masking a decision to kill. The point is that even with breathing stabilized, A is about to die.

But there will be other cases that are much less clear-cut – cases, for example, where a treatment does have a chance of being effective, though it is a very slim chance, and the treatment will be burdensome to the patient. Here disagreements about whether the treatment is futile are likely to turn not so much on the clinical effectiveness of the treatment in question as on the balance between burdens and benefits. Sometimes, in discussions about futility, the cost of treatments is also brought into play. But this does seem to be a cheat. While it is perfectly reasonable for excessive costs to be a reason for denying someone a treatment, it is a cheat to make out that a treatment would be futile when the truth is that it *would* be effective, only it costs too much.[3]

The difference between intending and merely foreseeing a patient's death

Case 5   A is a premature baby in an intensive care unit. A is now in a stable condition, comfortable and with good long-term prospects of survival. But A is also profoundly impaired and will continue so: blind, deaf and paraplegic. A's case is reviewed, and it is decided to 'let A die'.

Here, of course, we need to ask what 'letting die' amounts to, seeing that the patient prior to this decision is not dying. A only begins to die *after* the decision is made to 'let A die', in consequence of which it will soon be true that A is dying. In other words, the decision in this case is plainly a decision to kill by omission.

Case 6   A is a terminally ill patient. A's doctor prescribes a pain-relieving drug which he realizes may shorten A's life. The doctor claims that this possible outcome is no part of his intention.

Here it may be complained: why should we take the doctor's word? How do we know that this is not simply a pretence? It would help if there were some test of intention to apply. In some cases there might be. Suppose that the doctor has deliberated whether to use this pain-relieving drug or that. He chooses this, which is more expensive. Both are reckoned equally effective pain-relievers, but the less expensive one carries more risk of shortening life. Now we have some evidence, independent of the doctor's mere say-so, that the doctor is not aiming to shorten life, even though the drug he chooses carries that risk. Indeed, would it not suffice to show that the doctor was not intending to shorten the patient's life had he sought a drug less likely to shorten death or if it were the case that, if he had known of such a drug, he would have chosen it. These examples show that there is a real difference between intending and merely foreseeing, even if we are often unable to put particular claims to the test, and may have no more to go on than the doctor's say-so.

Revisiting the case of Ms B

Let us return to the case of Ms B. We asked whether the law engaged in a cheating pretence in making out that the doctors who took her off the ventilator were only letting her die? To show that there was no cheat, it would not be enough simply to affirm that the doctors would not be doing this in order to kill her. There is another question that needs addressing: whether the doctors' actions themselves are correctly described as intentional killing. To pursue that question with regard to our case, it is instructive to compare it with another: the case of the conjoined twins, Mary and Jodie.

Jodie and Mary (not their real names) were born conjoined at St Mary's Hospital, Manchester, in 2000. Their parents had come to Manchester from their home on the Maltese island of Gozo for what was expected to be a difficult birth. When the children were born, they were found to each have their own brain, heart, lungs and other vital organs. They each had arms and legs. But Mary's heart and lungs were found to be too weak to sustain her. She depended on Jodie's heart to survive. Yet Jodie's heart would eventually fail under the strain of supporting Mary (within, it was estimated, three to six months) unless the common artery shared by the twins was severed. Severing the artery would result within minutes in Mary's death. Jodie would survive without mental impairment, though probably with some significant physical impairments, like being in a wheelchair and incontinent. The parents, faced with this dilemma, would not consent to the operation. They believed that the operation meant killing the one child to save the other. That, in their view, could not be justified. The hospital sought a court declaration to permit surgeons to operate. The initial court ruling granted the hospital its declaration and this was upheld (unanimously) on appeal.[4]

Clearly, the procedure for which court guidance was sought was not proposed in order to benefit Mary – euthanasia was not the issue. But the case is instructive for us to consider here by way of testing our understanding of what counts as intentional killing. If the law unequivocally prohibits doctors from killing their patients, can it consistently permit the surgical separating of Jodie from Mary?

Separating the twins involved cutting off Mary's blood supply in circumstances which would inevitably bring about her death. The surgeons might well say that while this was true, they were not proposing to do this *in order to* kill Mary, but merely to save Jodie. If Mary were miraculously to survive the procedure, the surgeons would be delighted. Be it so, this alone would not suffice to show that the surgeons would not be intentionally killing Mary. Is not the killing of Mary the very means they would be proposing to take in order to save Jodie? The means you choose to achieve your ends, as we have noted, are always intended. But here the surgeons might say, 'The means we propose involve detaching Mary from Jodie, by cutting the blood supply. We foresee Mary's death as a result, but that is simply a regretted incidental side-effect.' Well, is it? Or is cutting the blood supply in these circumstances itself intentionally killing? (That appears to be, indeed, how the surgeons themselves must have felt, even though they had legal authorization to proceed: why else did the surgeons both place their hands on the knife, making the lethal cut their joint act?)

The Mary and Jodie case corresponds to Case 1 above. Here, as there, we cannot simply bracket off the death that results from what the surgeons do as a merely regretted, quite incidental side-effect – hence, unintended. In both cases, it rings false to say that the death that resulted was not meant to happen. Indeed, the honest response of surgeons if asked, 'Why did you decide to kill Mary?', would not repudiate the implication that this was intentional – done for a reason, but would defend the deed, probably by pointing out that regrettably they 'had to' kill her in order to save Jodie – and since Mary was going to die soon anyway. The 'had to' in this context would clearly indicate that what they did, they intended to do.

If we say that the surgeons who deliberately cut off Mary's blood supply intentionally killed her, must we say likewise that the doctors who detached Ms B from the ventilator on which they knew she was dependent intentionally killed her? There is a significant difference between the two cases. The decision of the doctors complying with the court order in the case of Ms B is a decision to let die, to cease to rescue. Here again we may take note that the duty of rescue is qualified. In this case, the relevant qualification is that medical rescue ceases to be a duty if the patient withdraws consent. Thus, the case of Ms B corresponds to Case 2 above. There is no cheat in describing the doctors' action here as letting die, not killing. The same cannot be said of the death of Mary. The doctors did not 'cease to rescue Mary'. Her life was not under any immediate threat before it was decided to do the operation to separate the twins.

Might a defence of the killing of Mary be mounted appealing to notions of self-defence and necessity? That the law does not allow private citizens to engage in pre-emptive killing makes sense where a civil authority is available to protect citizens whose lives are threatened by fellow citizens; and no doubt this is the teaching we need. But, arguably, the obligation to refrain from pre-emptive killing in self-defence does not apply if there is no civil authority to hand – as in the early pioneering days in the Wild West. Since civil authorities can offer no protection against the kind of threat Mary posed to Jodie, a case might be made that Jodie was entitled to defend herself against this threat, and that her doctors were entitled to come to her rescue.[5]

Taking stock

Where patient A dies as a result of a doctor's decision, there are three possibilities:

1 The doctor intends to kill A (as in Cases 1 and 5 above),
2 The doctor intends not to kill, but to save A (as in Cases 3 and 6 above),
3 The doctor has no intention either way regarding A (as in Cases 2 and 4 above).

While in Cases 2 and 4 the decision which leads to A's death shows that the doctor did do something intentionally, this is not to say that the doctor killed. To say that the doctor only let die is sometimes a cheat, but not in these cases. When is it a cheat?

1 When the doctor administers an analgesic not in order to relieve pain but in order to speed up the patient's dying (as with King George V),
2 When the doctor alters treatment in order to bring it about that the patient is dying (as with the baby, John Pearson),
3 When the doctor subjects a patient who was not dying to a procedure which the doctor knows will immediately and inevitably cause death (as with Mary and Case 1), but which is chosen in spite of this as a means to some further end (like saving someone else's life).

There will, needless to say, be many cases that do not slot clearly into one category or another. Compare, for example, Case 6, where a doctor administers a drug to relieve pain or agitation, knowing that it may (but may not) hasten death, with a case where the doctor expects this result as pretty well certain and immediate. We can expect many cases to be borderline between these. And the borderline cases are bound to be fuzzy.

14

Moral Issues in Reproductive Medicine

Since so many of the controversial new possibilities in the field of reproductive medicine have sprung from the development of *in vitro* fertilization (IVF),[1] let us look first at this procedure. Infertility is a bane in the lives of many people. Some 10–15 per cent of couples are infertile for one reason or another. Is it not altogether welcome news if reproductive medicine comes up with ways of helping them?

In vitro fertilization as a morally unproblematic solution to infertility

Louise Brown was born in Manchester in 1978: the world's first 'test tube baby'. Mrs Brown had been trying for nine years to become pregnant, and then learned that her fallopian tubes had been damaged by an earlier ectopic pregnancy. Professor Edwards (a physiologist) and Mr Steptoe (an obstetrician) combined Mrs Brown's ovum and Mr Brown's sperm *in vitro* to produce an embryo which was then implanted in Mrs Brown's womb.

IVF is now a well-established technique. Twenty years on, there were some 200,000 more births worldwide resulting from IVF, including a sister to Louise. The procedure, however, is expensive, and the price is rising. The cost of a cycle of IVF on the NHS in 2004 is about £2,770.[2] According to the Human Embryology and Fertilization Authority, about 24,000 infertile couples in the UK undergo IVF treatment, and about 8,000 babies are born as a result. One in four women under 30 using their own eggs is successful; only 1 in 10, by the age of 40 (HFEA Patient Guide 2003–4).

Plainly, in view of the expense and the poor success rate,[3] IVF is not an easy solution to the problem of infertility. But is it, at least in itself, a morally unproblematic solution – a neat and innocent way of circumventing common causes of infertility: tubal damage and low sperm counts? It simply enables couples like the Browns to do what healthy couples of child-bearing age can do naturally. How could there be anything morally amiss with this procedure? How could the mere location of where fertilization takes place, in a Petri dish rather than in a woman's body, have any significance?

There are, though, two objections to the procedure which are bound up with features of IVF as it is usually conducted at present. These features are, however, merely incidental to IVF treatment – usually present, but not essential to it. Naturally, if not many people wanting IVF are troubled by these features, there is not much incentive to developing alternative economical procedures for those few who are. One objection has to do with the usual means used to obtain spermatozoa, viz. masturbation. The other has to do with the creation of surplus embryos, which may subsequently be disposed of or used in research – research that results in their being destroyed. Let us consider these two objections in turn.

Masturbation and sexual morality

Most seekers of IVF do not mind about masturbating to provide sperm. The man's role in the IVF procedure is the easy bit: the activity can be carried out quickly, cheaply and agreeably. But is masturbation morally objectionable?

To answer this question would necessitate our venturing into the field of sexual morality. This I am reluctant to do, not seeing my way too clearly. It is, all the same, a field which deserves more considered attention than it tends to get in the medical ethics literature. We should not suppose that this neglect indicates that sexual morality is more difficult, more mysterious, than other topics in medical ethics that philosophers boldly undertake to shed light on. In chapter 10 we considered some of the answers that go the rounds to the question of what makes it wrong (when it is wrong) to kill another human being. We did not seem to see our way clearly there either.

It is possible to think of sex as purely recreational. And for those who take this view, there would be no possible objection to masturbation. No one has moral objections to playing patience. Yet, if that is the correct way to think of sexual activities, it is curious that so much opprobrium attaches to forcing someone to engage in this play who does not want to do so. Schoolchildren are forced to play sports, like it or not. Why, then, is it thought to be so abhorrent if they are forced to take part in sexual recreation? Again, why is it more or less universally thought that sexual intercourse should be done in private? The peculiar form of our objection to rape and paedophilia, and our sense of privacy, all tell strongly against the liberal view of sex as simply recreational.

Sex affects human happiness very deeply. Consider, for instance, how it, unlike our other appetites, is a major preoccupation of literature and art. Superficially, there is no sex in *Pride and Prejudice*. No bodices get ripped. But, of course, sex is the dominating theme. We do not have to be Freudians to recognize how much human happiness is in one way or another bound up with sexuality. True, some people are able to live flourishing lives without sexual activity. That said, people can be profoundly distressed, even devastated, by matters to do with sex. It is not just one appetite among others that needs managing. Hence, we should not be surprised to see that, traditionally, it has been hedged about with protective teachings. Naturally, we quarrel over which teachings are appropriate, and it is difficult to find the core of understanding from which these quarrels can be adjudicated. We need to understand more about the good of marriage, and what is needed for the protection of children – for the contraceptive revolution seems paradoxically to have increased the incidence of unwanted pregnancy.

Perhaps part of the difficulty we face in trying to talk sense about sexual morality is that different aspects of sexual conduct involve different virtues. One aspect involves considerations of temperance – wise handling of a physical appetite. Another aspect involves keeping faith (contractual justice) – as with the solemn commitment of sexual fidelity bound up in marriage vows. And another aspect may bring certain ideals into play. Maybe, too, the virtues and vices we are accustomed to delineate do not encompass well the concerns that people have about sex. Consider, for example, the indignity of nakedness – of parading naked prisoners, for example. Which of the vices is involved in such treatment? The treatment is degrading – a violation of human dignity, we say. The place of dignity in regard to sexual conduct needs to be explored. It is easy to see how there could be Kantian doubts about masturbation that turn on this notion.

These are admittedly sketchy remarks. Fortunately, for seekers of fertility treatment who do have some moral objection to masturbation, it is actually possible to obtain sperm for IVF treatment without recourse to it. In Israel, for example, some fertility clinics, working within certain religious (halachic) restrictions that forbid masturbation, collect the husband's sperm after intercourse, using a condom that has not been treated with spermicide.[4]

The 'selecting' of embryos for implantation

Let us turn now to the other objection to IVF, which might seem, to many, to be more serious – that it involves *selecting* embryos for implantation. Remembering the sinister selecting (by doctors) of those fit to work that went on among the new arrivals at the concentration camps of Birkenau and Buchenwald, we need to pay attention to what is up when people talk about 'selecting'. We should always ask: what is to happen to those who are not selected?

Now in the case of IVF, selection is a routine part of the procedure, as more embryos are normally produced than can safely be implanted. While the more embryos that are implanted at one time, the better the mother's chances of becoming pregnant, multiple pregnancies are more liable to result in babies being born with handicaps and needing intensive care. In the UK, the current National Institute for Clinical Excellence (NICE) guidelines recommend that a maximum of two are implanted.[5] What happens, then, to those 'surplus' embryos that are not selected for implantation? They may be frozen and stored for later use by the couple, donated for use by another couple, donated for research, or discarded. In the UK their fate is settled in accordance with the couple's wishes, though the storage period for frozen embryos is restricted – usually in the first instance to five years. Thus, the practice of IVF commonly involves the deliberate destruction of some embryos. Needless to say, objection to this aspect of IVF is made by those who maintain that these early embryos are human beings and, accordingly, that the duty we are under not to kill one another applies to them too. Those who take this view, naturally, consider IVF as it is usually conducted to be unconscionable. But this has not been our view. The conclusion we reached in chapter 10 was that it is incorrect to suppose that the very early embryo, pre-implantation, is already a human being.

There are, in any case, some ways round the problem of surplus embryos, for those who object to their wanton destruction. The Irish Medical Council, for instance, approves IVF, but not the deliberate destruction of embryos.[6] This implies that the one is possible without the other. There is what is called 'natural-cycle-IVF'. No drugs are used to stimulate the ovary, and the ova that are harvested are implanted. The success rate of this method is said to be very much less than where surplus embryos are created (10 per cent as opposed to 25 per cent). Italy has recently introduced a new law requiring that no more than three oocytes may be fertilized at a time and that any embryos created must be implanted.[7]

Suitable parents?

Doctors with the necessary know-how can help women to get pregnant who are having difficulties doing so. Assuming that the means employed to this end are not in themselves morally problematic, should those who offer this kind of service be willing to give it to *all* who ask for it? Or should they take into account before agreeing to help whether the prospective parents would make suitable parents?

It may be said that there is a basic right to marry and found a family. This, though, does not entail a right to be helped to do so. Forbidding a marriage on the ground that the couple would not make suitable parents would surely be a tyranny (despite what Mill says).[8] But giving assistance in such a project is something of a favour. After all, no one, surely, has an obligation to search out a partner on behalf of someone who would like to have a baby. Granted that a doctor need not provide this service, would there be occasions where it would be wrong to do so? And would it be wrong for a state to require those providing this kind of assistance to vet prospective parents for suitability?

Let us consider, first, the role of the state: whether imposing such a duty on doctors would constitute an infringement of people's liberty rights – in this case, a private contract between would-be parents and the doctors who are willing to provide the service they seek. In defence of the state's right to impose a vetting requirement on doctors, analogy might be drawn with the state's regulating of adoption and fostering proceedings. People seeking to adopt or to provide foster care have to satisfy the authorities that children placed in their care will not be neglected or abused. Does the state not have the same duty to safeguard the welfare of future children?

Here, however, there is a difficulty: do merely possible children *have* welfare needs? Let us imagine a case where the seeker of fertility assistance seems conspicuously ill-suited for parenthood. Suppose the applicant is a single woman who has a history of mental illness, alcoholism and, in addition, a criminal record of child abuse. Suppose that, in spite of all this, she manages to secure assistance from a fertility clinic and in due course gives birth to a child. Could we accuse the clinicians who have assisted her of having done this child harm? To be harmed is to be made worse off than you previously were. But for *this* child there will have been no better alternative. It is not as if this child could have been given a better mother.

By the same argument, it seems that we must also concede that this feckless mother cannot be accused of having harmed her child either. All the same, she may have acted unjustly in setting about having a child, and likewise the clinic that chose to help her do so. David Hume, as we noted in chapter 3 (pp. 28–9), points out that an action which we can see will not harm anyone may still be unjust. Thus, we cannot assume that merely because the feckless woman, and her willing assistants, have not harmed the child they have brought into the world, they have done no wrong. Well, would they have done wrong?

Indeed, they would have. With certain roles, that are not in themselves unjust, go responsibilities and duties. To take on these roles voluntarily without being prepared to fulfil these responsibilities is a kind of injustice. It shows an unwillingness to give others their due. So, for example, if you become a car driver, you take on duties to make sure that your car is roadworthy, and to make sure that you are sober when you drive it. And if you help someone else to become a car driver, although it is obvious to you that they will not act responsibly behind the wheel, you are assisting their wrongdoing – and are a party to it. Likewise, if you take on the role of parenthood, you undertake a commitment to take good care of your children. Otherwise, if you are either unwilling or unable to commit to their care, you act unjustly – as do those who assist you and who know or should know of your lack of commitment.

Commitment is obviously a matter of degree. How committed to the welfare of children are parents obliged to be? That is hardly a sensible question to pose in the abstract. But we might roughly distinguish three levels of commitment and ask which level corresponds to what parents owe their offspring: a commitment to maximum welfare, to reasonable welfare, or to a minimal threshold of welfare.[9] Let us understand commitment to maximum welfare to imply that children are entitled to the best possible care, reasonable welfare to imply that they are entitled to adequate care, and minimal threshold of welfare to imply that they are entitled not to be put at high risk of serious harm.

Which level of commitment are children-to-be owed? I suggest that parents' duties to their prospective children are of a piece with parents' duties to their actual children: no more and no less. On that basis we can dismiss as an extravagance the idea that parents or prospective parents are obliged to aim at maximum welfare. Even supposing that we have some clear notion of what constitutes maximum welfare, it is plainly absurd to suggest that responsible parenting involves avoiding choices that disadvantage our children in any foreseeable way. Were that high standard to be taken seriously, we would have to denounce the conduct of Dr Lukwiya (see chapter 3, pp.30–1), who stayed at his post caring for patients and colleagues, foreseeing that as a result of his choice his young children might be left fatherless (as indeed happened). Not only that, but we would have to denounce the mother who casually puts her child in the car to go on a shopping spree, even though she knows that it would be safer to put the child in a pram and walk to the shops.

Commitment to maximum welfare is too high a standard, but isn't the minimum threshold standard too low? People, it will be said, should not be having babies if they are *not* prepared to look after them. That suggests at least an obligation to meet the minimum threshold – and maybe that *is* pitching the commitment on the low side. It might, even so, be the appropriate standard of commitment for doctors to apply (and for the law to impose) – assuming, for the moment, that doctors should impose some standard. These doctors, after all, can only be asked to act within their competence. That should enable them to exclude would-be parents whose children would be at high risk of serious harm. But if doctors were called upon to assess parents on finer points as to whether they would be adequate parents, their judgements would quite likely be simplistic and often prejudiced. It is not, after all, as if we have to hand a reliable fund of general knowledge regarding who are or would be adequate parents.

But is it wrong of doctors to undertake to vet prospective parents for their parental suitability? Let us suppose that what the vetting doctors do is confined to what is well within their competence; they are vetting only for commitment that meets what we are calling the minimum threshold of welfare. Even this may be objected to, for three reasons: (1) doctors ought to be strictly non-judgemental towards their patients; (2) it is unfair to vet would-be parents needing help to have children when would-be parents who don't need help are not subject to any vetting; (3) if doctors impose this vetting, they are violating people's rights of procreative autonomy. Let us consider each objection in turn.

It is true that doctors are expected to treat all comers non-judgementally. Thus, army surgeons are supposed to patch up the enemy wounded with as much care and attention as they bestow on their own wounded. This important tradition is not undermined, though, if doctors refuse to aid and abet injustice at a patient's request. Suppose that you are a cosmetic surgeon and a child molester who has escaped from prison seeks your help to alter his physiognomy so that he can escape detection, are you obliged to give it? If, instead, you report him to the police, have you betrayed the duty to do no harm? Recall that on my account of that duty (in chapter 7) I said that it does not stand in the way of doctors performing their citizenly duties. Suppose that this escapee comes to you needing first aid. Then, of course, you have a duty to provide for his needs with the same care that you would give to anyone else needing first aid. But you would not be betraying your duty to do no harm if you also contacted the police.

Is it unfair of doctors to impose any vetting of would-be parents on those who need help to have babies, when those who do not need medical help are not subjected to any such vetting? It may be said that for doctors to take advantage of those needing help in this way is simply opportunistic.

To this we may agree. Still, that is not to say it is unjust. Is it unjust for policemen opportunistically to patrol around pubs at closing time on the look-out for drunken drivers? Is it unjust for a Vehicle Licensing Bureau opportunistically to invite applicants to say if they would wish to be kidney donors if they met with a fatal accident? Isn't such opportunism plain good sense? True, the infertile, through mere ill luck, face a hurdle that the fertile do not face. But, as I argued in chapter 8, people cannot complain that they are victims of injustice merely because they are (brute) unlucky.

But do doctors who impose any vetting on people seeking their help to have babies infringe these people's rights of procreative autonomy? Let us grant that there are some rights that may be so described: the right not to be compulsorily sterilized and the right not to be forced to become pregnant would seem to fall under this description. Both these rights, let us note, protect a person's bodily integrity, whereas people's bodily integrity is not violated merely because they are denied fertility services. If the doctors who refuse to offer help believe (with good reason) that they would be helping the would-be parents to act unjustly, they are not infringing rights. There is no right that entitles people to do wrong or to be helped to do so.

In the light of these considerations, it seems not only reasonable for doctors to vet prospective parents, but wrong for them not to do so, provided that they confine their attention to what should be within their competence, screening out prospective parents who conspicuously do not measure up to the minimum threshold: where children would be at high risk of serious harm.[10]

A suitable child?

By combining IVF and pre-implantation genetic screening of embryos, it is now possible to select among embryos according to their genetic profile (so far as that can be discerned). The question then arises: what genetic traits among those that are identifiable should determine which embryos to implant? And is that a decision to be made by the parents-to-be or by the fertility clinician? Does the state have any business laying down restrictions on what criteria may or may not be used? It is already possible, for example, to select embryos of the preferred sex for implantation. Should this be allowed only where there is a need to avoid passing on a gender-related genetic disease like haemophilia? Should it be used only for screening out very serious diseases that blight life from the outset – like Tay Sachs – or should it be used also to screen out for late-onset diseases like Alzheimer's and Parkinson's? Why, if the procedure is not in itself morally problematic, should its use be restricted to serious diseases or, indeed, restricted in any way? What if some would-be parents want to use this technology in order to select for what most parents would want to select against? Suppose, for example, deaf parents are keen to have a deaf child.

Selecting for deafness

Candy McCullough and Sharon Duchesneau, a lesbian couple living in Maryland, were both deaf. Sharon obtained sperm from a deaf friend and inseminated herself. In due course she gave birth to a deaf daughter. She repeated the procedure again a few years later using the same sperm donor and gave birth to a deaf son (reported in the *Washington Post*, 31 March 2002).

Sharon, as it happened, did not need the help of a fertility clinic. But if a fertility clinic were approached with a request of this kind, would it be acting wrongly in complying? As we have already remarked, there could be no objection based on an appeal to the child-to-be's welfare, since that child would not have been harmed. For *it* the alternative would not be a life with hearing, but no life. All the same, it may be argued that choosing to select *for* deafness is wrong. Does it not show an irresponsible attitude on the part of the parents?

Some people will condemn such a proceeding both because they object to this particular preference for deafness being indulged and because they object anyway to what the method of accommodating the preference, pre-implantation genetic diagnosis, involves – selecting which embryos to kill off as not fit to see the light of day. So let us keep these issues separate. We are concerned here to explore just the former issue. So let us suppose that the parents think that they have other ways of achieving their preference. Maybe they are offered a pill (by a quack) which they are assured will cause any child they conceive to be deaf. Or maybe they read that if they follow a particular diet, it will have the desired effect. They act accordingly, presumably in the belief that it will be easier for them and easier for the child if it is deaf. Thus, if in due course a child is born, and to their disappointment it turns out to have hearing, they will see nothing wrong with using surgery to make it deaf, supposing the surgery involved is simple and safe. Suppose they cannot find a surgeon willing to oblige, but that the infant happens to develop a condition which can easily be put right, but which will make the child deaf if not treated. In that case they will refuse treatment, believing that allowing the child to become deaf will do it no harm. The parents, we may suppose, insist that deafness is no defect. They may argue that being deaf is being 'differently abled', not disabled – so that there is no harm in leaving their child untreated.

Is this a credible claim? Does it correct a widespread prejudice? 'Defect' implies that something is missing, lacking, that is supposed to be present. Thus defects are characteristically disadvantageous – making the subjects that have them less able to perform as they are supposed to. (Of course, they may be advantageous incidentally. You might escape the draft thanks to your having flat feet.) Defects in tools and instruments make them less serviceable for the job they are supposed to do: leaking is a defect in an electric kettle, but not in a colander. Defects in plants and animals relate likewise to how they are supposed to be as members of a species with its own life form: 'Pliability is good in a reed though a defect in an oak.'[11] There are, however, defects that are so easy to correct for that they are no disadvantage. Short-sightedness is a defect. We nowadays wear glasses or contact lenses to correct for this. We don't say that there is nothing *to* correct. But in our modern world there is nothing missing in the life of short-sighted people. They might even have advantages inasmuch as wearing spectacles protects the eyes. The important issue here is whether a defect means that you miss out on things that make life fortunate. Short-sighted people nowadays, generally speaking, it may be argued, do not – as they surely did in Roman times.

Now those who protest that deafness is no defect may say that there need be nothing missing in the lives of deaf people, that deaf people are able to live very full and worthwhile lives. Let us agree that this can be so, and might be so more often if more effort were made in hearing societies to lessen difficulties that are carelessly imposed on the deaf minority because their particular needs get ignored or overlooked.

All that granted, deafness none the less is a defect. Suppose a factory owner facing a charge of neglecting to provide equipment to workers to protect their hearing defends his inaction by arguing that deafness is no defect. Won't this defence rightly get laughed out of court? Deafness in a rabbit or a cat is clearly a defect. For something to be a defect in particular individuals, it need not in anyway be disadvantageous to them. The farmer's sheepdog that is too lame to fetch the sheep may be allowed to curl up by the fireside while its nimble-footed companions have to go out and about in all weathers. And it is quite remarkable how individual humans with various impairments manage to adapt and compensate so as not to miss out on good things. Lameness is a defect in mouse and man. But man is equipped to cope better. While, as we have said, much could be done to lessen the difficulties for deaf people in a hearing society, it still remains the case that deafness is a serious disadvantage for human beings – and not just in their dealings with other humans.

Given that deafness is a defect, is it wrong for parents to choose to have a deaf child? That depends. It would be irresponsible of parents to go out of their way to have a deaf child – for example, using IVF and pre-implantation genetic diagnosis specifically in order to have a deaf child. Wrong too, if they casually allow a child to acquire this defect when they could easily take steps to prevent it, say by consenting to a minor operation to insert grommets to correct for 'glue ear,'[12] or when they could easily remedy the condition of profound deafness – say, by consenting to the insertion of a cochlear ear implant.[13]

But it is another matter if parents who are deaf decide to have children in the natural way, knowing that any child they have is likely to inherit their deafness. Suppose that, with assisted conception, these parents could improve the chances of having a defect-free child of their own, but that they would need to re-mortgage their house to pay for the treatment. Would they then be morally obliged to do that? Not so. We have already dismissed as ridiculous the notion that parents have a duty to choose the best option for their (actual or potential) children.

Genetically modified babies

Suppose that advances in reproductive medicine make it possible to enhance healthy embryos by inserting genes that simply confer benefits without having any disruptive effects on other genes. Needless to say, as with any pioneering new treatment, there will be concerns about safety and efficacy. For this reason a cautious approach makes sense: trying out the modifying techniques first on somatic cell lines rather than on germ lines (since the former affect only the individual who is treated, whereas the latter become part of the genome of the individual and are transmitted to all its progeny). For the same reason, it makes sense to start with corrective modifications for serious conditions not otherwise treatable, before attempting merely enhancing ones. Corrective treatment aims to improve the situation of someone who is already in a bad way. Enhancing treatment aims to improve the situation of someone who is not in a bad way but could be in a better way. It stands to reason that the case for letting well enough alone carries more weight in regard to enhancing treatments where the *status quo* of the individual to be treated is already well enough.

In 1992, the UK government appointed a committee to advise on the ethics of gene therapy. It was chaired by Sir Cecil Clothier – hence became known as the Clothier Committee. In its report (*Report of the Committee on the Ethics of Gene Therapy*) it advised that somatic cell gene therapy aimed at alleviating disease 'posed no new ethical problems' (4.23). As to the possibility of using enhancing therapy, the committee observed: 'We are alert to the profound ethical issues that would arise were gene modification ever to be directed to the enhancement of normal human traits' (2.16). The committee did not elaborate on what these 'profound' issues were. It contented itself with approving the cautious application of gene therapy to alleviate disease, remarking that this is 'a proper goal of medicine' (8.4). Was this to imply that enhancement is *not* a proper goal? Doesn't cosmetic surgery straddle both corrective and enhancing surgery?[14]

The American Medical Association's Code of Ethics advises: 'genetic manipulation should be utilized only for therapeutic purposes. Efforts to enhance "desirable" characteristics through the insertion of a modified or additional gene, or efforts to "improve" complex human traits, "the eugenic development of offspring", are contrary not only to the ethical tradition of medicine, but also to the egalitarian values of our society' (E-2.11). The Code goes on to lay down some conditions that would be necessary, though maybe not sufficient, to render enhancing ethically unproblematic. One of these conditions is that all citizens would have equal access to the technology, 'irrespective of income or other socioeconomic characteristics'. The Code does not elaborate on why this stipulation should apply to genetic enhancement when it does not apply to corrective therapies, genetic or otherwise.

Here let us explore whether, safety and efficacy considerations aside, there are any good reasons for regarding enhancing modifications as inherently more problematic than corrective modifications. On the face of it, a line drawn between ethically permissible and impermissible therapies according to whether they are corrective or enhancing seems rather arbitrary. It would permit interventions to correct for shortness that was the result of a deficiency of human growth hormone, but not for shortness that was simply the result of having normally short parents. But, in so far as shortness is a bane for children, does it matter what is the cause of it? Is it not reasonable for parents to choose to spare their offspring that bane – assuming the technique is proved safe and they foot the bill themselves?

Since our purpose here is to examine enhancing, as opposed to corrective, treatments, we should ignore ethical concerns that would seem to apply to both. Thus, for example, there may be special concerns about protecting people's rights of privacy, specifically confidentiality, in regard to genetic interventions. If so, these will apply to both forms of intervention, not just to those aimed at enhancing. Similarly, we can ignore concerns about unequal access, which apply to both forms. Likewise, any concerns about applying these treatments to children will arise in regard to corrective as well as to enhancing treatments. In short, we want to see whether there are any particular concerns that arise only in regard to enhancing, which would explain why it might be more problematic than corrective treatments.

Let us suppose that the method of enhancing is not in itself a ground for disquiet (safety and efficacy considerations aside, of course). Suppose that it is simply a matter of inserting the desirable gene. That sounds innocent enough. Now, if the means are innocent and the procedure is safe, that seems to leave only the end aimed at as a possible source of disquiet. But the end aimed at is to improve the individual treated. The procedure involves making some embryos better than they would otherwise be and making none worse. How can anyone object to that?

There are, however, some troubling aspects to the project specifically of enhancing human embryos. Here I will examine two worries about the project. (1) Do the parents who might be seeking to have their offspring enhanced know what kinds of modifications would be genuinely beneficial? (2) For whom, anyway, would and should the enhancements sought be beneficial: the children themselves? their parents? the wider community? (The American Code asserts that 'there would have to be a clear and meaningful benefit to the person' treated. Is that right? Why is it not enough that the one treated does not suffer harm, while others benefit?) These same two questions arise with regard to any treatments, genetic or otherwise, aimed at enhancing patients who are not competent to consent on their own behalf. For example, they arise with regard to cosmetic dentistry on children's teeth – say, to straighten them. Let us consider the questions in turn, beginning with the anxieties about what people may suppose is truly enhancing.

John Harris protests against there being a total ban on enhancements. He says: 'either such traits as hair colour, eye colour, gender and the like are important or they are not. If they are not important, why not let people choose? If they are important, can it be right to leave matters to chance?'[15] Yet once we move away from correcting for diseases to improving on the healthy normal child, how can we be sure that what we do is an improvement at all: big or little? John Habgood, formerly Archbishop of York, in the course of a public lecture delivered at the University of York in 1995, warned: 'be very suspicious about improving human nature; and even more suspicious of those who think they know what improvements ought to be made'. This worry about improving human nature might seem a little odd coming from a man of the cloth. Isn't improving human nature very much his business? But Habgood's worry may be more about the kinds of enhancements that some people might see fit to bestow on their offspring.

The Habgood worry seems especially relevant to enhancements that involve adding a novelty feature to children (for example, enabling them to see in the dark, or to glow in the dark, or giving them extra fingers). It is also relevant to the project of bestowing some advantage that enhances beyond the normal scale (for example, giving a child exceptionally strong muscles or outstandingly acute hearing). We do not have experience of what it is like to live with these novelty features or with features intensified beyond the normal ranges. It might turn out, for example, that exceptionally acute hearing would be more bane than blessing. A harpist might be eager to add an extra finger to her child, thinking of how advantageous it would be for playing the harp and assuming that any child of hers will naturally want to do that. Her own enthusiasm might blind her to the possible down side for the child of being regarded by its schoolfellows as a freak. But suppose that the enhancements sought are merely to prevent offspring from inheriting some disadvantageous though not abnormal or health-compromising features of their parents: a father might wish not to pass on to sons his baldness; a mother might not want to pass on to daughters her hirsutism. In such cases, the Harris defence of parental choice seems apposite.

The Catholic bishops in their report on genetic interventions for the Linacre Centre, contemplating the possibility that some day parents might be able to have the intelligence of their offspring enhanced by genetic modification, declare that altering their child's potential with a technical 'fix' is less satisfactory than their doing so by eliciting the child's cooperation.[16] But, then, why shouldn't parents try both? What, anyway, is wrong with making use of technical fixes, when they work – candles, corkscrew, curtains (three essentials for a romantic evening): where would we be without them?

It may be argued that allowing enhancing treatments to be performed on a child violates what Joel Feinberg calls the child's 'right to an open future'.[17] Feinberg has in mind what he also calls certain 'rights-in-trust' – rights that the child has not the capacity to choose to exercise yet, but which should be saved for the child to be able to exercise later. These rights would be violated if parents made choices that would close off certain 'key options' for the child when it grows up: for example, closing off or restricting the child's future choice of career.

What this alleged right amounts to, though, is not so clear. Feinberg supposes that it is threatened if children do not have access to education. 'Education', however, seems, by definition, a matter of leading out or away from something to something. Isn't that a matter of closing some doors and opening others? Doubtless, some types of education are less intent on closing doors than others. But even liberal education will strive to close some. Won't it aim to inculcate tolerance and other citizenly values? If so, isn't it closing doors on intolerant and uncitizenly ones? There is nothing on the curriculum for the child who wants to learn how to pick locks – a useful skill for some careers.

But let us suppose, for the sake of argument, that children do have some such right. Even so, we need not also suppose that all forms of genetic enhancing would be of a nature to impede a child's freedom. Parents choosing a modification to make their children glow in the dark would no doubt be closing off certain future careers for their offspring – careers not only in thievery, but also in detective work or the military. But other modifications might be chosen in order to widen the child's freedom – modifications, for example, to make a child more agile, to have a better memory, or to be better at mathematics. None of these would seem to close any doors on future choices.

Thus far we have been thinking about how parents might aim to benefit their offspring by conferring some genetic modification on them. We have found no reason why enhancements *per se* might not genuinely be of benefit. Obviously, though, we should bear in mind the Habgood worry, and be cautious about what parents take to be genuinely enhancing – especially as some people have very eccentric tastes (like the man who has tried to make himself into a lizard as far as possible, covering his body with lizardly tattooings and having his tongue made forked – he might want to have his offspring genetically modified to become little Lizzies).

Let us now turn to our second question. What if the enhancement is an improvement, not for the individual who is treated, but for others – for parents, carers or the wider community? Is this necessarily unjust to the individual? Because of the usual broad convergence of interests between child and parents or carers it may typically be the case that what is beneficial for one is so for the other as well. Thus, if a child is treated in a way that makes it easier for parents to cope – is given a drug, say, that makes the child more tractable – this *may* be 'win-win'.

What, though, if the treatment to enhance is imposed for the benefit of the wider community? Is this necessarily unjust? Is it not of the essence of education that it aims to influence, to modify, children? This is done partly with a view to benefiting the children, but partly with a view to benefit the community – to turn the children into good citizens. Assuming that we regard education as part of every child's birthright and approve of education pursuing this aim, we cannot condemn as unjust the project of imposing enhancements on children in pursuance of the very same aim. Why should the particular method of enhancing be ethically concerning, provided it is proved safe and reliable?[18]

It is instructive to compare the genetic enhancements that are made on animals. Typically, the aim behind these is not to benefit the individual animal but to meet various human interests or needs. Some of the modifications performed on animals to benefit humans do not in anyway impinge on the welfare of the animals. Some may even be to their advantage. Others, however, do adversely affect their welfare.

Compare the following examples. During the 1980s the Roslin Institute in Edinburgh researched the introduction of human proteins into sheep. A gene was introduced into one ewe called Tracey, which enabled her to produce a protein which could be used to treat human emphysema sufferers. Tracey suffered no deleterious effects whatsoever. In fact, she was rather cosseted. On the other hand, inserting growth genes into pigs and sheep in order that they will grow bigger or faster or provide leaner meat has not proved harmless for the animals treated: 'The "Beltsville" pigs – named after the US Department of Agriculture research station where they were born – were given a human growth hormone. As intended, the animals did grow faster and proved leaner too . . . However, the animals were arthritic, had ulcers, were partially blind.' Sheep treated with human growth hormone have 'proved to be diabetic and have suffered high mortality'.[19]

Isn't it only the latter kind of example of genetic modification that is problematic? What makes it so has to do quite simply with the adverse impact of the treatment on the animal's own welfare. It has nothing to do with genetic manipulation *per se*. The same concern arises with other treatments of animals that do not involve the new genetic technology. Compare the docking of the tails of sheep and of pigs. The former practice seems to be win-win: it protects sheep against fly-strike, which causes infested animals acute misery. The practice of docking pigs' tails is more controversial, just because it is not clear that this does not have an adverse effect on the pigs' welfare. It does stop pigs biting each other's tails – a source of suffering in a pig herd. But, arguably, the propensity to bite is symptomatic of other welfare problems (like, perhaps, overcrowding or poor diets) in the herd, that may get ignored if the tail biting is solved by docking.[20] As above, here too, it is the impact on the animal's welfare that makes the way it is treated problematic, and not that the procedure is carried out to meet certain human interests.

In short, provided a modification of an animal either benefits it somewhat or at least does not harm it, there is no injustice in the procedure merely because the aim is to benefit others. Likewise, with regard to modifying children. True, this involves treating children not exclusively with a view to *their* best interest. But I have already argued that parents are not obliged to do that. Indeed, they may do no wrong if they sometimes put their own convenience before the best interests of their children (recall our example, conveying their child to the shops by car rather than by pram, though the latter is a safer mode of travel) – provided they are still providing a good standard of care. So, too, we may suppose that the state does not act badly if it imposes some enhancements aimed at benefiting the community, provided these do not harm those who are treated. Immunization programmes, for example, confer a big benefit on the community and are not intended to harm individuals (though, predictably, some will be harmed). Of course, each individual as a member of the community stands to benefit indirectly by the existence of the programme.

It may be objected that this, however, would not be treating the child as 'an end in itself'. Suppose we fall in line with those who think that this elevated but obscure description captures something of importance for us to consider. Presumably, this objection applies only where someone is said to be treated as a *mere* means. We need not, then, suppose that it applies here – any more than we should say that a child is being used as a mere means when directed to put away toys, to make a bed, or to help wash up.

Taking stock

Any new technology that is developed increases our powers and widens our choices. Increased powers and more choice are always a mixed blessing. Couples able to choose the sex of their prospective offspring have something else to quarrel about. But where a new technology is not bad in itself, and where it has some good uses, it seems reasonable to look for ways of regulating rather than banning it – especially if banning would be difficult to enforce. None of the new reproductive technologies we have discussed (IVF, pre-implantation genetic diagnosis, and genetically enhancing embryos) seems bad in itself. Each can be used in good ways as well as bad.

What policies should clinics adopt by way of regulating use of these technologies? Let us not assume that the same policies are necessarily appropriate regardless of local circumstances. But we might expect there to be some underlying guiding principles that should inform the choice of policies everywhere. The mere commitment to do no harm seems necessary, but not sufficient. Clinics should also commit to doing no wrong. The commitment to act always in the best interests of children-to-be is, however, extravagant. Parents have a duty to give a good standard of care to their children. They are not obliged always to act in their best interests, whatever sense can be attached to that catch-phrase.

15

The Old and the New

In this final chapter, instead of merely synopsizing and repeating, it might be more useful to reflect on a very different approach to many of our problems. In the last chapter of his *Rethinking Life and Death,* Peter Singer contrasts what he takes to be the 'old' and the 'new' ethic. Since in this book we have often turned sympathetically to the Hippocratic teachings, it might seem that we must be siding with the old. We shall find, however, that matters are not quite so straightforward.

Singer, like us and surely pretty well everyone else, is dissatisfied with the present state of public thinking on these subjects. We can all readily agree that some 'rethinking' is in order. And indeed, as we all know, the task will never be finished. The mass of received opinion at any one time is bound to represent an untidy patchwork of the good, the bad and the indifferent. This conglomerate of the accepted can be expected to be corrupt in ways to which the glare of convention blinds us.

However, when Singer talks disparagingly about 'our traditional ethic' or 'our conventional ethic of life and death', we do well to ask which aspects he has in mind. It is perfectly conventional to suggest that we should not go around shooting our neighbours. One might call this *an unexamined opinion*. It is also perfectly conventional to insist that a woman 'has the right to do what she likes with her own body', and to say that sincere and conscientious conduct cannot be wrong. Talk of 'conservatism' as a defect represents a *code* familiar within a circle of the initiated. Those who adopt this code will always in practice want to 'conserve' this or that element of the current teaching, often – and this is not a complaint – without being able to present a clear rationale for their choice.

At any rate, we may readily fall in with the quite unsurprising view that 'our conventional ethic' is unsatisfactory. The question must then be faced: What we are to do about it? Singer's response is characterized by a combination of two attitudes, not uncommonly found together: philosophical confidence of a somewhat Benthamite cast, coupled with hostility to the lingering influence of religion. Our conventional ethic is too far gone, in his opinion, to be patched and mended. 'The patching could go on, but it is hard to see a long and beneficial future for an ethic as paradoxical, incoherent and dependent on pretence as our conventional ethic of life and death has become.'[1] The task is urgent, he says; doctors and nurses otherwise struggle on, applying an ethic which causes unnecessary misery for patients and their families. This is, we may agree, a serious matter, for though any reasonable ethic would *also* cause much misery – a point we should not forget – it would not, we may assume, cause misery in a way rightly judged to be unnecessary.

However, the presumption that a radical rethink can confidently be guided by the latest philosophical theorizing may seem to fly in the face of experience. Misgivings on this score, as I mentioned in the Introduction, are not unreasonable, and should make us wary of claims that the conventional ethic of the future is going to be any more 'coherent' than the conventional ethic it replaces. And there is a further difficulty. What would *count* as a truly radical rethink, a casting aside of the old? If someone comes to us pressing for a more Benthamite approach to questions of life and death, as would seem to be the case here, would it be relevant to point out that Jeremy Bentham's *An Introduction to the Principles of Morals and Legislation* was published way back in 1789? If we are truly to think afresh, shouldn't we be trying to purge our present-day attitudes of confusing utilitarian elements unthinkingly inherited from those far-off days, attitudes which, if acted upon, might cause unnecessary suffering?

What particularly troubles Peter Singer is the influence of religion upon the present patchwork of opinion. He speaks of 'a set of ideas we have inherited from the period in which the intellectual world was dominated by a religious outlook'.[2] There seems to be something not quite right about this. European thought from the Greeks onwards has been a critical and quarrelsome tradition (unlike some traditions elsewhere). Greek quarrelled with Greek; Jew quarrelled with Jew, Christian with Christian. Aquinas may now be thought of as a perfect model of orthodoxy, but the Catholic Church initially found it quite difficult to accommodate his teachings, to say nothing, of course, of what the Reformers made of them.[3] Hence, the notion that there is a 'set of ideas' which consists of a body of canonical (religious or indeed secular) teaching that has been handed down, received and adopted uncritically by successive generations until the present day is somewhat misleading.

Ironically, in so far as there has been agreement, Singer does not characterize it well, and this is quite significant for his approach as a whole. He talks about 'the Judeo-Christian view of human beings as the pinnacle of creation', a thought he associates with the 'cherished' pre-Copernican idea 'that we are the centre of the universe'.[4] This view of the chain of being (as it was once called), and of the significance of our being at the centre, is a popular error. The traditional view of the sanctity of life was evidently *not* based upon the idea that we are simply the best thing around. It would not, for instance, account for the difference of attitude that supporters of sanctity of life have towards the duty not to kill and the duty to rescue.

Singer dismisses the elements of the old ethic that he wishes to replace as mere 'religious relics'. This is somewhat surprising in view of the enormous influence of Plato and Aristotle, not least upon the biblical religions themselves. Plato and Aristotle begin with reflections on human nature, on human needs, and what makes for living well: acquiring virtues and avoiding vices. We can sensibly enter on *this* discussion even if we do not have religious presuppositions.

Singer does not think much of an ethic that takes its origin from reflections upon human nature and the virtues. Commenting on Aristotle and natural law theory, Singer, writing with his colleague Helga Kuhse, observes that 'there is no reason to believe that living according to nature will produce a harmonious society, let alone the best possible state of affairs for human beings'.[5] They go on to reel off some of the unsavoury characteristics of our human nature. But does Aristotle – do natural law theorists – advocate 'living according to nature'? What, anyway, are we to understand by this idea? Thomas Hobbes speaks of laws of nature.[6] But he hardly suggests that we should live *according* to nature. On the contrary, he makes out that life according to nature is just what we should strive most to escape from. As for Aristotle, he too is well aware of the troublesome aspects of human nature. Indeed, the virtues, as we have noted, are plausibly glossed as necessary correctives to the flaws to which we are naturally prone. On his account, our vices are every bit as natural as our virtues. He recommends the latter over the former not, as more natural, but as the better bets for our chances of living well.

Singer and Kuhse also challenge the notion that ethics should be based on virtues *rather than* principles or rules.[7] What use is it, they ask, saying that virtuous choice is 'whatever the virtuous person would choose', if we do not have some prior independent notion of what it is right to do – what that person *would* choose in a specific situation? 'Cultivate the virtues!' seems unhelpful as a directive towards resolving the problems of medical ethics unless we are able to supplement this with an account of 'right action'.

This is one of the complaints about virtue ethics to which I responded in chapter 2 (pp. 25–6). I pointed out how very implausible is the suggestion that an ethics based on virtues is not *also* based on principles or rules. There is no such dichotomy in regard to the cardinal virtue of justice – the virtue that is so much bound up with the issues of concern in medical ethics. In fairness to Kuhse and Singer, they may be commenting on virtue ethics as it is so often presented these days. We have noted the tendency in many accounts to marginalize this virtue. But the remedy for this may be not to give up on the virtues but to reinstate justice.

The thought that a new ethic which Singer would be able to accept can be established quite independently of religious doctrines familiar in our history is an interesting one. This may not have received the attention it deserves. If Singer is really resolute, if he knocks away every distinctively religious underpinning, might he not bring the whole house down upon this head – especially since the modifications he wants to make to the old house are 'radical'? Modern writers tend not to notice the danger they might be in, partly because it has become a respectable practice to stipulate one's way out of difficulties;[8] but partly also because of an unexamined thought that it would be fair by now to call 'traditional'. For many years it has been the custom, even among those with religious beliefs, to say that disobedience to a divine commandment *could not of itself* render an action bad. In every case, either God would be reinforcing an obligation stemming from an independent moral law, it would be said, or his commandments would simply be 'arbitrary'.

Must we accept that this dichotomy exhausts the possibilities? Does it do so in regard to secular authority? Consider the kinds of constraints that the laws of the land put us under. Some of these laws prohibit our doing things that are independently wrong – like raping or stealing. Others prohibit our doing things that are wrong only because the law prohibits them – like one-way street restrictions or car parking ordinances. Such prohibitions as these are, of course, not arbitrary. In fact, it is not clear what an 'arbitrary' prohibition could be, for prohibiting is an action which calls for a reason, if only 'I wanted to see if you would obey'.

My approach, like Singer's, aims to provide an ethic of life and death that does not draw on religious teachings. Even someone who has religious beliefs will be interested to see how far it is possible to go in this 'secular' way. Singer is particularly keen to excise religious teachings from the thinking that governs life-and-death decisions concerning patients. The notion of a 'religious teaching', however, is pretty indeterminate. Does the teaching of the brotherhood of man or the injunction to 'love your neighbour' count as religious?

Peter Singer's new commandments

Let us turn now to consider Singer's specific proposals for a new ethic. They take the form of five new 'commandments' to replace what he takes to be five 'commandments' of the older, 'traditional' ethic. In each case we must ask whether the old commandment truly represents the older view of things when considered with reasonable intelligence and moderate sympathy. And we must ask what the corresponding new commandment would mean, and whether we would be well advised to follow it.

1   The old commandment: 'Treat all human life as of equal worth' is to be replaced by the new: 'Recognize that the worth of human life varies.'

The first thing to notice here is a point of logic: that injunctions of the form 'act as if p' and 'recognize that not-p' are compatible. They can be obeyed simultaneously. And there need be no dishonesty or even irrationality in adopting both. Thus, we may recognize that people are of 'unequal worth to society', as the phrase goes, but still choose to treat them as if they were of equal worth to society.

Compare, for example, Sherlock Holmes with his brother Mycroft: the former endeavouring with some effect to see justice done, the latter, brilliant but leading an utterly idle life. Nevertheless, it might be good policy for doctors to turn a blind eye to such a difference when a Sherlock and a Mycroft arrive in Casualty – that is to say, to adopt the fiction that the social good will be served alike if either is saved. This is called *deeming*: we *deem* that their value to society is equal, if the question comes up at all. The deeming can be done quite openly, and no one need suppose that there is anything to be ashamed of. We would not have to claim that this kind of deeming is always appropriate, but only that it is sometimes so. Similarly, we might agree to live by the fiction that all patients are equally deserving of

treatment, even though some of them may be very unattractive crim-
inals, or may have carelessly put themselves in need of costly treatment. Doctors (including those who are in private practice) might
want to observe this kind of 'equality' in their approach to their
patients. After all, the attempt to make comparisons of desert among
patients might be time-consuming and would involve much indeterminacy: wouldn't it be better for the doctors just to get on with the
healing task, 'making the care of their patients their first concern' (as
directed on the aforementioned GMC card which lists the essential
duties of doctors.

Let us suppose, then, that the old commandment is to be read:
'Recognize that the worth of human life does not vary.' So understood, the old is obviously incompatible with the new. But notice how
obscure both are in sense. Both seem to imply that there is some
notion of *abstract* worth. At the very least, we must agree that this
notion is unclear, though we might not want to dismiss it altogether.

Singer, however, gives a certain slant to this notion of *worth*, which
those who talk of *equal* worth would not for a moment recognize. He
says: 'The best argument for the new commandment is the sheer
absurdity of the old one.' He proceeds to interpret the old to imply
that doctors and nurses should regard every patient's life as equally
worth *saving* regardless of its prospects. Thus, a team of surgeons who
followed this commandment and who received a liver for transplant
would consider it quite wrong to select which of their patients to give
it to by comparing the patients' chances of surviving the surgery for
five years or more. Let us agree that a teaching which implies anything
so silly as that is insupportable. But who has ever taught a doctrine of
'equal worth' *of this kind*?

Consider now how Singer interprets his new replacement commandment. He lists the characteristics that he takes to be relevant to
estimating the worth of an individual – this being directly relevant to
whether care to keep the individual alive should continue. Aside from
considerations about how much, if at all, the individual is enjoying life
or wants to go on living, other relevant considerations include 'having
relatives who will grieve over your death, or being so situated in a group
that if you are killed, others will fear for their own lives.'[9] He adds: 'All
of these things make a difference to the regard and respect we should
have for a being.'[10] Thus, it would appear, someone who has relatives
who would grieve has more worth, is owed more respect, other things
being equal, than someone who has not. It would be something for
doctors to take into account before deciding to withdraw care, or
indeed kill. For all the obscurity of the old commandment, we might

well have misgivings about the effect on medical and nursing students
if it were replaced by the new.

2 The old commandment: 'Never intentionally take innocent
human life' is to be replaced by the new: 'Take responsibility for the
consequences of your decisions.'

Here again, we might note that the two injunctions do not seem to be
incompatible. Leaving that aside, let us consider each commandment
on its merits. The old in this case does indeed seem recognizable as a
teaching of long standing. Its hold on us nowadays has been consid-
erably undermined, though, by the general acceptance of elective
abortion. To persuade us to repudiate this teaching entirely, Singer
calls to our attention its grim implications in some circumstances. For
those who stood by the old commandment, the following dilemma
used to occur occasionally. Sometimes when a woman was in labour,
the head of the baby would get stuck. The only way of saving the
mother's life in such cases was to crush the baby's skull. If this procedure was not followed, both mother and baby would die. The traditional teaching, says Singer, forbade killing the baby even so. Those
who uphold the teaching may not face this particular dilemma any
more, thanks to advances in obstetrics, but the 'appalling' teaching,
Singer observes, still stands in conservative quarters.

   It seems to me that there might have been a way round this dilemma,
though, even for those who accepted this second commandment.
'Innocent' (as we noted on p. 121) in the traditional Christian teaching was construed to mean 'not threatening harm' – and this quite irrespective of any question of culpability. So understood, someone who
was in no way to blame for threatening your life, someone who was
helplessly a threat (as Mary was to her conjoined twin Jodie), would
not count as innocent in the relevant sense. Hence, it might be argued
that intentional killing in these special circumstances could be justified. As I have already suggested (in chapter 13, p. 168), intentional
killing is normally ruled out, since we live in a civil society and expect
the police to defend us. But the police would obviously be no help with
regard to Jodie's peril or with that of the woman in labour.

   Suppose, however, that this line of argument is defective in some
way or other, and that Singer is right to say that, according to this old
teaching, doctors faced with the dilemma he describes had no choice
but to let mother and baby die. Would this demonstrate that the
teaching never to kill the innocent was 'appalling'? Why 'appalling',
rather than just 'severe'? Someone who stands by the teaching here
might concede that the *situation* is appalling but not that the doctor

might be at fault. What the dilemma does show is that this teaching had harsh implications. It would be a bad teaching to preserve if we could replace it with a better teaching. A better teaching would not have these harsh implications, but would still keep us from wrongful killing. In order to produce that better teaching, though, we need to gain more insight than we have managed thus far into what makes killing wrong when it *is* wrong.

Meanwhile, we should observe yet again that the teachings of any ethical theory or approach, including notoriously the teachings of those, like Singer, whose basic ethical position is utilitarian,[11] will have harsh consequences in some situations. According to Singer, as we noted in chapter 10, p. 120, you may be morally obliged to drive over a person trapped and in your way in order to get five others to hospital.

Let us turn now to the new commandment: 'Take responsibility for the consequences of your decisions.' 'Taking responsibility' means, according to Singer, that we must answer not only for the intended consequences of our actions but also for their foreseen consequences, and not only for our decisions to do but also for our decisions to omit to do. But who says otherwise? As we have noted in our discussion of double effect teachings, those who attach significance to the distinction between consequences that are intended and consequences that are merely foreseen do not say that we only have to answer for the consequences that are intended. Does the teaching 'Never intentionally kill' imply that doctors are answerable only for their decisions to do and not for their decisions to omit? Not so. Intentional killing can be by omission (as with the Dr Arthur case we discussed in chapter 12, pp. 153–4).

There may, though, be more at issue here than is immediately obvious from the wording of Singer's replacement command. What does he have in mind by 'taking responsibility'? Is taking responsibility simply a matter of having an answer, a response, to account for taking decisions which have bad consequences, or is it a matter of having an *adequate* answer? And what is to count as adequate? Is it only a utilitarian-style answer that is to be deemed adequate?

Consider the scenario conjured up by Bernard Williams, in his well-known and widely reprinted discussion of 'Jim and the Indians'.[12] Jim, a botanist, while on an expedition in South America, happens upon a scene in a small town where twenty Indians have been tied up against a wall by some soldiers. The captain in charge explains to Jim that after recent acts of protest against the government, these Indians, a random group of villagers, have been rounded up to be shot. Jim is invited 'as an honoured visitor from another land' to shoot one of them himself. If Jim accepts, the captain will let the rest go. If Jim declines, they will all be shot.

Now suppose Jim, faced with this dilemma, refuses to kill an Indian. He says simply: 'I would have to kill one man, in order to save the rest. I cannot do that.' Thus, he recognizes the bad consequences of his decision, and produces an answer (response) to explain it. Singer might insist that this explanation is inadequate. And, no doubt, from a utilitarian point of view, so it is. Moreover, from *any* point of view, Jim's answer is not very explanatory. But suppose he is unable to say more – other than that he assumes there is a deeper answer – a story – which others wiser than he might be able to supply. Is *he* then failing to 'take responsibility'?

For sure, when people's decisions result in bad consequences, it may be reasonable to expect them to 'take responsibility' in the sense that they recognize these consequences and are prepared to respond – explain. Needless to say, *that* kind of expectation is nothing new – nothing that would not be shared equally by advocates of the so-called old ethic. If, however, we are to understand 'taking responsibility' to imply being prepared to offer a utilitarian-style explanation for our decisions, that does seem difficult to square with some traditional teachings.

3   The old commandment: 'Never take your own life and always try to prevent others taking theirs' is to be replaced by the new: 'Respect a person's desire to live or die.'

This old commandment is double-barrelled. The first part of it does indeed match a long-standing teaching that condemns suicide. And this, as I have argued in chapter 11, is not so very unreasonable. But it is easy to see how someone might want to qualify the rigours of the 'never'.

However, what about the add-on? Who is there who has supposed that we must 'always try to prevent others taking their lives'? How many people, we may wonder, have actually been taught this? What would you have to do to comply? Join the Samaritans? Raise money for the Samaritans and for no other cause? Spend your nights patrolling the Golden Gate, Niagara Falls or Beachy Head? Maybe the teaching should be taken in a more qualified way: for example, that one should do something to prevent suicide *when one is in a special position to do so*. The commandment would hardly be basic. It would have to be an inference from some *other* teaching – like the popular teaching that we are to take the interests of others into account, and thus, when the occasion particularly arises, discourage rash decision making. At any rate, this commandment as it stands is neither old nor sensible – at least in regard to the preventing segment of it.

Consider now Singer's replacement: 'Respect a person's desire to live or die.' It conjoins two commands: respect a person's desire to live and respect a person's desire to die. Let us examine each in turn. Consider first the idea that you should respect a person's desire to live. If that means simply that you should not *kill* your patients against their wishes, that is hardly a new teaching. If, on the other hand, it means that you should always grant their wishes for life-saving treatment where doing so is in your power, that is not a sensible teaching. Patients obviously do not have a right to rescue regardless of cost. And sometimes saving life would involve wronging others.

What are we to say of the other idea, that you must respect a person's wish to die? Here again we need to clarify if showing respect means complying with patients' wishes to be killed or if it means merely not forcing life-saving treatment on them against their wishes. If it means the latter, it is no replacement of what is generally taught and considered obligatory. If it means the former, it does, of course, mark a radical departure from a traditional teaching. Singer advocates the former. He refers approvingly to Mill's defence of a person's liberty right, particularly against state paternalism. Yet, even if state paternalism is somewhat objectionable for the reasons Mill gives, medical paternalism, I have argued (in chapter 6), is another matter. Post-operative patients, for example, may predictably be disorientated, confused, despairing and uncooperative. Doctors and nurses know from experience that they can be tided over into happier frames of mind with some judicious doses of paternalist cajolings and manipulative encouragings. Might not the same reasons that Mill has for allowing paternalism *vis-à-vis* children also apply to these post-operative patients?

Singer might happily allow some such qualification to be added to this commandment, restricting it to respect for the settled wishes of patients who are clearly competent to weigh things up for themselves. He does not, after all, say that we must *always* respect a person's desire to live or die. And in fairness to Singer, we should bear in mind that in this exercise of mapping out new commandments, he is aiming to write simply and briefly. He describes his new commandments as a 'preliminary' and 'rough' sketch.[13] And he is much more confident that the old ethic needs completely replacing than that the particular new commands he proffers are appropriate.[14] As it stands, though, Singer's replacement, 'Respect a person's desire to live or die', is very vague. We have been taking 'respect a person's desire' here to mean: 'Grant it!' Maybe it is only meant to imply: 'Take note of it!' But then the replacement commandment would turn out to be nothing new and nothing radical. Nor, even, would it be incompatible with the old commandment that it is supposed to replace.

4   The old commandment: 'Be fruitful and multiply' is to be replaced by: 'Bring children into the world only if they are wanted.'

Here again, we have to ask whether what is presented as the old commandment really does match a teaching that has been part of our traditional ethic. Even if such a teaching once held sway, it hardly seems to do so nowadays. Despite the dramatic decline in childbirth in various Western countries, there seems to be very little by way of propaganda urging people to do their duty and produce more children. The only recent philosopher I know of who has held that we have a (*prima facie*) duty to bring more people into the world is the utilitarian, R. M. Hare. He makes out that we have duties to merely possible people (to make them actual): otherwise they are left out in the cold, so to speak, endlessly waiting their turn to be allowed on-stage.[15] But Hare's curious view on this matter does not seem to have caught on, even among other utilitarians.

Well, then, has this commandment been significant in our past? And might it have a lingering (and bad) influence on attitudes still? Singer traces it to some teachings of Augustine, Luther and Calvin – teachings against intercourse without procreative intent or against Onan's act of 'spilling his seed on the ground' (Gen. 38: 9). Is it plausible, though, to explain these teachings as driven by the thought that we need to bring more children into the world? If that had been the underlying thought of Augustine, Luther or Calvin, we might expect them also to have encouraged intercourse outside of marriage and to have criticized religious orders whose members were required to forgo having children. Anyway, whatever we should make of the views of Augustine, Luther and Calvin on the matter, do *contemporary* followers of these Christian teachers hold that we have an obligation to bring more children into the world?

For sure, 'Be fruitful and multiply' does come from the Bible, but has it really been part of the tradition that Singer is attacking? What, in any case, would make people think of 'Be fruitful and multiply' as an order rather than as an encouragement, a counsel, a recommendation? Were people threatened with punishment for not obeying an order of this kind? In its biblical context it sounds just like an encouragement. 'Work hard, buy a farm, make a success of it, raise a family . . .' Even here we would not think of a recommendation to each and every fertile person, but let us say to a people rather generally. To interpret it as a commandment seems on a par with treating 'Go on! Enjoy yourself! And don't forget your walking boots!' as a commandment.

Christian teaching does not encourage every fertile person to be fruitful – not the unmarried, for example, at least while in that condition. And it does not urge everyone to marry. Furthermore, those who wish to marry are not urged to marry early so as to have more children. It is possible to live a Christian life as a monk or a nun, or indeed as a celibate layperson. And turning to the Greek root of our tradition, there seems to be nothing in the Hippocratic ethic to support such a command. Its prohibition on abortion need involve nothing other than the assumption that one must not kill.

Let us now consider Singer's replacement: 'Bring children into the world only if they are wanted.' We need to reflect on just what he has in mind here. It might be supposed that this commandment is of a piece with the pronouncement that people should not acquire a pet if they are not prepared to look after it – 'A dog is for life, not just for Christmas.' The idea, anyhow, that people who have children have a duty to cherish them is hardly new, hardly a corrective to conventional thinking.

Is Singer's new commandment directed only at people who contemplate reproducing, or is it also directed at people who have reproduced and now may regret it? When exactly is a child 'brought into the world'? Some might think of this as happening only when a child is born. But that is not Singer's view. He makes no bones about the fact that abortion generally involves killing *babies*. A baby in the womb is *in* the world just as your liver and your gut are.

Singer, however, is not merely directing his new commandment at those who have not yet reproduced. What he actually advocates requires a more complicated formula – something like: 'Bring children into the world only if they are wanted *and let them live only if they continue to be so.*' And this view does indeed 'radically' challenge certain old teachings. Thus, he is not simply thinking antecedently about people considering whether or not to create a child, but also about people who, having created a child, would now rather that it did not exist. If the child is not wanted – maybe, for example, because it is discovered, before or after birth, that it has Down's syndrome – then, Singer maintains, the parents' wishes should be accommodated. In his view, the newly born are not yet 'full members of the moral community'.[16] They do not yet have a right not to be killed.

Incidentally, leaving aside Singer's radical add-on concerning children already in the world that are no longer wanted, should we agree with the *initial* formulation of the new commandment: 'Bring children into the world only if they are wanted'? Is it always remiss to have a child that you do not want? Suppose, for example, that you personally would prefer not to have a child, but you decide to have one because you know that your spouse very much does want to have a child? Mightn't this be a worthy undertaking on your part – assuming, of course, that if you decide to have this child, you mean to cherish it as parents should? Isn't the important question not whether you particularly want a child but whether you are prepared to give a child good care – as its parent. Many children are brought into the world by people who did not particularly want to have them. Luckily, it by no means follows that the children are neglected or unloved.

5   The old commandment: 'Treat all human life as always more precious than any non-human life' is to be replaced by: 'Do not discriminate on the basis of species.'

What is here portrayed as the old does seem roughly to capture a teaching that has actually been promulgated and still is. But it is by no means easy to explain what the commandment means – in particular, in what sense we are to treat all humans as 'more precious'. Do people who could do medicine but choose instead to go in for veterinary studies disobey this command? The teaching seems to be particularly bound up with our attitude to homicide. But it is not at all clear how the link is made. Needless to say, Singer does not quarrel with our generally putting people-interests before, say, mouse-interests. What he does object to is the blanket preference for the interests of every human individual, including those who are very impaired or undeveloped, to the interests of individual animals of other species. This preference he labels 'speciesist', and to understand what he means by this and why he is against it, we should examine his replacement command, 'Do not discriminate on the basis of species'.

According to Singer, what has come to be known as 'speciesism' (the exercise of mere partiality for the members of one species over those of another) is analogous to racism. Is this analogy persuasive? Racism is a kind of injustice: its victims are denied their rights on spurious grounds. Is there some corresponding injustice if people show partiality for the members of one species over those of another: favouring cats over mice, rare birds over feral mink? Personal preferences do not necessarily call for justification: your preference, say, for coffee over tea, for ice hockey over cricket, for tulips over daffodils. The last of these examples shows that the alleged injustice of 'speciesism' needs clarifying. Does it arise only in regard to partialities in respect of (some) animal species? Can there be injustice in partiality towards members of plant species or of insect species? Of course, if by some independent argument it is established that (some) animals have rights, then we can proceed to criticize the exercising of those specific partialities that ignore these rights. But in the absence of that argument as to the rights and as to the significance of those partialities, doesn't the analogy between speciesism and racism break down?

So-called speciesism, I suggest, is either impossible or innocent. It is impossible if someone's partiality is held to be *merely* on the basis of species, with a certain stress on the 'merely'. For this would not be an intelligible reason for partiality. Compare how people have sometimes said that racists discriminate *merely* on the basis of colour (though, of course, this was not supposed to involve some aesthetic preference, in the way that gentlemen are said to prefer blondes). People have said this sort of thing to underline the irrationality of racism. But if we make out that our opponents are very irrational indeed, we run the risk of attributing to them attitudes which are not even intelligible *as* attitudes.

That so-called speciesism can be innocent comes out when we reflect that you can admire, say, otters simply because they are otters. If you have this partiality, you may, but need not, be able to offer some explanation as to why you specially like them. Maybe you remember otters from your childhood days. Or maybe you remember reading 'Tarka the Otter'. The point is that acting from this kind of ordinary human partiality, acting as your enthusiasm prompts, is patently innocent. It is as innocent as preferring the Alps to the Rockies. Other people will have different partialities – and will act to promote the welfare of the species they happen to prefer. That too is innocent.

So, it seems, speciesism is either impossible or innocent. If this is so, it has an important consequence. It is not necessary or obligatory or even a sign of virtue to maintain 'an impartial concern for the good of every sentient being'. This, of course, is important only because the requirement of impartiality has been promoted as something of a moral axiom. It is an advance to be rid of it.

Leaving aside the foregoing exercise in rethinking 'our conventional ethic of life and death', Peter Singer does, however, present an interesting criticism of the current ethic; and it has some force. He thinks that the current ethic involves us in a kind of dishonesty or pretence in regard to the sanctity of life. Doctors make use of various stratagems to disguise, maybe even from themselves, how much deliberate killing they do. There is the pretence underlying redefinitions of death designed to enable doctors to harvest vital organs from the nearly dead. Prenatal screening may be offered to women as a 'health check' for their baby. The fact that this is not screening to treat, but screening to filter out, defective babies is not something anyone involved cares to dwell on. Consider, too, the practice mentioned above, pp. 137–8, of 'selective non-treatment' of spina bifida babies, which, Singer says, 'has been normal practice in many paediatric hospitals in most of the developed world'.[17] This practice may no longer be 'normal', because nowadays so much more can be done for even the severest cases. But isn't 'selective non-treatment' in this context just a euphemism for infanticide? The language used disguises what is actually going on.

Singer speculates that 'selective non-treatment' is 'probably more common still' in regard to elderly people.[18] Whether decisions not to treat in respect of the elderly are analogous to what was going on when selective non-treatment was applied to spina bifida babies may be questioned. It rather depends on *why* decisions not to treat are taken. As I argued in chapter 12, although the decision to withhold treatment may indicate intent to kill, it need not. It does not, for example, if a doctor withholds a treatment only because the elderly patient declines it. In that case it would of course be quite wrong to insinuate that the patient has been 'selected' to die. Nor in that case is there any euphemistic cheat in describing what transpires as 'allowing' the patient to die.

In so far as there is an element of dishonesty and pretence of the kind that Singer points up, it does indeed signify something unsatisfactory about current practices and attitudes.[19] Yet, in a way, such pretence, unsatisfactory though it is, may signify something good about those involved. At least, if they are having to pretend, not just to the world but to themselves as well, that they are only letting die and not killing, that shows a reluctance to kill.

Concluding observations

If there is a general lesson to be drawn from our enquiries in this book, it is, perhaps, this: that our understanding of the ethical issues in medicine (as elsewhere) continues to be very imperfect and tenuous. In view of this rather sombre conclusion, we should be wary of claims by philosophers that they can provide some firm framework, 'ethical grid', or set of commandments for health professionals to apply to the problems they encounter. We have found quite simple and central notions on which we draw in thinking about ethical issues to be tricky and troublesome to handle: like the notion of what is harmful or of what is wrongful (unjust) or of what is in someone's interests. We have found that even the answer to the basic question as to why it is wrong to kill another person in circumstances where we all agree it is wrong, cases of plain murder, eludes us. The answers that go the rounds are not adequate.

Notwithstanding the difficulty of advancing our understanding of ethics in medicine, we must not give up trying. Nor, obviously, should we suppose that we do not, after all, know that plain murder is wrong, simply because we cannot provide a satisfactory understanding of its wrongness beyond perhaps a few halting steps. As I have said before, there are many things we know which have a deeper aspect which eludes us. This is nothing peculiar to ethics. Much of philosophy involves the attempt to understand more deeply what we believe.

We should not, however, exaggerate the importance of ethics in medicine. In particular, we should not suppose that a difficulty which arises in the professional life of doctors and nurses which is not technical must somehow be ethical or can usefully be thought of as such. Nor should we suppose that where a problem is ethical, ethicists should be wholly trusted as philosophical consultants. Our subject, as I have said, is a wayward one, and philosophers are often the last people to be taken seriously on any important question, despite the obligatory display of the apparatus of reason, the endless professions of 'rigour', and the enthusiasm to follow the argument wherever it leads, no matter what that might lead us to do.

Nor, obviously, should we imagine that putting ethics on the curriculum in medical and nursing schools will do something to prevent bad conduct – a perfectly comical supposition. People often display a touching faith in ethics courses. Recently, a judge in Wisconsin had to deal with a pharmacist who had been found guilty of refusing to dispense a birth control prescription on grounds of conscience. The defendant was ordered to pay costs *and to take a course in ethics*.

Obviously, too, many instances of bad conduct on the part of doctors or nurses arise not from their failing to have learned how to tell right from wrong, so to speak, but from their failure to do the one and avoid the other. In such cases, it is not corrective instruction that is needed, but honest avowal. Such a thing can even pay. A certain Dr Fordyce, as Boswell relates, did not need to be told that he was acting badly. He told himself, fortunately within earshot.

Dr Fordyce, who sometimes drank a great deal, was summoned to see a lady patient when he was conscious that he had had too much wine. Feeling her pulse, and finding himself unable to count its beats, he muttered, 'Drunk, by God!' Next morning . . . a letter from her was put into his hand. 'She knew too well', she wrote, 'that he had dis-covered the unfortunate condition in which she was when he last visited her; and she entreated him to keep the matter secret in consideration of the enclosed (a hundred-pound bank-note).'[20]

Notes

Introduction

1 Singer, *Rethinking*, p. 1.
2 *Lancet* editorial, p. 897.
3 Beauchamp and Childress, *Principles*, p. 377, cf. p. 387.
4 Singer in conversation with Hyun Hochsmann, *On Peter Singer*, p. 98.
5 Engelhardt Jr. and Wildes, 'The four principles'.
6 Geach, *Virtues*, p. 13.

Chapter 1   Virtues and Vices

1 Recall Peter Geach's observation (above, p. 5) that even if we disagree about what ultimate ends are worth pursuing, we may still agree about what ills are worth avoiding.
2 But, as Georg von Wright observes (*Varieties of Goodness*, p. 144), the terminology is somewhat misleading. What Aristotle means by 'moral' is not quite the same as what is meant by it nowadays. Cf. Foot, *Virtues and Vices*, p. 2.
3 Foot, *Natural Goodness*, p. 14.
4 Ibid., p. 12.
5 Ibid., p. 72.
6 Foot, *Virtues and Vices*, p. 6.
7 Ibid.
8 Foot, *Natural Goodness*, p. 68.
9 Ibid., pp. 79–80.
10 Hursthouse, *On Virtue Ethics*, pp. 172–4.
11 Ibid., p. 8.

Chapter 2   Justice – A Problematic Virtue?

1 *Institutes of Justinian*, p. 3. Book 1 opens with this sentence. (Book 1, Title 1: 'Of Justice and Law'.)
2 Foot, *Virtues and Vices*, p. 3.
3 Foot, 'Moral beliefs', p. 99.
4 Plato, *Republic*, 343C.
5 Ibid., 357E.
6 Plato, *Protagoras*, 321D–323C.
7 See especially the opening paragraph of sect. 2 in Hume, *Treatise*, Book III, part ii.
8 We might remember that Mill chose to translate *Protagoras* into English.
9 Hume, *Treatise*, Book III, part ii, sect. 2.
10 According to the sixth and final inquiry under the chairmanship of Dame Janet Smith, <http://www.the-shipman-inquiry.org.uk/6r_page.asp>
11 Dr Theodore Dalrymple recalls: 'he has always been remembered, or misremembered, as a murderer. Indeed, he was successful in more than one libel suit because newspapers forgot both that he was still alive and that he had been acquitted rather than convicted of murder'. 'Our lives in their hands', *Guardian*, 2 Feb. 2000.
12 Kinnell, 'Serial homicide'.
13 Anscombe, 'On promising', p. 18.
14 Hume, *Enquiry*, Sect. III, part i.
15 Hobbes, 'Questions', p. 116.
16 On the implications for justice where there is basic inequality between ourselves and others, see von Wright, *Varieties of Goodness*, pp. 212–14.
17 Jeremy Bentham speaks of the 'imperious duty to be tender with the feeble, and to spare those who cannot resist'. 'The first index of a dangerous character is *oppression of the weak*': *Theory of Legislation*, p. 258.

Chapter 3   Benevolence – A Problematic Virtue?

1 Rosalind Hursthouse (as we noted in ch. 1, p. 13) says: 'all virtue ethicists assume it is on the list [of virtues] now': *On Virtue Ethics*, p. 8. Cf. Philippa Foot, 'Utilitarianism and the virtues', pp. 224, 235; cf. *idem*, 'Morality, action and outcome', pp. 31.
2 Geach, *The Virtues*, p. 81.
3 Hume, *Enquiry*, Sect. IX, part ii.
4 Ibid.
5 A minor virtue might, though, be especially appealing. Aristotle says that 'the liberal are almost the most loved of all virtuous characters': *Nicomachean Ethics*, 1120a.

6 'The operation of benevolence is circumscribed by justice': Foot, 'Morality, action and outcome', p. 32.
7 Hume, *Treatise*, Book III, part ii, sect. 2.
8 Ibid.
9 Geach, *The Virtues*, p. 86.

Chapter 4   Benevolence – The Only Virtue?

1 Mill, *Utilitarianism*, p. 218.
2 Scheffler (ed.), *Consequentialism and its Critics*, p. 2.
3 Foot, in 'Morality, action and outcome' and in 'Utilitarianism and the virtues'.
4 Foot, 'Utilitarianism and the virtues', p. 224.
5 Ibid., pp. 224–5.
6 Scheffler (ed.), *Consequentialism and its Critics*, p. 1.
7 Ibid., Scheffler should, of course, say 'permits' rather than 'tells', though *sometimes* morality does tell. It tells us to pay our bills before we bestow our money on someone who would be more pleased to have it.
8 Foot, 'Utilitarianism and the virtues', p. 227.
9 Thomson, *Goodness and Advice*, p. 19.
10 Foot, 'Morality, action and outcome', p. 32.
11 Ibid., p. 34.
12 Foot, 'Utilitarianism and the virtues', pp. 233–6.
13 Beauchamp and Childress, *Principles*, p. 341.
14 Nussbaum, in Thomson, *Goodness and Advice*, p. 100.
15 Ibid., p. 105.
16 Thomson, in *Goodness and Advice*, pp. 156–7.

Chapter 5   The Dictates of Conscience

1 The nature, scope and depth of our dependency is brought out in Wittgenstein's *On Certainty*.
2 Aquinas, *Summa Theologica*, Ia2ae. 5, 6.
3 Ibid., Ia2ae. 4.
4 Ellen Goodman, 'Dispensing morality'.
5 See McHale and Fox, *Health Care Law*, pp. 747–50.
6 See Blustein on New York State's Do-Not-Resuscitate Law, in 'Doing what the patient orders', p. 290.
7 Kennedy, *Treat Me Right*, p. 29.
8 Watt, *Life and Death*, pp. 68–71.
9 Quoted by Ellen Goodman, approvingly, in 'Dispensing morality'.
10 Naomi Wolf, 'Our bodies, our souls'.

Chapter 6   The Duties to Obtain Consent, Give Information
and Respect Autonomy

1 BMA, *Medical Ethics Today*, p. 321.
2 McHale and Fox, *Health Care Law*, p. 317. Cf. 'the idea of autonomy has emerged as a central notion in the area of applied moral philosophy, particularly in the biomedical context': Gerald Dworkin, *The Theory and Practice of Autonomy*, pp. 4–5.
3 Faden and Beauchamp, *Informed Consent*, p. 18.
4 For a broader overview of the history of the law on consent, see ibid., part ii; cf. Mendelson, 'Historical evolution'; for a comparison of current trends in the USA and in England, see Robertson, 'Informed consent'.
5 *Re F (Mental Patient: Sterilisation)* [1990] 2 AC 1.
6 *Collins* v. *Wilcock* [1984] 1 WLLR 1172.
7 Mendelson, 'Historical evolution', p. 8.
8 *Sidaway* v. *Bethlem Royal Hospital* [1985] AC 871.
9 Bentham, *Theory of Legislation*, p. 269.
10 See Brazier, *Medicine, Patients and the Law*, p. 75. Cf. BMA, *Medical Ethics Today*, p. 7.
11 This is true in English law. But in *Salgo* v. *Leland Stanford Jr. University Board of Trustees*, 317 P.2d 170, 181 (1957) failure to disclose was actually held to vitiate consent.
12 154 Cal. App. 2d 560, 317 P. 2d 170 (1957).
13 186 Kan. 393, 350 P. 2d 1093 (1960).
14 [1981] 1 Q.B. 432, 443.
15 HMC [1957] 2 All E.R. 118. In *Sidaway*, the courts had the opportunity to embrace the legal concept of informed consent and chose instead to apply Bolam.
16 464 F. 2d 772 (D.C. Cir. 1972).
17 8 Cal. 3d 229, 104 Cal. Rptr. 505 (1972).
18 295 A. 2d 676.
19 Beauchamp and Childress, *Principles*, p. 82.
20 48 BMLR 118.
21 In *Chester* v. *Afshar* [2004] UKHL 41, the question arose as to whether if a patient is not properly informed of a risk which eventuates, she needs to show that she would not have undergone the operation at all, or merely that she would not have undergone it at a particular time, preferring, perhaps, to go away and think about it first. It was held that she need not show that she would not have undergone the operation at all. This judgement signals the trend towards fuller disclosures.
22 Mason and McCall Smith, *Law and Medical Ethics*, p. 288.
23 Percival, *Medical Ethics*, p. 91.
24 Hutcheson, *Collected Works*, vol. 6, p. 33.
25 Mason and McCall Smith, *Law and Medical Ethics*, p. 279.
26 See Ian Kennedy, *Treat Me Right*, p. 178: 'Consent, in short, is an ethical doctrine about respect for persons and about power. It seeks to transfer

some power to the patient in areas affecting her self-determination, so as to create the optimal relationship between doctor and patient, which is the same as that between any professional and his client – namely, a partnership of shared endeavour in pursuit of the client's interests. Good medical ethics strives for a relationship which is neither one of "medical paternalism" nor "patient sovereignty", but one of "shared decision-making".' Likewise, McHale and Fox, *Health Care Law*, p. 317, trace the duty to get valid consent and the duty to inform (adequately) back to the same human right: 'the right to have one's autonomy and self-determination respected'. So too does the Department of Health in its *Reference Guide to Consent for Examination or Treatment* (2001). So too do Faden and Beauchamp. See also, Mason and McCall Smith: 'Looked at from the ethical point of view, the matter is one of self-determination. A person should not be exposed to a risk of damage unless he has agreed to that risk and he cannot properly agree to – or, equally important, make a choice between – risks in the absence of factual information': *Law and Medical Ethics*, p. 278; cf. p. 286. Mason and McCall Smith are putting forward this principle that we should only be exposed to risks to which we agree in the context of obtaining consent to treatment. As a general principle, it would be less persuasive. Aeroplanes fly over our homes, subjecting us to risks. We never agreed to this.

27 Engelhardt, *Foundations of Christian Bioethics*, p. 28.
28 Ibid., p. 128.
29 Engelhardt Jr. and Wildes, 'The four principles', p. 137.
30 Ibid., p. 147.
31 Engelhardt, *Foundations*, p. 354.
32 G. Dworkin, *Theory and Practice*, p. 6.
33 Feinberg, 'The idea of a free man', p. 21.
34 Compare this case outlined by Beauchamp and Childress: a physician obtains the results of a myelogram (a graph of the spinal region). Although the test is inconclusive and needs repeating, it suggests a serious pathology. But the physician withholds the information, not doubting that the patient would consent to another myelogram but simply not wishing to cause possibly unnecessary anxiety: *Principles*, pp. 185–6.
35 In a sense this is not exactly true. If information is deliberately kept from you, for paternalistic reasons, say, of an alternative treatment that is available, you are none the less, strictly speaking, at liberty to choose it. Still, you are being prevented by the contrived ignorance from exercising your liberty.
36 Feinberg, 'Legal paternalism', esp. pp. 113, 116. Cf. *Moral Limits*, esp. pp. 12ff.
37 See Joel Feinberg, *Moral Limits*, pp. 12–13.
38 Geach, 'Plato's Euthyphro', in *Logic Matters*, p. 37; originally published in *The Monist*, 50 (1966).
39 See ch. 3, pp. 30–1.
40 *ReB (Adult Refusal of Medical Treatment)* [2002] 2 All E.R. 449; [2002] 2 F.C.R.1. This case is discussed in ch. 12.

41 Orr, 'Hippocratic Oath', p. 3.
42 Beauchamp and Childress, *Principles*, p. 186.

Chapter 7 'First, Do No Harm'

1 For examples of how we can harm others by 'doing nothing', see Davis, 'The priority of avoiding harm', pp. 309–10.
2 See Jonsen, 'Do no harm', in *Philosophical Medical Ethics*, ed. Spicker and Engelhardt.
3 Translation from the Greek by Ludwig Edelstein, from *The Hippocratic Oath*. See <http://www.pbs.org/wgbh/nova/doctors/oath_classical.html>. I have deviated from Edelstein's translation at one point. His reads: 'I will keep them from harm . . .'. I omit 'them'. It is not in the Greek, and it implies a duty not only to avoid harming patients but to prevent their being harmed.
4 Statement by the Council of the British Medical Association for submission to the World Medical Association, June 1947, <http://www.donoharm.org.uk/leaflets/war.htm>.
5 Orr, 'Hippocratic Oath', p. 3. Just as this book goes to press, the BMA at its annual conference (June 2005) has voted to adopt a neutral stance in relation to euthanasia.
6 *The Care of Women Requesting Induced Abortion*, National Evidence-Based Clinical Guidelines, no. 7, March 2000.
7 Raanan Gillon edited the *Journal of Medical Ethics* for over 20 years and took the lead in Britain in getting ethics firmly on to the curriculum in medical schools.
8 Gillon, *Philosophical Medical Ethics*, ch. 13.
9 Ibid., p. 85.
10 Beauchamp and Childress appear to be expressing the same view in this not so clear passage: 'A beneficial action does not necessarily take second place to an act of not causing harm. In cases of conflict, nonmaleficence is typically overriding, but the weight of these principles – like all principles – vary in different circumstances': *Principles*, p. 115.
11 Gillon even includes vaccination programmes among his examples of practices that the pledge would rule out – on the grounds that those administering vaccinations know that some will be harmed. But of course this assumes that the pledge rules out unintentional harming, which we have already dismissed as an unreasonably unsympathetic way of interpreting it.
12 The American Medical Association Code of Ethics prohibits doctors from participating in executions. But lethal injection (which was conceived by an anaesthesiologist, Dr Stanley Deutsch, at the University of Oklahoma and was first used on a condemned man in Texas in 1982) is the main method of execution, and many doctors see nothing wrong in their assisting. (See Farber et al., 'Physicians' attitudes about involvement in lethal injection for capital punishment'.) Some see it as a civic duty to do so. And some who are opposed to the death penalty still believe that

they have a duty to assist so as to prevent executions being botched. Because of the objections over doctors participating, Missouri now hires nurses to assist. But if it is wrong for doctors to assist, how can it be all-right for nurses to do so? The American Nurses Association is 'strongly opposed' to participation, declaring that it is 'contrary to the fundamental goals and ethical traditions of the profession'.

13 It is especially chilling to learn that the 'medical inspections' of new arrivals to the Auschwitz-Birkenau concentration camp in 1943 were examined by five men who were indeed all doctors. These doctors selected those they deemed fit 'for light work only' to be led off 'to the showers' to be sprayed with Zyclon B. My source: Elkins, *Forged Fury*, p. 113.

14 The American Medical Association adopts a neutral stance on the morality of capital punishment, but objects to doctors assisting in any way in administering it. The thought is presumably that it is in some way unbecoming for *doctors* to participate – as in some countries it is deemed unbecoming for doctors to advertise their services.

15 See Weiner, 'The real Doctor Guillotin'.

16 In fact, one of the earliest and most used statins has recently (August 2004) been approved in the UK for over-the-counter sale at the pharmacist's discretion for those willing and able to pay the true cost and treat themselves.

17 A doctor who could have saved your sight entirely, but who through carelessness left you only partially sighted, could hardly fend off criticism on the grounds that you have not been harmed, since you have not been made worse off than you would have been without treatment. In such a case you have been harmed in spite of being made better off than you would have been. The proper baseline here is not how things would have been for you without any treatment, but how things would have been for you with competent treatment. Still, competent treatment is not necessarily the best possible treatment.

18 Hursthouse, *Beginning Lives*, p. 335.

19 See Elliott, 'A new way to be mad'.

20 There are, of course, Sermon on the Mount precedents: Matt. 5: 29–30. This seems to be contradicted, though, in Catholic teachings according to which amputations are only licit if for medical purposes: *Catechism of the Catholic Church*, s. 2297.

21 Foot, *Natural Goodness*, p. 94.

22 'A loving parent would often be puzzled if told "You should just consider your own good" if the good of the children were at stake. Naturally, there can be consideration of advantages on one side or the other, having to do, for instance, with an interesting job for a parent in one country and better schooling for the children elsewhere. But there is a way in which a loving parent does not really separate *his or her good* from the good of the children. And I think it is wrong to suppose that this is only because one will affect the other': ibid., p. 102.

23 Reported on CNN.com 29.12.04.

24 445 SW 2d 145 (Ky App 1969).
25 But in the nature of such cases, firm, reliable evidence may be difficult to secure. Those best positioned to provide it are likely to be interested parties.
26 Would failure to assist the Pattersons to find willing surgeons fall foul of the duty listed by the GMC as one of the essential duties of a doctor: 'make sure that your personal beliefs do not prejudice your patients' care'?
27 Foot, 'Killing, letting die, and euthanasia: a reply to Holly Smith Goldman', p. 160.
28 Marco et al. conducted a survey of emergency physicians which suggests that the majority of decisions to attempt to resuscitate after cardiac arrest are made out of fear of litigation or criticism, despite the expectation that the intervention is futile: 'Ethical issues of cardiopulmonary resuscitation'.

Chapter 8   Duties to Give, and Rights to Get, Health Care

1 Suppose you are a retired GP, and over a drink in the pub an acquaintance asks your advice about a spot on his arm: might it be malignant? You reassure him, saying you think it is not. Then it turns out you were wrong. Have you acted unjustly, even if your advice was freely bestowed? I think not – though it would, no doubt, have been sensible to warn the enquirer that you were no longer so up-to-date and to advise the enquirer to consult his own GP.
2 Imagine that an emergency arises and only you, who are a recently retired GP, are available to attend a patient. In that case, would you not be entitled (morally speaking) to reassure the patient and relatives, saying: 'Trust me, I'm a doctor!'? At least, if you were only recently retired, there is a sense in which you *would* still be a doctor – still have the skills and understanding to cope in the situation that has arisen.
3 The example is worded to exclude the kind of screening where coming up positive leads to the elimination of the affected individual. Whatever the merits of this weeding-out type of screening service, it is a little odd to describe it as 'health care'.
4 And besides, the duty to offer health care has about it a further indeterminacy that does not attach to the duty to rescue. Whereas the need for rescue arises in face of threats that are not always present, our needs for health care may be more or less continuous, ongoing, standing needs.
5 See Webster, *The NHS*; cf. Barnett, *The Lost Victory*; cf. Owen, *In Sickness and in Health*.
6 See Owen, *Our NHS*, p. 9.
7 My source for this information is Loudon (ed.), *Western Medicine*, pp. 281–2.
8 R. Dworkin, *Sovereign Virtue*, p. 73.
9 The first inroad on the free-at-point-of-use comprehensive health service in the UK was in 1949, when a small charge for prescriptions

was imposed. The next was to impose a charge for spectacles and false teeth – whereupon Aneurin Bevan resigned from the Cabinet.

Chapter 9   Distributive Justice in Health Care

1 As the seventeenth-century philosopher Thomas Hobbes points out, 'Many times the injury [wrong] is received by one man, when the damage redoundeth to another. As when the master commandeth his servant to give money to a stranger; if it be not done, the injury is done to the master, whom he had before covenanted to obey; but the damage redoundeth to the stranger, to whom he had no obligation; and therefore could not injure him': *Leviathan*, ch.15, pp. 114–15. Thus, it may be pointed out that nurse A, by neglecting the patient, acts unjustly to her employer. That is true. But I think it is reasonable to suppose that in our two cases nurse A wrongs *both* her employer *and* the neglected patient. Hobbes's example to illustrate his point carefully singles out a stranger as the person who suffers. The stranger has no claim on the master. Patients, surely, do have claims on the nurses who are supposed to be attending them.
2 Sometimes, of course, providing a service is not, or not quite, in a person's gift. You might, for example, have a debt of gratitude to a certain patient. Here it may be not only permissible, but, in a way, dutiful, for you to be partial.
3 See, e.g. Rachels, *The Elements of Moral Philosophy*, p. 19: 'The conscientious moral agent is someone who is concerned impartially with the interests of everyone affected by what he or she does'.
4 Schroeder, 'Rationing medical care – a comparative perspective', pp. 1089–91.
5 R. Dworkin, *Sovereign Virtue*, p. 310.
6 Williams, 'The idea of equality'.
7 For witty and pointed criticism of Williams on this matter, see Nozick, *Anarchy, State and Utopia*, pp. 233–5.
8 Gutmann, 'For and against equal access to health care'.
9 Walzer also claims that in contemporary life it is 'degrading' to be cut off from medical services. See *Spheres of Justice*, p. 89.
10 Davies, *Discoveries: Early Letters 1938–1975*, p. 26.
11 Daniels, *Just Health Care*; cf. Beauchamp and Childress, *Principles*, pp. 237, 240, who endorse Daniels's rule; cf. Alastair Campbell et al., *Medical Ethics*, p. 193. The inspiration behind this line of thought in Daniels and others is Rawls's *Theory of Justice*.
12 Walzer, *Spheres of Justice*, p. 98.

Chapter 10   Abortion

1 See our earlier discussion of conscience in ch. 5.
2 Hursthouse, 'Virtue theory and abortion', p. 234.

3 Ibid., p. 238.
4 Beauchamp and Childress, *Principles*, p. 144.
5 Marquis, 'An argument that abortion is wrong'.
6 Ibid., p. 96.
7 Jamieson (ed.), *Singer and his Critics*, p. 313.
8 Mill, *Utilitarianism*, p. 255.
9 Ibid., pp. 250–1. While David Hume, as we noted in ch. 2, tends to portray the duties of justice as largely to do with property and promising, he, like Mill, locates the importance of observing the rules dictated by the duties of justice in our basic, standing need for social peace and order. See his *Treatise*, Book III, part II.
10 Bentham, Theory of Legislation, p. 265. Less well known is Bentham's own condemnation of infanticide. While he considers it 'barbarous' for the law to inflict 'an ignominious death upon an unhappy mother' seeking to avoid disgrace, he does approve censure of infanticide, that it should be 'branded with disgrace'. 'It is commonly the fear of shame which is its cause; it needs a greater shame to repress it.' For, he says, 'It is not possible to fortify too strongly the sentiments of respect for humanity, or to inspire too much repugnance against everything that conduces to cruel habits': ibid., pp. 264–5.
11 This was the point at issue in Thucydides' account of the Melian debate, when Athens sent a deputation ahead of its force to persuade the island of Melos to join the Athenian empire or else be vanquished. The Melians wanted to remain neutral and appealed to considerations of justice. The Athenian deputation scorned this appeal: what relevance could it have in dealings between the mighty and the weak?
12 Thomson, 'A defense of abortion'.
13 Pence, *Classic Cases*, p. 167.
14 If, however, euthanasia is defensible (we will come to this issue in chs 11 and 12), a case could be made for foetal euthanasia (with the mother's consent). Some prenatal screening and abortion for serious handicap with the aim to kill might be defended in this way. Of course, the serious handicap would have to be of such a nature as to justify the presumption that the killing was in the interests of the child that was killed.
15 Thomson, 'A defense of abortion', p. 47.
16 Tooley, 'Abortion and Infanticide'.
17 Sadler, *Langman's Medical Embryology*, p. 63.
18 Anscombe, 'Were you a zygote?', p. 113.
19 See Norman Ford, *When Did I Begin?*, p. 84.
20 Ibid., p. xvii.
21 Unlike the cake batter that the cook puts in the oven, where the batter is already distinguishable from its container.
22 Ford, *When Did I Begin?*, p. 181.
23 Figures taken from a national survey carried out prior to the publication of the Royal College of Obstetricians and Gynaecologists' *The Care*

of Women Requesting Induced Abortion: 2000, Evidence-Based Clinical Guidelines, <http://www.rcog.org.uk>

24 See *Doe* v. *Bolton,* 410 U.S. 179 (1973): 'We agree . . . that the medical judgment may be exercised in the light of all factors – physical, emotional, psychological, familial, and the woman's age – relevant to the wellbeing of the patient. All these factors relate to health', Mr Justice Blackmun, delivering the opinion of the court regarding a 22-year-old Georgian woman who already had three children, two in foster homes and one up for adoption and who was living with her indigent parents and their eight children.

25 McMahan, *The Ethics of Killing,* p. 189.

26 British Medical Association, *Medical Ethics Today,* p. 103. The BMA, as of June 2005, has moved from 'unreserved' rejection of enthanasia to neutrality. See p. 210, n. 5 above.

27 'In Romania, for example, the number of abortion-related deaths increased sharply after November 1966 when the government tightened the previously liberal abortion law. Abortions were legalized again in December 1989, and by the end of 1990, maternal deaths caused by abortions dropped to around 60 per 100 000 live births' *Report of the World Health Organization,* 'Unsafe abortion'.

Chapter 11   Suicide, Assisted Suicide and Euthanasia

1 *Roe* v. *Wade,* 410 U.S. 113 (1973).

2 Quoted by Rachels in 'Active and passive euthanasia', p. 78.

3 British Medical Association, *Medical Ethics Today,* p. 103, cf. n. 26 above.

4 Foot, 'Euthanasia', in *Virtues and Vices,* p. 56.

5 Perhaps we should not let pass without comment the casual juxtaposition of 'very old' and 'soon to die', seeing that the presumption that the very old are soon to die is so unreliable and smacks of ageism.

6 Foot, 'Euthanasia', p. 56.

7 *Report of the Select Committee on Medical Ethics,* vol.11, para.21.

8 McMahan, *The Ethics of Killing,* p. 456.

9 The notion of posthumous benefits or harms has long been a matter of controversy. Epicurus maintained that death cannot be bad for you, assuming it annihilates you, since once you are dead, there is no you left to be the subject of misfortune. Epicurus also maintained that nothing bad can happen to you unless you experience it as bad – unless you suffer it. Cicero accused Epicurus of inconsistency, since Epicurus took some trouble over making his will. Why should he have bothered if he really believed that it would be no misfortune for him if the will were not honoured? For a more contemporary discussion of the issue, see Nagel, 'Death', in *Mortal Questions,* and for a detailed discussion which comments on the history of the controversy, see Warren, *Facing Death.*

10 Harris, *The Value of Life,* p. 85.

11 Ibid., p. 82.

12 Ibid., p. 34. See John Lorber, 'Ethical problems in the management of myelomeningocele and hydrocephalus', *Journal of the Royal College of Physicians*, 10 (1975), pp. 47–60.
13 Flew, 'The right to death', p. 4.
14 Hare, 'Why I am only a demi-vegetarian', p. 221.
15 Found from Chaucer to Macaulay, according to Gormally (ed.), *Euthanasia, Clinical Practice and the Law*, p. 52.
16 Quoted in Keown, *Euthanasia, Ethics and Public Policy*, p. 66.
17 The same explanation has been offered to account for the decriminalization of suicide elsewhere. See e.g. Kamisar, 'Physician-assisted suicide', p. 229.
18 'Except in certain fairly rare cases, for instance of great suffering in a terminal illness, suicide is contrary to the virtue of hope. It may surprise some people that I call hope a virtue, but of course it is; in part because we are often tempted to think that all is lost when we cannot really know that it is so. In view of the appalling number of young suicides in our present society, I suggest that hope should be among the first of a fairy godmother's gifts at the cradle of a child' Foot, *Natural Goodness*, p. 74.
19 Seneca, *Epistle 70*, trans. Richard M. Gummere, <http://www.molloy.edu/academic/philosophy/sophia/seneca/epistles/ep 70.htm>
20 Kant, *The Doctrine of Virtue*, p. 86.
21 Admittedly, the protective teaching is not cost-free. For isn't it also true that sometimes just knowing the option is available allows a person to hang on?
22 Hume, 'On suicide', p. 595.
23 See Keown, *Euthanasia, Ethics and Public Policy*. Cf. discussion in Biggar, *Aiming to Kill*, pp. 124–51.Cf. M. Moller and R. Huxtable, 'Euthanasia in the Netherlands', p. 1600.
24 See ch.6, pp. 66–7 on the absurd ambition of being totally self-reliant in what one believes.

Chapter 12   Killing and Letting Die

1 At any rate, no one whose thinking has not been reconstructed by a philosopher. John Harris, as we noted in the last chapter (p.137), maintains that case 2 is *not* a mere letting die, but a killing by omission. We should also note that if what is in question is withdrawing a life-saving measure (rather than just withholding it) for any of these reasons, it is maybe not so clear that the doctor is not killing. We will take up this point shortly in discussion of the case of Ms B.
2 The case is discussed by Helga Kuhse and Peter Singer in *Should the Baby Live?*, pp. 11–17. The *R* v. *Arthur* case that came before the courts in England in 1981 will be discussed shortly (pp. 153–4 ff). Another English case, *Re B* [1990] 3 All E.R. 927 concerned a Down's syndrome baby born with an intestinal blockage. The parents would not authorize surgery. The child was made a ward of the Court. The Court authorized the surgery, and this authorization was upheld on appeal – as in the child's best interests.

3 Burleigh, *Death and Deliverance*, pp. 45–6.

4 In the early 1990s a similar pair of cases came before the courts in Canada and met with the same response. One case, *Nancy B.* v. *Hotel-Dieu de Quebec et al.* (1992), 69 C.C.C. (3rd) 450 closely resembled that of Ms B. The other case, *Rodriguez* v. *British Columbia (Attorney General)* 107 D.L.R. (4th) 342 (1993); *Rodriguez* v. *Attorney General of Canada* [1994] 2LRC 136, was similar to that of Pretty, except that Sue Rodriguez was claiming the right to physician-assisted suicide, whereas Pretty was seeking immunity from prosecution for her *husband* if he assisted her. Rodriguez's defence appealed to the Canadian Charter of Rights and Freedoms. Counsel for Pretty appealed to the European Convention on Human Rights, seeking to connect the right to assisted suicide with other less controversial rights such as (among others) the right to life (Article 2), the right of the disabled not to be discriminated against (Article 14) and the right of privacy (Article 8).

5 The court in the analogous case of Nancy B emphasized that it was not permitting physician-assisted suicide, which is prohibited under Quebec law. Admittedly, simply *saying* that you are not assisting suicide does not of itself make it true.

6 Anscombe, *Intention*.

7 The example is Anscombe's. See 'War and murder', p. 54.

8 Anscombe remarks that the idea that the man could make it true simply by saying to himself that he is not intending to poison, only to earn his living is 'obvious bosh': *Intention*, p. 42, 25.

9 Ibid., p. 45, 25.

10 Anscombe maintains that the distinction is essential to Christian ethics, inasmuch as this involves absolute prohibitions (which prohibitions she describes as 'bedrock' in Christian ethics). The idea of certain types of actions being absolutely forbidden breaks down if you are answerable for the foreseen consequences of your actions or refusals as much as for doing the forbidden actions. See 'War and murder', p. 58.

11 Kenny, 'Philippa Foot on double effect', p. 85.

12 Here is an instance of doctor killing which in a way, considered in isolation, seems a small matter. And there would not be much risk of Lord Dawson making a practice of speeding up the death of kings or other eminent patients. It is only under the aspect of intentional killing of the innocent that what he did may be seen as an instance of a seriously bad practice.

13 Anscombe, 'Action, intention and "double effect" ', p. 23.

Chapter 13   Patients' Deaths and Doctors' Decisions

1 Compare the case of baby Charlotte Wyatt, whose parents sought unsuccessfully through the courts to compel her doctors to attempt resuscitation if she stopped breathing. Her doctors maintained that her chronic respiratory and other problems rendered repeated resuscitations cruel

and futile. See *Portsmouth NHS Trust* v. *Wyatt & Ors* [2004] EWHC 2247 (Fam) (7 Oct. 2004).

2 *Airedale NHS Trust* v. *Bland* [1993] 2 WLR 316.

3 See *R.* v. *Cambridge Health Authority, ex p B* [1995] 1 WLR 898. In this case the father of a child who had a recurrence of leukaemia, which the doctors deemed futile to treat (the chance of success was estimated at from 1–4 per cent), sought through the courts to compel the health authority to provide the treatment. The father maintained that the refusal to treat was driven by considerations of cost. The doctors did not deny that costs were a consideration, though they insisted that, costs aside, further treatment was not in the child's best interests. See the discussion of this case in Christopher Newdick, *Who Should We Treat?*, pp. 131–3.

4 My account is based on *Re A (children) (conjoined twins: surgical separation)* 4 All E. L. R. 961 [2000].

5 It was precisely the concepts of private defence and of necessity on which the Appeal Court judges relied to justify authorization of the surgery to separate these twins – to rescue Jodie from the lethal threat posed by Mary.

Chapter 14   Moral Issues in Reproductive Medicine

1 Fertilization 'in vitro' means literally: in glass. It refers more generally to fertilization performed in a laboratory. Ova are removed from the woman (using a laparoscope), and these are mixed with spermatozoa from her partner or a donor. They are incubated until embryos (blastocysts) are formed, and then some are implanted, and the others are discarded or frozen for later use.

2 Figure from the National Institute for Clinical Guidance, Clinical Guideline no. 11. Fertility Feb. 2004. For details of costings see <www.nice.org.uk> in Appendix B.

3 The success rate of natural succession, though, is comparable (about 20 to 30 per cent each cycle). See *HFEA Guide to Infertility*.

4 There are also techniques such as PESA (percutaneous epididymal sperm aspiration) and TESE (testicular sperm aspiration). Since these are invasive and painful, they are generally used only where it is not possible to obtain sperm by ejaculation (e.g. as in cases of azoospermia – where there may be a blockage in the ducts that conduct sperm).

5 The HFEA Code of Practice stipulates a maximum of three in the case of women aged 40 or more using their own eggs; otherwise, no more than two. But the HFEA has just announced (28.7.05) that it is now considering whether to follow certain other countries such as the Netherlands, Sweden and Finland in limiting the transfer of embryos to one.

6 Irish Medical Council, 'A guide to ethical conduct and behaviour', #26.4.

7 *British Medical Journal*, 328 (2004) 1334.

8 'The laws which, in many countries on the continent, forbid marriage unless the parties can show that they have the means of supporting a

family, do not exceed the legitimate powers of the state . . . they are not objectionable as a violation of liberty': J. S. Mill, *Liberty*, p. 304.

9 In the UK, the HFEA has a statutory obligation to give guidance to fertility clinics on how to apply and interpret section 13 (5) of the HFE Act 1990, which states: 'a woman shall not be provided with treatment services unless account has been taken of the welfare of any child who may be born as a result of treatment (including the need of a child for a father) . . .'. It is currently reviewing its guidance and has published a public consultation document, 'Tomorrow's Children', in which it demarcates three possible levels of commitment: maximum welfare, reasonable welfare and a minimum threshold of welfare: HFEA, 'Tomorrow's Children', Jan. 2005, sect. 2.4 <http://www.hfea.gov.uk>

10 For a robust denunciation of welfare vetting of would-be parents, however, see Jackson, 'Conception'.

11 Foot, *Natural Goodness*, p. 35. Foot draws on the notions of natural defects and natural goodness in plants and animals to cast light on how we should explore human virtues and vices.

12 Grommets are small ventilation tubes placed in the eardrum of children whose ears glue up from repeated colds and ear infections.

13 A cochlear ear implant consists of an electrode that is permanently implanted in the inner ear. The implant is connected to an externally fitted microphone and electronic unit which is powered by batteries.

14 The 1996 *Working Party of the Catholic Bishops' Joint Committee on Bioethical Issues* declares that medicine is concerned with health in a narrow sense only: to meet a need created by some functional defect, or by the possibility of some functional defect, either by curative or preventative treatment, or by palliation of symptoms.

15 Harris, *Clones, Genes, and Immortality*, p. 191.

16 Working Party of the Catholic Bishops' Joint Committee on Bioethical Issues, *Genetic Interventions on Human Subjects*, p. 39–40.

17 Feinberg, 'The child's right to an open future'.

18 Admittedly, a bad education might be easier to correct than a genetic intervention that turned out to be unfortunate. But here we are interested in establishing if, *safety aside*, there are other reasons for repudiating enhancing interventions.

19 Reiss and Straughan, *Improving Nature?*, p. 174.

20 Gatward, *Livestock Ethics*, pp. 230–2.

Chapter 15   The Old and the New

1 Singer, *Rethinking*, p. 189.

2 Ibid.

3 See Kenny, *Aquinas*, pp. 26–7.

4 Singer, *Rethinking*, p. 187.

5 Kuhse and Singer (eds), *Bioethics*, p. 4.

6 Hobbes, *Leviathan*, pp. 13–16.

7 Kuhse and Singer, *Bioethics*, p. 5.
8 I do not mean to insinuate, though, that *Singer* does this.
9 Singer, *Rethinking*, p. 191.
10 Ibid.
11 See Singer, *Unsanctifying Human Life*, p. 112, where he declares that his 'basic position' is utilitarian. If it is our duty to maximize preference satisfaction, it is hard to underestimate the appallingness of what we might 'have' to do. See the second of the three common objections to utilitarianism in ch 4.
12 Williams, in Smart and Williams, *Utilitarianism*, pp. 96–100, 110–17.
13 Singer, *Rethinking*, p. 206.
14 Ibid., p. 190.
15 Hare, 'Possible people'.
16 Singer, *Rethinking*, p. 131.
17 Ibid., p. 118.
18 Ibid., p. 156.
19 Not that Singer sees the need for dishonest pretence as *necessarily* showing an ethic to be unsound. As I mentioned in the Introduction, he advocates dishonest pretence about lying to patients.
20 *Boswell's Life of Johnson*, vol. 2, p. 274, n. 6.

Bibliography

Anscombe, G. E. M., *Intention* (Basil Blackwell, Oxford, 1957).

Anscombe, G. E. M., 'On promising and its justice, and whether it need be respected *in foro interno*', in *The Collected Papers of G. E. M. Anscombe*, vol. 3 (Basil Blackwell, Oxford, 1981), pp. 10–21.

Anscombe, G. E. M., 'War and murder', in *The Collected Papers of G. E. M. Anscombe*, vol. 3 (Basil Blackwell, Oxford, 1981), pp. 51–61.

Anscombe, G. E. M., 'Were you a zygote?', in *Philosophy and Practice*, ed. A. Phillips Griffiths (Cambridge University Press, Cambridge, 1985), pp. 111–17.

Anscombe, G. E. M., 'Action, intention and "double effect"', in *Human Life, Action and Ethics: Essays by G. E. M. Anscombe*, ed. Mary Geach and Luke Gormally (Imprint Academic, London, 2005), pp. 207–26.

Aquinas, *Summa Theologica*, tr. Fathers of the English Dominican Province (Benziger Brothers, New York, 1947).

Aristotle, *Nicomachean Ethics*, tr. Sir David Ross (Oxford University Press, London, 1925).

Atiyah, P. S., *The Rise and Fall of Freedom Of Contract* (Clarendon Press, Oxford, 1979).

Barnett, Correlli, *The Lost Victory* (Macmillan, London, 1995).

Beauchamp, Tom L. and James F. Childress, *Principles of Biomedical Ethics* (Oxford University Press, New York, 2001).

Beecher, Henry K., *Research and the Individual: Human Studies* (Little, Brown, Boston, 1970).

Benson, John, 'Who is the autonomous man?', *Philosophy*, 58 (1983), pp. 5–17.

Bentham, Jeremy, *An Introduction to the Principles of Morals and Legislation* (Clarendon Press, Oxford, 1823; originally published 1789).

Bentham, Jeremy, *The Theory of Legislation*, tr. Etienne Dumont (Trench, Trubner, Paul, London, 1931).

Biggar, Nigel, *Aiming to Kill* (Darton, Longman & Todd, London, 2004).

Blustein, Jeffrey, 'Doing what the patient orders: maintaining integrity in the doctor–patient relationship', *Bioethics*, (1993) pp. 284–314.

Boswell's Life of Johnson, ed. George Birkbeck Hill, rev. L. F. Powell (Clarendon Press, Oxford, 1971).

Brazier, Margaret, *Medicine, Patients and the Law* (Penguin, London, 1992).

British Medical Association, *Medical Ethics Today: Its Practice and* Philosophy, from the BMA's Ethics, Science and Information Division (BMJ Publishing Group, London, 1993).

Burleigh, Michael, *Death and Deliverance: 'Euthanasia' in Germany 1900–1945* (Cambridge University Press, Cambridge, 1994).

Campbell, Alistair, Max Charlesworth, Grant Gillett and Gareth Jones, *Medical Ethics* (Oxford University Press, Auckland, 1997).

Catechism of the Catholic Church, rev. ed (Geoffrey Chapman, London, 1999).

Cross, F. L. (ed.), *Oxford Dictionary of the Christian Church* (Oxford University Press, London, 1958).

Daniels, Norman, *Just Health Care* (Cambridge University Press, Cambridge, 1985).

Davies, Robertson, *Discoveries: Early Letters 1938–1975*, selected and ed. Judith Skelton Grant (McClelland & Stewart Ltd., Toronto, 2002).

Davis, N. Ann, 'The priority of avoiding harm', in *Killing and Letting Die*, 2nd edn, ed. Bonnie Steinbock and Alastair Norcross (Fordham University Press, New York, 1994), pp. 298–354.

Dworkin, Gerald, *The Theory and Practice of Autonomy* (Cambridge University Press, Cambridge, 1988).

Dworkin, Ronald, *Sovereign Virtue: The Theory and Practice of Equality* (Harvard University Press, Cambridge, Mass., 2000).

Edelstein, Ludwig, *The Hippocratic Oath: Text, Translation, and Interpretation* (Johns Hopkins Press, Baltimore, 1943).

Elkins, Michael, *Forged Fury* (Piatkus, Loughton, Essex, 1981).

Elliott, Carl, 'A new way to be mad', *Atlantic Monthly*, 286 (2000), pp. 72–84.

Engelhardt, H. Tristram Jr., *Foundations of Christian Bioethics* (Swets & Zeitlinger, Lisse, 2000).

Engelhardt, H. Tristram Jr. and Kevin William Wildes, 'The four principles of health care ethics and post-modernity: why a libertarian interpretation is unavoidable', in *Principles of Health Care Ethics*, ed. Raanan Gillon (John Wiley & Sons, Chichester, 1994), pp. 135–47.

Faden, Ruth R. and Tom L. Beauchamp, *A History and Theory of Informed Consent* (Oxford University Press, New York, 1986).

Farber, Neil, Elizabeth B. Davis, Joan Weiner, Janine Jordan, E. Gill Boyer and Peter A. Ubel, 'Physicians' attitudes about involvement in lethal injection for capital punishment', *Archives of Internal Medicine*, 160 (2000), pp. 2912–916.

Feinberg, Joel, 'The idea of a free man', in *Rights, Justice and the Bounds of Liberty* (Princeton University Press, Princeton, 1980), pp. 3–29.

Feinberg, Joel, 'Legal paternalism', in *Rights, Justice and the Bounds of Liberty* (Princeton University Press, Princeton, 1980), pp. 110–29.

Feinberg, Joel, *The Moral Limits of the Criminal Law: Harm to Self*, vol. 3 (Oxford University Press, New York, 1988).

Feinberg, Joel, 'The child's right to an open future', in *Whose Child? Children's Rights, Parental Authority, and State Power*, ed. William Aiken and Hugh LaFollette (Rowman & Littlefield, Totowa, NJ, 1980); repr. in Joel Feinberg, *Freedom & Fulfilment* (Princeton University Press, Princeton, 1992), pp. 76–97.

Flew, Antony, 'The right to death', <www.libertarian.co.uk/lapubs/legan008.pdf>, pp. 1–4.

Foot, Philippa, 'Moral beliefs', *Proceedings of the Aristotelian Society*, 59 (1958–9), pp. 83–104; repr. in Foot, *Virtues and Vices*, pp. 110–31.

Foot, Philippa, *Virtues and Vices and Other Essays in Moral Philosophy* (Basil Blackwell, Oxford, 1978).

Foot, Philippa, 'Killing, letting die, and euthanasia: a reply to Holly Smith Goldman', *Analysis*, 41/3 (1981), pp. 159–60.

Foot, Philippa, 'Morality, action and outcome', in *Morality and Objectivity: A Tribute to J. L. Mackie*, ed. Ted Honderich (Routledge & Kegan Paul, London, 1985), pp. 23–38.

Foot, Philippa, 'Utilitarianism and the virtues', in *Consequentialism and its Critics*, ed. Samuel Scheffler (Oxford University Press, New York, 1988), pp. 224–42.

Foot, Philippa, *Natural Goodness* (Clarendon Press, Oxford, 2001).

Ford, Norman M., *When Did I Begin? Conceptions of the Human Individual in History, Philosophy and Science* (Cambridge University Press, Cambridge, 1988).

Gatward, Gordon, *Livestock Ethics* (Chalcombe Publications, Lincoln, 2001).

Geach, P. T., *Logic Matters* (Basil Blackwell, Oxford, 1972).

Geach, P. T., *The Virtues* (Cambridge University Press, Cambridge, 1977).

General Medical Council, *Guidance on Consent: The Ethical Considerations* (GMC, London, 1985).

General Medical Council, *Good Medical Practice* (GMC, London, 2001).

Gillon, Raanan, *Philosophical Medical Ethics* (John Wiley & Sons, Chichester, 1985).

Goodman, Ellen, 'Dispensing morality', *Washington Post*, 8 April 2005.

Gormally, Luke (ed.), *Euthanasia, Clinical Practice and the Law* (Linacre Centre, London, 1994).

Gutmann, Amy, 'For and against equal access to health care', *Millbank Memorial Fund Quarterly/Health and Society*, 59 (1981), pp. 542–60.

Habgood, John, Heslington public lecture, University of York, 1st February, 1995.

Hare, R. M., 'Possible people', in *Essays on Bioethics* (Clarendon Press, Oxford, 1993), pp. 67–83.

Hare, R. M., 'Why I am only a demi-vegetarian', *Essays on Bioethics* (Clarendon Press, Oxford, 1993), pp. 219–35.

Harris, John, *The Value of Life* (Routledge, London, 1989).

Harris, John, *Clones, Genes, and Immortality* (Oxford University Press, Oxford, 1998).

Hobbes, Thomas, *Leviathan* (Clarendon Press, Oxford, 1909; originally published 1651).

Hobbes, Thomas, *The Questions concerning Liberty, Necessity and Chance*, in *The English Works of Thomas Hobbes*, ed. Sir W. Molesworth, vol. 5 (John Bohn, London, 1841).

Hochsmann, Hyun, *On Peter Singer* (Wadsworth/Thomson Learning, Inc., Belmont, Calif., 2002).

Human Fertilisation and Embryology Authority, 'Tomorrow's Children', January 2005, <http://www.hfea.gov.uk>

Hume, David, *A Treatise of Human Nature*, ed. L. A. Selby-Bigge (Clarendon Press, Oxford, 1958; originally published 1739).

Hume, David, *An Enquiry Concerning the Principles of Morals*, ed. L. A. Selby-Bigge (Clarendon Press, Oxford, 1902; originally published 1777).

Hume, David, 'On suicide', in *Essays, Moral, Political and Literary*, The World's Classics edn. (Grant Richards, London, 1904).

Hursthouse, Rosalind, *Beginning Lives* (Blackwell, Oxford, 1987).

Hursthouse, Rosalind, 'Virtue theory and abortion', *Philosophy and Public Affairs*, 20 (1991), pp. 223–46.

Hursthouse, Rosalind, *On Virtue Ethics* (Oxford University Press, Oxford, 2001).

Hutcheson, Francis, *Collected Works*, ed. B. Fabian (George Olms, Hildesheim, 1969), vol. 6. (originally published 1755).

Institutes of Justinian, tr. J. B. Moyle (Clarendon Press, Oxford, 1913).

Irish Medical Council, *A Guide to Ethical Conduct and Behaviour*, <http://www.medicalcouncil.ie/publications.htm (1998)>

Jackson, Emily, 'Conception and the irrelevance of the welfare principle', *Modern Law Review*, 65, 2 (2002), pp. 176–203.

Jamieson, Dale (ed.), *Singer and his Critics* (Blackwell, Oxford, 1999).

Jonsen, A. R., 'Do no harm', in *Philosophical Medical Ethics: Its Nature and Significance*, ed. S. F. Spicker and H. T. Engelhardt (Reidel, Dordrecht, 1977), pp. 27–41.

Kamisar, Yale, 'Physician-assisted suicide: the last bridge to active voluntary euthanasia', in *Euthanasia Examined*, ed. John Keown (Cambridge University Press, Cambridge, 1995), pp. 225–60.

Kant, Immanuel, *The Doctrine of Virtue: Part II of the Metaphysics of Morals*, tr. Mary J. Gregor (Harper & Row, New York, 1964; originally published 1797).

Kennedy, Ian, *Treat Me Right* (Clarendon Press, Oxford, 1988).

Kenny, Anthony, *Aquinas* (Oxford University Press, Oxford, 1980).

Kenny, Anthony, 'Philippa Foot on double effect' in *Virtues and Reasons*, ed. Rosalind Hursthouse, Gavin Lawrence and Warren Quinn (Clarendon Press, Oxford, 1995), pp. 77–87.

Keown, John, *Euthanasia, Ethics and Public Policy: An Argument Against Legalisation* (Cambridge University Press, Cambridge, 2002).

Kinnell, Herbert G., 'Serial homicide by doctors: Shipman in perspective', editorial in *British Medical Journal*, 321 (2000), pp. 1594–7.

Kuhse, Helga and Peter Singer, *Should the Baby Live?* (Oxford University Press, Oxford, 1985).

Kuhse, Helga and Peter Singer (eds.), *Bioethics: An Anthology* (Blackwell, Oxford, 1999).

Lancet editorial, 'The ethics industry', 350 (1997), p. 897.

Lorber, John, 'Ethical problems in the management of myelomeningocele and hydrocephalus', *Journal of the Royal College of Physicians*, 10 (1975), pp. 47–60.

Loudon, Irvine (ed.), *Western Medicine: An Illustrated History* (Oxford University Press, New York, 1997).

Marco, C. A., E. S. Bessman, C. N. Schoenfield and G. D. Kelem, 'Ethical issues of cardiopulmonary resuscitation: current practice among emergency physicians', *Academic Emergency Medicine*, 4 (1997) 894–904.

Marquis, Don, 'An argument that abortion is wrong', in *Ethics in Practice*, ed. Hugh La Follette (Blackwell, Cambridge, Mass., 1997), pp. 91–102. This article is an updated version of an earlier article which appeared in the *Journal of Philosophy*, 86 (1989), pp. 183–202.

Mason, J. K. and R. A. McCall Smith, *Law and Medical Ethics* (Butterworths, London, 1999).

McHale, Jean and Marie Fox, *Health Care Law* (Sweet & Maxwell, London, 1997).

McMahan, Jeff, *The Ethics of Killing: Problems at the Margins of Life* (Oxford University Press, New York, 2002).

Mendelson, Danute, 'Historical evolution and modern implications of concepts of consent to, and refusal of, medical treatment in the law of trespass', *Journal of Legal Medicine*, 17 (1996), pp. 1–71; repr. in *Medical Law and Ethics*, ed. Sheila McLean (Ashgate, Dartmouth, 2002), pp. 111–81.

Mill, John Stuart, *Utilitarianism*, in *Essays on Ethics, Religion and Society*, in *Collected Works of John Stuart Mill*, ed. J. M. Robson, F. E. L. Priestley and D. P. Dryer (University of Toronto Press, Toronto, 1969), vol. pp. 203–59). Originally published in 1861.

Mill, John Stuart, *On Liberty*, in *Essays on Politics and Society*, in *Collected Works of John Stuart Mill*, ed. J. M. Robson (University of Toronto Press, Toronto, 1977) vol. 18, pp. 213–310.

Moller, M. and R. Huxtable, 'Euthanasia in the Netherlands: the case of "Life Fatigue"', *New Law Journal*, 151 (2001), pp. 1600–1.

Nagel, Thomas, *Mortal Questions* (Cambridge University Press, Cambridge, 1979).

Newdick, Christopher, *Who Should We Treat?* (Clarendon Press, Oxford, 1995).

Nozick, Robert, *Anarchy, State and Utopia* (Blackwell, Oxford, 1974).

Orr, Robert D., 'The Hippocratic Oath: is it still relevant?', *Center for Christian Bioethics*, 14 (March 1998), pp. 2–4, <http://www.llu.edu/llu/bioethics/update/u141b.htm>

Owen, David, *In Sickness and in Health: The Politics of Medicine* (Quartet Books, London, 1976).

Owen, David, *Our NHS* (Pan, London, 1988).

Pappworth, M. H. *Human Guinea Pigs: Experimentation on Man* (Routledge & Kegan Paul, London, 1967).

Pence, Gregory E., *Classic Cases in Medical Ethics* (McGraw-Hill, New York, 1995).

Percival, Thomas, *Medical Ethics; or a Code of Institutes and Precepts, Adapted to the Professional Conduct of Physicians and Surgeons* (S. Russell, Manchester, 1803).

Plato, *Crito*, tr. Hugh Treddennick, in *The Last Days of Socrates* (Penguin, London, 1954) pp. 79–96.

Plato, *Republic*, tr. H. D. P. Lee (Penguin, London, 1955).

Plato, *Protagoras*, tr. W. K. C. Guthrie (Penguin, London, 1956).

Rachels, James, 'Active and passive euthanasia', *New England Journal of Medicine*, 292 (1975), pp. 78–80.

Rachels, James, *The Elements of Moral Philosophy* (McGraw-Hill, Boston, 1999).

Rawls, John, *A Theory of Justice* (Harvard University Press, Cambridge, Mass., 1971).

Reference Guide to Consent for Examination or Treatment (Department of Health, London, 2001).

Reiss, Michael J. and Roger Straughan, *Improving Nature?* (Cambridge University Press, Cambridge, 1996).

Report of the Committee on the Ethics of Gene Therapy (HMSO, London, 1992).

Report of the Select Committee on Medical Ethics, chaired by Lord Walton (HMSO, London, 1994).

Report of the World Health Organization, 'Unsafe abortion: global and regional estimates of incidence of morality due to unsafe abortion' (WHO, Geneva, 1997).

Robertson, Gerald, 'Informed consent to medical treatment', *Law Quarterly Review*, 97 (1981), pp. 102–26; repr. in *Medical Law and Ethics*, ed. Sheila McLean (Ashgate, Dartmouth, 2002), pp. 85–109.

Royal College of Obstetricians and Gynaecologists, *The Care of Women Requesting Induced Abortion*, Evidence-Based Clinical Guidelines, no. 7 (London, March 2000).

Sadler, T. W., *Langman's Medical Embryology*, 7th edn. (Williams & Wilkins, Baltimore, 1995).

Scheffler, Samuel (ed.), *Consequentialism and its Critics* (Oxford University Press, New York, 1988).

Schroeder, Steven A., 'Rationing medical care – a comparative perspective', editorial in *New England Journal of Medicine*, 321 (1994), pp. 1089–91.

Seneca, Epistle 70, tr. Richard M. Gummere, <http://www.molloy.edu/academic/philosophy/Sophia/Seneca/epistles/ep 70.htm>

Singer, Peter, *Rethinking Life and Death* (Oxford University Press, Oxford, 1995).

Singer, Peter, *Unsanctifying Human Life*, ed. Helga Kuhse (Blackwell, Oxford, 2002).

Smart, J. J. C. and Bernard Williams, *Utilitarianism* (Cambridge University Press, Cambridge, 1973).

Thomson, Judith Jarvis, 'A defense of abortion', *Philosophy and Public Affairs*, 1 (1971), pp. 47–66.

Thomson, Judith Jarvis, *Goodness and Advice* (Princeton University Press, Princeton, 2001).

Tooley, Michael, 'Abortion and infanticide', *Philosophy & Public Affairs*, 2 (1972), pp. 37–65.

von Wright, Georg Henrik, *The Varieties of Goodness* (Routledge & Kegan Paul, London, 1963).

Walzer, Michael, *Spheres of Justice* (Basic Books, New York, 1983).

Warren, James, *Facing Death* (Clarendon Press, Oxford, 2004).

Watt, Helen, *Life and Death in Healthcare Ethics* (Routledge, London, 2000).

Webster, Charles, *The NHS: A Political History* (Oxford University Press, Oxford, 1998).

Weiner, D. B. 'The real Doctor Guillotin', *Journal of the American Medical Association*, 220 (1972), pp. 85–9.

Williams, Bernard 'The idea of equality' in *Philosophy, Politics and Society*, ed. Peter Laslett and W. G. Runciman, 2nd edn (Blackwell, Oxford, 1962), pp. 110–31.

Wittgenstein, Ludwig, *On Certainty*, ed. G. E. M. Anscombe and G. H. von Wright, tr. Denis Paul and G. E. M. Anscombe (Blackwell, Oxford, 1969).

Wolf, Naomi, 'Our bodies, our souls', *The New Republic*, 16 Oct. 1995; <http://www.priestsforlife.org/prochoice/ourbodiesoursouls.htm>

Working Party of the Catholic Bishops' Joint Committee on Bioethical Issues, *Genetic Interventions on Human Subjects* (Linacre Centre, London, 1996).

Index